Blake's Illustrations

TO THE

Divine Comedy

Blake's Illustrations

TO THE

Divine Comedy

———

BY ALBERT S. ROE

PRINCETON UNIVERSITY PRESS

PRINCETON · NEW JERSEY

1953

FOREWORD

〜〜〜〜〜〜〜〜〜〜〜〜〜〜〜〜〜〜〜〜〜〜〜〜〜〜〜〜〜

I rest not from my great task!
To open the Eternal Worlds, to open the immortal Eyes
Of Man inwards into the Worlds of Thought, into Eternity
Ever expanding in the Bosom of God, the Human Imagination.
Jerusalem 5, 17-20.

〜〜〜〜〜〜〜〜〜〜〜〜〜〜〜〜〜〜〜〜〜〜〜〜〜〜〜〜〜

THE particular concern of this study is William Blake's series of drawings and engravings which illustrate the *Divine Comedy* of Dante. Blake the lyric poet, Blake the
journeyman engraver, Blake the composer of long and complex religious prophecies
in unrhymed verse, Blake the visionary—the mere word has been the origin of endless
misconceptions about him in many minds—now turns to drawing and watercolor to
make a series of designs based upon the masterpiece of a fellow poet. Blake the illustrator is not a separate figure, but merely another aspect of an extraordinarily complex
and yet remarkably integrated artistic personality. The many other facets of his
nature and talents, above all the endless creative urge which never deserted him in
spite of some fluctuations in its intensity, will constantly assert themselves in this new
undertaking. As he proceeds with his task, Dante's poem will not be for him an im-
personal story to serve as the framework for turning words into pictures; rather, he
will relive Dante's journey in terms of his own creative experience. His illustrations
will frequently be not merely literal, but will embody his own ideas at the same time
as they portray the events of Dante's poem—and yet, this will be done with such skill
that Blake's personality will rarely intrude itself in an obvious way. Only on the
basis of a thorough knowledge and comprehension of Blake's thought, as revealed in
his writings, and of familiarity with the whole body of his other work in the visual
media, will we be enabled to discern the counterpoint of Blake's own beliefs as they
blend with the dominant theme provided by the incidents and personalities of the
Divine Comedy.[1]

It is important to realize, therefore, that we are not dealing with the usual relationship between author and illustrator, but with a very rare instance of one creative mind
observing, interpreting, and commenting on the work of another. We must remember
that Blake, since his youth, had spent his life in seeking to organize an over-all view
of the totality of human experience, and in striving to present his beliefs through the

---

[1] The skill with which Blake is able to mingle appropriate illustration of a text with elaborate
symbolism of his own contriving was first fully demonstrated by Joseph Wicksteed in his study,
Blake's Vision of the Book of Job (London and New York, 1910; 2nd edition, 1924). For over
eighty years the Job designs had been admired at their face value and it was not suspected that
in reality they are filled with Blake's own symbolism. Wicksteed showed—and his conclusions
are now fully accepted—that we must think of the designs on four levels: as literal illustration
of the biblical narrative; as portraying the entire cycle of cosmic history as Blake conceived it;
as showing the fall, regeneration, and salvation of the individual soul; and as being to a considerable extent autobiographical.

two art forms in which he was gifted, poetry and painting. Before he took up the task of illustrating Dante's work, he had written three monumental philosophical poems—of which at least one, *Jerusalem*, is comparable in scope with the *Divine Comedy*—in addition to a dozen or so lesser poems of a prophetic nature. He had also created many drawings based upon the Bible and Milton, as well as designs to illustrate and decorate his own prophetic poems, and was just bringing to a conclusion what has since become his most famous contribution to the visual arts, the engravings based upon the Book of Job. Thus his creative experience had been a long and varied one, and had included previous projects of a nature similar to that to which he now addressed himself.

Considering as he did that creative imagination is a perception which God grants to man of ultimate truth, and regarding that truth as eternal and indivisible, Blake was convinced that the visionary perceptions of all really inspired artists must approach the same unity. He and Dante had been travellers in the same land—the land of every man's eternal self—and in different times, countries, and languages had striven to set down the memory of eternity which had been preserved in their immortal imaginations. Believing himself to be in a fallen world, Blake sought to find in the points of similarity between his own vision and that of another poet a confirmation for his faith in an eternal order. Thus his illustrations are not so much an attempt to render incidents from the *Divine Comedy* in pictorial terms as they are a visual commentary by Blake on Dante's vision. "Man Passes on, but States remain for Ever; he passes thro' them like a traveller who may as well suppose that the places he has passed thro' exist no more, as a Man may suppose that the States he has pass'd thro' Exist no more. Every thing is Eternal."[2]

[2] *Vision of the Last Judgment*, p. 640.

ACKNOWLEDGMENTS

THIS work is made possible in its present form by the generosity of the Trustees of the National Art-Collections Fund, London, in giving permission to reproduce all of the plates in the portfolio published by them in 1922 under the title *Illustrations to the Divine Comedy of Dante by William Blake*. I wish to record here my gratitude to the Trustees for their kindness in making their publication available.

The engravings, which are not included in the above mentioned portfolio, have been reproduced directly from an original set in the possession of Philip Hofer, Esq., of Cambridge, Massachusetts. Mr. Hofer's interest in this work and his willingness to make his fine set of engravings available to the printers of the plates are deeply appreciated. His contribution to the book has been a major one, for which I wish to express my thanks.

I am also grateful to the Syndics of the Fitzwilliam Museum, Cambridge, for permission to reproduce the two pencil drawings of Blake by John Linnell and to the authorities of the City Art Gallery, Manchester, who kindly gave permission for the reproduction of Blake's tempera portrait of Dante, which appears as plate 103.

This publication represents a revision and condensation of a study undertaken originally as a doctoral dissertation at Harvard University. Over the period during which it has been in preparation, in this country and in England, many individuals and institutions have given assistance and placed facilities at my disposal. To all of them I am most grateful for their help which has always been most generously forthcoming.

Finally, I wish to record my thanks to those who have supervised the work during publication, and especially to Miss Margot Cutter and Mrs. Helen Van Zandt of the Princeton University Press and to Mr. Harold Hugo of the Meriden Gravure Company. Their interest has been a great source of encouragement and I am much indebted to all of them for their help and advice on numerous matters in connection with the preparation of the work in its present form.

BIBLIOGRAPHICAL NOTE

A selected Bibliography will be found at the end of the text.

ALL REFERENCES to Blake's literary works are to the text as given in the one-volume edition edited by Geoffrey Keynes, published in London by the Nonesuch Press and in New York by Random House under the title *Poetry and Prose of William Blake*. Page references are to the fourth edition, 1939, and later editions. For the convenience of readers who may have access to an earlier edition in which the pagination is different, a table is given as Appendix A which will make it possible to locate passages in those editions without difficulty.

As the lines of Blake's poems in Keynes' edition are not numbered, all references to them include not only the line numbers but also the page on which the appropriate passage will be found. The only exception is in the case of *Milton* and *Jerusalem*; as the pagination of Blake's own editions of these works is indicated, further page references are unnecessary. Thus *Four Zoas* II, 398 (p. 278), refers to line 398 of the "Second Night" of *The Four Zoas*, and will be found on p. 278 of the fourth or later editions of *Poetry and Prose of William Blake*, edited by Geoffrey Keynes. *Jerusalem* 10, 20, refers to line 20 of plate 10 of *Jerusalem* and the passage will be readily found by turning to the text of *Jerusalem* in the same edition.

When reference is made to the page numbers of the original works as engraved and published by Blake himself, these are as given in the descriptions of the various works in Geoffrey Keynes, *A Bibliography of William Blake*, New York, 1921.

The numbers assigned to the Illustrations to Dante are those given in the portfolio, *Illustrations to the Divine Comedy of Dante by William Blake*, published in London by the National Art-Collections Fund in 1922.

After due deliberation, it was decided to give all quotations from the *Divine Comedy* in accordance with the translation of the Rev. Henry Francis Cary rather than in the Italian original or in some more recent English translation. First published in its entirety in 1814, this has remained, in spite of many shortcomings, the most familiar and readily accessible translation. The decision to employ it was based chiefly on the fact that it is the translation which was used by Blake, although he was familiar with at least some, if not all, of the poem in Italian as well. For purposes of this work, the Everyman's Library edition of Cary's translation, as reprinted in 1948, has been used.

CONTENTS

Purgatorio

Paradiso

Additional Drawings

PART I

INTRODUCTION

CHAPTER 1

HISTORY OF THE DESIGNS AND ENGRAVINGS

General Knowledge is Remote Knowledge; it is in
Particulars that Wisdom consists & Happiness too.
Vision of the Last Judgment, p. 645

WILLIAM BLAKE commenced work upon his illustrations to Dante's *Divine Comedy*
in the autumn of 1824, some two or three months before his sixty-seventh birthday.
He died three years later on August 12, 1827, leaving a complete series of designs,
the greater number of which, however, were only preliminary sketches. From these
drawings, he had at the time of his death made seven engravings, most of them unfinished in certain details, although nearing completion.

The task was undertaken at the instigation of John Linnell, a young artist whom
Blake had met in 1818 and with whom he remained on close terms of friendship for the
remainder of his life. The kindness which Linnell showed to Blake is well known. Not
only the loneliness but the extreme poverty of the most difficult years of Blake's life,
those from 1810 onward, came to an end with the development of this association. Linnell introduced Blake to a number of younger kindred spirits whose friendship greatly
brightened the older man's last years, and he also provided for him a steady, though
small income, through the purchase of his works. It was Linnell who suggested that
Blake engrave a series of plates based upon the drawings which Blake had made to
illustrate the Book of Job, and who undertook to give him regular payments as the
work progressed. When the Job project was drawing to a close, Linnell conceived the
idea of a Dante series as a means of providing Blake with continuing employment.

While the progress of the Job engravings can be followed very exactly on the basis
of a number of recently discovered documents, comprising the original agreement
between Blake and Linnell and some account of their transactions kept by Linnell,[1]
we are unfortunately not on such sure ground with regard to the history of the production of the Dante illustrations. The Blake-Linnell papers contain only one reference to them, a record of the payment of five pounds to Blake in 1825 "for sketches
of subjects from Dante."[2]

There is, however, good evidence for determining the date when the undertaking
was begun. One of the young artists introduced to Blake by Linnell was Samuel
Palmer, later to become Linnell's son-in-law. In a note written shortly after the interview, Palmer stated: "On Saturday, 9th October, 1824, Mr. Linnell called and went

[1] Edwin Wolf II, "The Blake-Linnell Accounts in the Library of Yale University," *Papers of
the Bibliographical Society of America*, XXXVII, 1943, pp. 1-22. Geoffrey Keynes, *Blake Studies*,
London, 1949, pp. 125-144.
[2] Keynes, *op. cit.*, p. 144.

with me to Mr. Blake. We found him lame in bed, of a scalded foot (or leg). There, not inactive, though sixty-seven years old, but hard-working on a bed covered with books sat he up like one of the Antique patriarchs, or a dying Michael Angelo. Thus and there was he making in the leaves of a great book (folio) the sublimest designs for his (not superior) Dante. . . . He designed them (100 I think) during a fortnight's illness in bed!"[3]

Aside from this, we get only occasional glimpses of Blake at work on the Dante designs. Henry Crabb Robinson, lawyer, journalist, and friend of many eminent literary figures, noted in his diary that on two occasions when he called on Blake in his rooms at Number 2, Fountain Court, Strand, he found him at work on the illustrations to Dante. Robinson informs us that Blake used the translation made by the Rev. Henry Francis Cary.[4] Blake's obituary and the account of a friend, Frederick Tatham, further inform us that he learned Italian in the course of only a few weeks in his sixty-seventh year in order to be able to read the *Divine Comedy* in the original as well.[5] It is impossible to say exactly when Blake commenced the engravings from his designs, although it seems unlikely that he would have begun a new set of engravings until he had finished those after the Book of Job which were completed at the very end of 1825.[6] The first evidence we have concerning the engravings occurs in a letter from Blake to Linnell dated July 2, 1826. During the next ten months there are a number of references to them in letters which have been preserved, the last on April 25, 1827, when Blake mentions that proofs have been taken of six plates and that he is about to start the engraving of the seventh.[7]

As to the amounts paid to Blake by John Linnell for the Dante designs, and to the method of payment, we have the account of Linnell's biographer: "The agreement between the two was to the effect that Blake was to proceed with the designs, doing as much or as little as he liked, and that Linnell was to go on paying him, as here-

[3] A. H. Palmer (ed.), *The Life and Letters of Samuel Palmer, Painter and Etcher*, London, 1892, p. 9. G. Grigson, *Samuel Palmer, the Visionary Years*, London, 1947, pp. 18-19 and p. 142n.

[4] These visits took place on Saturday, December 17, 1825, and on Friday, February 2, 1827. Thomas Sadler (ed.), *Diary, Reminiscences, and Correspondence of Henry Crabb Robinson*, Boston, 1869, II, pp. 28-30, 74. We shall have more to say later concerning the opinions of Dante which Blake expressed to Robinson on these occasions. Aside from that of Cary, completed in 1814, the only other translation of the entire *Divine Comedy* into English available at the time was that of Henry Boyd, published in 1802. While at work on his designs, Blake became acquainted with Cary.

[5] *The Literary Gazette*, August 18, 1827, pp. 540-541. Archibald G. B. Russell, *The Letters of William Blake together with a Life by Frederick Tatham*, London, 1906, p. 32. The former also informs us that the Italian edition of Dante used by Blake was that of "Sessi Velutello." This would appear to refer to *Dante con l'espositione di Christoforo Landino et di Alessandro Vellutello, Sopra la sua Comedia dell'Inferno, del Purgatorio, & del Paradiso, Venetia, Appresso Giovambattista, Marchiò Sessa, & fratelli, 1564* (another edition, 1578).
With reference to Blake's knowledge of Italian, see also the account given in the biographical sketch of Blake in John Thomas Smith's *Nollekens and His Times*, London, 1828, as reprinted in Arthur Symons, *William Blake*, London, 1907, p. 385.

[6] Keynes, *Blake Studies*, pp. 132-133.

[7] In addition to those cited, Blake mentions the Dante illustrations in five other letters (see Keynes, *Poetry and Prose*, letters 74, 76, 82, 83, 84, 86, and 88 on pp. 921-928).

tofore, two or three pounds a week, according to his needs, until they were finished."[8] In a letter written to Edwin J. Ellis on January 7, 1893, John Linnell, Jr., states that from an examination of his father's papers he had found that Blake had been paid in all one hundred three pounds, five shillings, and sixpence; the last payment was made on August 2, 1827, just ten days before Blake's death. Linnell further states that his father paid Blake's widow an additional twenty-six pounds on account of the drawings.[9]

As Linnell had commissioned the Dante illustrations, after Blake's death the drawings and copper plates passed into his possession. There they remained for the rest of Linnell's life, but little known and seldom seen by any outside of Linnell's own circle. Late in 1862, William Michael Rossetti, who was then engaged in preparing a catalogue of Blake's drawings, paintings, and engravings for the second volume of Alexander Gilchrist's *Life of William Blake*, called upon Linnell at his home near London and saw the designs.[10] Linnell died in 1882, but the drawings and plates continued in the possession of the family. In all the years that they belonged to the Linnell family, there were only two occasions on which a limited selection was exhibited publicly: at the winter exhibition of the Royal Academy in 1893, and at the Tate Gallery in the autumn of 1913, the latter exhibition being shown also in the first half of 1914 at the Whitworth Institute, Manchester, at the Nottingham Castle Art Museum, and at the National Gallery of Scotland, Edinburgh.

The drawings were sold at the auction rooms of Messrs. Christie, Manson and Woods on Friday, March 15, 1918, when Linnell's heirs disposed of their Blake collection. The Dante designs brought 7,300 guineas. After the sale, the majority of the series was divided among a number of public galleries where they are now to be found: the National Gallery of Victoria, Melbourne, Australia (36), the Tate Gallery, London (20), the British Museum (13), the City Museum and Art Gallery, Birmingham (6), the Ashmolean Museum, Oxford (3), and the Royal Institution of Cornwall, Truro (1). Twenty-three were acquired privately by Grenville Lindall Winthrop of New York City who bequeathed them to the Fogg Museum of Art of Harvard University in 1943.[11] The copper plates were eventually sold by the Linnells, although not at the same time, and are now in the collection of Lessing J. Rosenwald of Jenkintown, Pennsylvania.

There are one hundred and two drawings in the Dante series. Of these sixty-nine are based upon the *Inferno*, twenty upon the *Purgatorio* and ten upon the *Paradiso*.

[8] Alfred T. Story, *The Life of John Linnell*, London, 1892, I, pp. 230-231. Story states that the Dante drawings were commissioned in 1825. However, the evidence for 1824 as given in the quotation from Samuel Palmer above, which agrees with the date given by Gilchrist, is undoubtedly more reliable. (Alexander Gilchrist, *Life of William Blake with Selections from his Poems and Other Writings*, 2nd edn., London, 1880, I, p. 375.)

[9] Edwin J. Ellis, *The Real Blake*, London, 1907, p. 410. John Linnell, Jr., gives as the date of the beginning of the payments to Blake "the latter end of 1825." It is possible that payments did not start until the *engravings* were commenced.

[10] William Michael Rossetti, *The Rossetti Papers, 1862-1870*, London, 1903, pp. 17-18; *idem.*, *Some Reminiscences of William Michael Rossetti*, New York, 1906, II, pp. 306-307.

[11] For the present location of each of the drawings, see Appendix B.

There are three additional drawings which do not relate to specific incidents in the poem. One of these (number 101) is a schematic diagram of the circles of the *Inferno*, and the other two (numbers 100 and 102) discussed in the analysis in Part II, also probably refer to the *Inferno*.

The drawings are on large sheets of watercolor paper measuring 20⅝ by 14½ inches (52 by 37 cm.). Although they are all on sheets of the same size, they are oriented differently; sixty-three of them occupy the page horizontally, while thirty-nine are vertical. Blake drew his original designs very sketchily with pencil. As the compositions began to take a form which pleased him, he would draw his lines more precisely and commence to add detail. When he was satisfied that a portion was as he wished it in the final form, he would begin to outline in india ink, usually with a pen, but sometimes with a fine brush, using thin lines made with long, sweeping strokes. Next, roughly massed washes in various colors would make their appearance, to be worked up eventually into carefully finished watercolors. Few of the drawings reached this final state. Some never passed the pencil stage; a number are in pencil and india ink only. The greater majority have the color begun in a rough way and are incomplete in detail. Most, but not all, are inscribed with the canto number, and occasionally with a line reference based upon Cary's translation. These inscriptions are mostly in india ink, although a few are in pencil. A small number are in addition signed with Blake's monogram. Several of the more unfinished designs have pencilled notations, occasionally of some length, which are of considerable importance for the insight which they give into Blake's ideas concerning the *Divine Comedy*. These are given in full in the discussion of the individual drawings on which they occur.[12]

As mentioned previously, Blake made engravings of seven of the designs, all of subjects taken from the *Inferno*. Neither numbered nor inscribed, the engraved surface measures 9½ by 13 inches, and the plate mark approximately 11 by 14 inches. The engravings are printed in black upon sheets measuring 13½ by 21 inches. They were issued as loose leaves or bound up in an oblong folio at two guineas a set, with an accompanying label headed "Blake's Illustrations of Dante" and giving for each plate an appropriate brief quotation from Cary's translation.[13] As Blake died before the plates were finished, very few impressions can have been made in his lifetime. Linnell doubtless printed others after the plates passed into his possession.[14]

A portfolio of excellent collotype reproductions of all the drawings was published in London in 1922 in a limited edition of 250 copies by the National Art-Collections Fund. This volume contains a one-page introduction, but no discussion of the individual designs. One plate is given in color. The size of the reproductions is reduced from that of the originals, being approximately that of the engravings which Blake made from the designs. Aside from this publication, reproductions of a few of the drawings are occasionally to be met with in books, articles, and catalogues,[15] but the

[12] It is, of course, very possible that more of the drawings had such notations originally, which Blake erased or covered over with watercolor as the design became further developed.

[13] Geoffrey Keynes, *A Bibliography of William Blake*, New York, 1921, pp. 182-185.

[14] Each copper plate has stamped on the back, "Pontifex & Co., 22 Lisle Street, Soho, London."

[15] The first selection of the drawings to be published, eight in all, appeared to illustrate an

great majority of them have not been published elsewhere. Reproductions of individual engravings are to be found more frequently, but they have been published as a group only twice.[16]

A complete list of important references to the Dante illustrations will be found in the Bibliography, where they are distinguished by an asterisk (*) placed in front of the appropriate entries. Considering the fact that ever since the appearance of Gilchrist's *Life* in 1863, the Dante designs have been recognized as among Blake's most important works, it is remarkable that the present vast amount of published material on Blake contains only the most scanty reference to them. Aside from brief and general notices in books and articles which treat of Blake's life and art, there are only two essays which have the Dante illustrations as their principal subject, those by William Butler Yeats (1896) and Guy Eglinton (1924). Even these are very general in scope, consisting of a brief stylistic appreciation of the designs, to which Yeats adds an interesting study of Blake's opinions concerning Dante's philosophy.

---

article by W. B. Yeats, "William Blake and his Illustrations to the Divine Comedy," *The Savoy*, II, 1896, no. 3, pp. 41-57; no. 4, pp. 25-41; no. 5, pp. 30-36. The greatest number reproduced at once, aside from the National Art-Collections Fund portfolio, was thirty-two, in an edition of Melville Best Anderson's translation of the *Divine Comedy* published in New York by the Heritage Press in 1944.

[16] In an edition of Cary's translation of the *Inferno* published in New York by Cheshire House in 1931 and in Geoffrey Keynes, *William Blake's Engravings*, London, 1950, plates 69-75. The first individual engraving to be reproduced was the last of the series, "The Circle of Traitors: Dante Striking Against Bocca degli Abati," in Gilchrist's *Life*, 1st edn., 1863, I, p. 334.

CHAPTER 2

BLAKE'S SYMBOLISM

~~~~~~

I must Create a System or be enslav'd by another Man's.

Jerusalem 10, 20

~~~~~~

IN SPEAKING of the basic aims of his art, Blake says: "The Nature of my Work is Visionary or Imaginative. . . . This world of Imagination is the world of Eternity. . . . There Exist in that Eternal World the Permanent Realities of Every Thing which we see reflected in this Vegetable Glass of Nature."[1] Thus art was to him not only a means of communicating his own beliefs to others, but actually a primary source of knowledge concerning the divine plan. He defined poetry, painting, and music as "the three Powers in Man of conversing with Paradise, which the flood did not Sweep away."[2] Imagination—he always calls it "the Divine Imagination"—he considered to be not mere fancy, but a means of visionary perception which God has granted to man to preserve in him a knowledge of his eternal self even while in his fallen state. Dealing with a theme of this character, he found—as other visionary poets have done—that language which has been devised for the everyday activities of this world will not adequately convey his message. He must rely to a large extent on images; these, by their very nature, demand not only perceptiveness on his part in the choosing of adequate symbols to suggest his meaning, but sympathetic imaginative understanding on the part of the reader.

Most poets in search of a readily comprehensible symbolism have employed a traditional mythology which, because of its historical or religious character, is generally known. Thus Dante and Milton drew their images principally from Christian and classical sources. Blake, however, did not choose to use an established mythology and the passage quoted at the head of this section tells us why. The age of neo-classicism had reduced much classical imagery to conceits and trivialities; the dogma of religious sects, he was convinced, had misconstrued much of the material provided by the Bible. Classical mythology he consequently rejected almost completely. From the Bible he drew continually. In most cases, however, his use of Biblical sources is not conventional, but based upon a richly symbolical interpretation of his own, the essence of which has been well set forth by a recent critic: "The Bible [to Blake] is not a moral code and a commentary on it: it is a series of visions."[3] Finally, as these two sources—and such other less familiar mythology as the nordic and the oriental from which he borrowed extensively—did not fully meet his needs, he created an

---

[1] *Vision of the Last Judgment*, pp. 638-639. [2] *ibid.*, p. 643.

[3] Bernard Blackstone, *English Blake*, Cambridge, England, 1949, p. 347. Blackstone gives a full discussion of the influence of the Bible upon Blake on pp. 346-366. For Blake and the classics, see Blackstone, pp. 205-207, 424-429, and Mark Schorer, *William Blake, the Politics of Vision*, New York, 1946, pp. 34-35.

involved mythology of his own.[4] To this mythology he left us no key and but few obscure hints, for reasons which he set forth in the following statement: "The wisest of the Ancients consider'd what is not too Explicit as the fittest for Instruction, because it rouzes the faculties to act."[5] Its structure can be pieced together only by a careful and perceptive reading of all his works and by a study of their accompanying designs. The reader is still called upon to provide for himself much of the insight necessary to understanding. Such a brief examination of the main points of Blake's mythology as that which follows can only serve as a general guide, and must be considered as such and not as a formula for solving a complex puzzle.[6]

When on the evening of Saturday, December 10, 1825, Henry Crabb Robinson and Blake dined at the home of the collector, Charles Aders, the discussion turned to religious questions. "I had suggested on very obvious philosophical grounds," Robinson says in his account of their conversation in his diary, "the *impossibility* of supposing an immortal being created—an eternity *a parte post* without an eternity *a parte ante*. . . . His eye brightened on my saying this, and he eagerly concurred— 'To be sure it is impossible. We are all co-existent with God—members of the Divine body. We are all partakers of the Divine nature.' . . . On my asking in what light he viewed the great question concerning the Divinity of Jesus Christ, he said—*'He is the only God.'* But then he added—'And so am I and so are you.' "[7] This is one of the few recorded instances of Blake's conversation concerning the nature of his beliefs, but it touches on a fundamental starting-point in a discussion of his ideas. All of Blake's philosophy stems from his acceptance of the statement in Genesis that God created man in His own image. There is, then, in every man the spark of the divine and the capacity to become one with God. But as man is the image of God, so is God the transcendent image of man. Jesus is referred to throughout Blake's poems as the "Divine Humanity."

> Thou art a Man, God is no more,
> Thine own Humanity learn to Adore.
> The Everlasting Gospel, p. 136

By the development of the understanding in its widest sense, under the guidance of the imagination, each of us may ultimately return to the perfect unity with God

---

[4] One cannot, of course, in a literal sense create a mythology, which is by definition traditional. Blake uses in his prophetic books characters with names of his own devising who are not to be thought of as individuals, but as personifications of human attributes. Symbolic in their intent, and freed in their actions from normal human limitations, they have many of the characteristics of the figures of ancient and widely-known mythologies. However, Blake wished to be sure that his symbolism would not be obscured by prior associations and thus chose to reject accepted mythology and create new personifications. Because of their nature, it is convenient to interpret the definition of mythology somewhat freely and to think of them as mythological personages.

[5] Letter to Rev. Dr. Trusler, August 23, 1799, p. 834.

[6] For those who wish to go into Blake's beliefs and symbolism more thoroughly, numerous excellent commentaries are now available and will be found listed in the Bibliography. The first extensive study of the subject was made by Algernon Charles Swinburne in *William Blake, a Critical Essay*, London, 1868; the next by E. J. Ellis and W. B. Yeats in *The Works of William Blake*, London, 1893.

[7] From Robinson's Diary as given in Symons, *William Blake*, p. 255.

which is eternal life. "He who sees the Infinite in all things, sees God."[8] Man, if he were enlightened, would realize this and would seek to develop his power of understanding rather than strive to establish his position in a worldly sense.

What, then, accounts for the present condition of man? The answer is that the world of our physical consciousness is a fallen world: "This Earth breeds not our happiness."[9] How humanity came to its present state; how salvation may be achieved; and a visionary realization of the nature of the Eternal World—these are the elements of Blake's epic. Blake announces this theme in his own characteristic phraseology in the opening lines of *Jerusalem*:[10]

> Of the Sleep of Ulro! and of the passage through
> Eternal Death! and of the awakening to Eternal Life.
>
> This theme calls me in sleep night after night, & ev'ry morn
> Awakes me at sun-rise; then I see the Saviour over me
> Spreading his beams of love & dictating the words of this mild song.
>
> Jerusalem 4, 1-5[11]

Blake thus states his intention quite clearly. Under the guidance of the Divine Humanity, Jesus—"the Poetic Genius" as he frequently calls Him, who through the Divine Imagination inspires men in creative moments—Blake proposes to explore the realms of human experience: the dark unknown out of which consciousness first comes; the tormented journey through a world of doubt which leads to the mysterious death of the body; the hope of ultimate salvation.

After the lines given above, the opening passages of *Jerusalem* continue in what at first seems an obscure vein, but one which on closer examination and with growing familiarity gives in brief compass much of the substance of the poem. The Saviour now addresses man:

> "Awake! awake O sleeper of the land of shadows, wake! expand!
> I am in you and you in me, mutual in love divine:
> Fibres of love from man to man thro' Albion's pleasant land.
> In all the dark Atlantic vale down from the hills of Surrey
> A black water accumulates; return Albion! return!
> Thy brethren call thee, and thy fathers and thy sons,
> Thy nurses and thy mothers, thy sisters and thy daughters
> Weep at thy soul's disease, and the Divine Vision is darken'd,
> Thy Emanation that was wont to play before thy face,
> Beaming forth with her daughters into the Divine bosom:

[8] *There Is No Natural Religion, II*, p. 148.

[9] Letter to Thomas Butts, November 22, 1802, p. 861.

[10] All of Blake's earlier prophetic books deal with certain aspects of this basic theme. Beginning with *The Four Zoas* (c. 1795-1804) a synthesis is sought, to be further developed in *Milton* (1804-1808). *Jerusalem* (1804- c. 1810) presents Blake's beliefs in their most complete form and is the basic source for any study of his mythology.

[11] The great influence upon Blake of his favorite poet, Milton, is readily apparent from these lines. Compare the first ten lines of *Paradise Lost*. The opening passages of both *Milton* and *The Four Zoas* announce the same theme with slightly varying phraseology.

Where hast thou hidden thy Emanation, lovely Jerusalem,
From the vision and fruition of the Holy-one?
I am not a God afar off, I am a brother and friend:
Within your bosoms I reside, and you reside in me:
Lo! we are One, forgiving all Evil, Not seeking recompense.
Ye are my members, O ye sleepers of Beulah, land of shades!"

But the perturbed Man away turns down the valleys dark:
"Phantom of the over heated brain! shadow of immortality!
Seeking to keep my soul a victim to thy Love! which binds
Man, the enemy of man, into deceitful friendships,
Jerusalem is not! her daughters are indefinite:
By demonstration man alone can live, and not by faith.
My mountains are my own, and I will keep them to myself:
The Malvern and the Cheviot, the Wolds, Plinlimmon & Snowdon[12]
Are mine: here will I build my Laws of Moral Virtue.
Humanity shall be no more, but war & princedom & victory!"

Jerusalem 4, 6-31

In these lines, the poet passes at once to the consideration of error and the Fall which follows its acceptance. Albion, the Eternal Man, symbol of mankind considered as a whole, has fallen into a state in which doubt is possible; this is the state which Blake calls "Beulah," upon which we shall enlarge later. On the one hand, the divine or imaginative aspect of man's nature, personified by the Saviour, keeps reminding him of his brotherhood with all men through their common kinship with God: "I am not a God afar off, I am a brother and friend: Lo! we are One, forgiving all evil, Not seeking recompense." Such is the way to eternal joy: love of all men as Sons of God through individual understanding and forgiveness. "Forgiveness of Sins. This alone is the Gospel, & this is the Life & Immortality brought to light by Jesus."[13] However, the purely rational side of man's nature replies to the imaginative by asserting the arguments of self-interest, often symbolized—though not directly here —as the Spectre or Satan. Other men are not brothers, but rivals; the fittest alone will survive and any means to that end are justified. The idea that complete liberty of the mind and spirit[14] will bring happiness is false since it will bring freedom to others

[12] We may agree wholeheartedly with S. Foster Damon (*William Blake: His Philosophy and Symbols*, Boston and New York, 1924, p. 186) that these constant geographical references "sully sadly the poetic dignity of *Jerusalem*." They seem to have been an attempt to parallel with English equivalents the listing of Hebrew place names found in the Bible. The result for both books is unfortunate, although the Bible may be excused as having the additional function of serving as an historical record, while *Jerusalem* is purely an epic poem. There is apparently little logical consistency in the use of English place names, except for a few instances such as "Tyburn's Brook." The meaning is, however, generally clear, even if the poetic effect is regrettable. For example, in this case the catalogue of mountains symbolizes the tendency of man to stick to his deeply-rooted prejudices and errors at all costs—prejudices which for most of us loom as large as our native mountains and to which we are as passionately and irrationally attached.

[13] *The Everlasting Gospel*, p. 131.

[14] "Jerusalem is called Liberty among the Children of Albion." (*Jerusalem* 54, 5) As will be seen, every male personification in Blake's myth has a feminine counterpart known as the "emanation." Hence the full title of Blake's major prophetic book is *Jerusalem, The Emanation*

as well as to one's self, while it is in one's interest to enslave them. Man can live only by trusting to the evidence of his senses to guide him to a practical knowledge and control over his environment; faith, being but a figment of the imagination, is an unreal passing fancy and no more. Man makes the choice offered him by selfhood. Error is embraced; truth rejected. The Fall takes place and man finds himself in the "valleys dark" of this world: a world where the divine light is almost shut out and we can perceive only the material; a world in which liberty must yield to the control of law; a world which deems love a sign of weakness and gives its applause to those who gain their triumphs at the expense of the death and suffering of others.

> All Love is lost! terror succeeds, & Hatred instead of Love,
> And stern demands of Right & Duty instead of Liberty.
> Jerusalem 22, 10-11

The world of our present experience is, therefore, a fallen world. By his acceptance of error, man has voluntarily surrendered his divinity and given himself over to the dark torment of mortal life. The sufferings of this world are not a punishment inflicted upon man for disobedience to God's law, for God knows no law but only love and forgiveness. Man has made his free choice, and in error has become a subject of Satan's realm of cruelty.

> . . . I called for compassion; compassion mock'd;
> Mercy & pity threw the grave stone over me, & with lead
> And iron bound it over me for ever.   Jerusalem 10, 53-55

In the eternal state, the perceptions of man had been infinite:

> . . . contracting their Exalted Senses
> They behold Multitude, or Expanding they behold as one,
> As One Man all the Universal family.
> Four Zoas I, 462-464 (p. 264)

With the Fall, however, the universality of man's vision is lost and only the imperfect organic senses remain: "For man has closed himself up, till he sees all things thro' narrow chinks of his cavern."[15] The omnipotent has now become the pathetically fragile mortal man, limited in perspective and preyed upon by forces of nature which he cannot control:

> Ah weak & wide astray! Ah shut in narrow doleful form,
> Creeping in reptile flesh upon the bosom of the ground!
> The Eye of Man a little narrow orb, clos'd up & dark,
> Scarcely beholding the great light, conversing with the Void;
> The Ear a little shell, in small volutions shutting out
> All melodies & comprehending only Discord and Harmony;
> The Tongue a little moisture fills, a little food it cloys,
> A little sound it utters & its cries are faintly heard.
> Milton 5, 19-26

---

of *The Giant Albion*. For what was doubtless the source of Blake's decision to use Jerusalem as a key symbol of his mythology, see Galatians iv, 26.

[15] *The Marriage of Heaven and Hell*, p. 187.

Man in this state, however, does not recognize nor admit his weakness. Rather he postulates that truth is to be learned by codifying the data of the senses; that which lies beyond the range of their observation must be ignored as unreal:

> In ignorance to view a small portion & think that All,
> And call it demonstration, blind to all the simple rules of life.
>
> Four Zoas VII b, 182-183 (p. 327)

Thus do man-made systems grow up. Based upon the limited knowledge available to the "Natural Man," they are at once endowed by him with divine authority, so that other men may be enslaved to his selfhood:

> No more could they rise at will
> In the infinite void, but bound down
> To earth by their narrowing perceptions
> They lived a period of years;
>
> . . . .
>
> And form'd laws of prudence, and call'd them
> The eternal laws of God.
>
> Urizen 499-502; 507-508 (p. 233)

Hence, in Blake's view, all accepted social systems become endowed sooner or later with tyrannical power that destroys human liberty. No other course could be possible in a world ruled by Satan. Most men will conform through ignorance or fear; those who do not will be ruthlessly destroyed by the "blind world-rulers of this life."[16] All accepted orders exist for the benefit of those who spend "their lives in Curbing & Governing other People's by the Various arts of Poverty & Cruelty of all kinds."[17] Since men cannot develop their selfhoods without hindering others, they are bound either to try to turn established systems to their own uses, or to be enslaved or destroyed by those systems. Governments establish their hold by rigid laws and increase their influence by wars. Social and economic systems give power and wealth to the few at the price of the degradation of the many. Society even perverts love: the alternative to rigid repression or a forced union of people who may prove incompatible is all too often either ostracism or disease. Organized religion is the worst of all, for it claims for itself divine authority and lends its sanction to the political and economic tyrannies which realize its usefulness as a repressive tool. Claiming to uphold the moral law as decreed by God, it in reality commits the supreme apostasy of setting Satan up for worship under the name of God.

Thus it was that Blake, devoutly religious in all his thought and works, exhibited the apparent paradox of vehemently opposing organized religion. All churches, he felt, based their doctrines upon human precepts and not upon those of God. Earthly religion preaches what it claims is God's law, and stresses not forgiveness of sins but punishment for transgression. But to Blake "The Gospel is Forgiveness of Sins & has No Moral Precepts," and further he believed that "Every Religion that Preaches Vengeance for Sin is the Religion of the Enemy & Avenger and not of the Forgiver

---

[16] Ephesians vi, 12. Quoted in Greek on the title page of *The Four Zoas*, because the King James version had modified the passage.

[17] *Vision of the Last Judgment*, p. 650.

of Sin, and their God is Satan, Named by the Divine Name."[18] To him it appeared that the churches exalted the Decalogue and its author, the "Angry God of this World," while presenting Jesus as a secondary figure, cast in a sentimental light, far removed from His revolutionary role as the advocate of forgiveness.[19] To Blake, this world is itself Hell, and its God, while called Jehovah by the churches, is in reality Satan. "In Hell all is Self Righteousness; there is no such thing there as Forgiveness of Sin; he who does Forgive Sin is Crucified as an Abettor of Criminals, & he who performs Works of Mercy in Any shape whatever is punish'd &, if possible, destroy'd, not thro' envy or Hatred or Malice, but thro' Self Righteousness that thinks it does God service, which God is Satan."[20] All of the blindness of human life to the true glory of the eternal world thus resolves itself into the essential error of subordinating the individual to man-made systems, while God intended for him no system, but only self-determination—liberty in its widest sense. Blake sums up his entire point of view in the pithy and marvelously striking and compact epigram in *The Marriage of Heaven and Hell*, "Prisons are built with stones of Law, Brothels with bricks of Religion."[21] Worldly institutions are thus "A pretence of Art to destroy Art; a pretence of Liberty to destroy Liberty; a pretence of Religion to destroy Religion."[22]

So far we have indicated the two main stages in Blake's "Circle of Destiny."[23] In eternity man was a perfect unity, coexistent with God, comprehending all things through divine intelligence, unrestrained by such limits as time and space. Through error the Fall has taken place, unity has been destroyed, and we—the fallen men—exist in a shrunken world of inert matter, enfeebled shadows of our eternal selves, guided by the imperfect perceptions of our five senses.

> Now the Starry Heavens are fled from the mighty limbs of Albion.
> *Jerusalem* 75, 27

The last words of Albion, as the Fall took place, were "Hope is banish'd from me."[24] However, he failed to take into account God's mercy and His infinite capacity for understanding and forgiveness.

[18] The first of these quotations is from Blake's annotations to *An Apology for the Bible in a Series of Letters Addressed to Thomas Paine* by Richard Watson, Bishop of London (Keynes, *Poetry and Prose*, p. 766); the second from plate 52 of *Jerusalem*.

[19] For Blake's own account of the contrast between his conception of Jesus and a conventional one, see the passages from his notebook which are now collected under the title of *The Everlasting Gospel (Poetry and Prose*, pp. 131-143).

[20] *Vision of the Last Judgment*, p. 651.

[21] One of the "Proverbs of Hell," p. 183. A major difficulty of Blake's symbolism is his frequent use of the same symbols with different meanings, requiring great discrimination on the reader's part as to what is intended. Thus "Hell" may be employed in a more usual sense to indicate our present world of suffering; on the other hand, as used here it signifies the mental attitude of the more radical and imaginative portion of humanity as viewed from the static "Heaven" of the conventional "angels."

[22] *Jerusalem* 43, 35-36.

[23] For a much more detailed account of the setting and characters of Blake's myth than can be given here, see Milton Percival, *William Blake's "Circle of Destiny,"* New York, 1938, pp. 5-76. The book takes its title from *Four Zoas* I, 83 (p. 254).

[24] *Jerusalem* 47, 17.

God is within & without: he is even in the depths of Hell!

Jerusalem 12, 15

Man has fallen through error; to be redeemed he must recognize error and cast it out. As the essence of the unfallen world is life in its most intense and vital form, so the opposite pole of the Fall would be annihilation. To save man from the pit of chaos from which there could be no return, God in His mercy has set limits to the Fall to grant man the time and opportunity to acquire understanding, and to reject the error into which his selfhood has betrayed him.

These limits are two. First there is "Adam," the Natural Man, the "limit of contraction." However far man may fall, he still has something of a mind and something of an imagination; a spark of divinity remains and thus hope of redemption is never lost. The second limit is the "limit of opacity," the state which Blake names "Satan." The error and evil of this Fallen World are so monstrous that even the contracted capacities of the Natural Man may eventually perceive them, and error once recognized can be cast out. Thus after the Fall, the possibility of regeneration remains. The second part of Blake's myth—following upon the account of the Fall, its origin, and the nature of the Fallen World—is concerned with the processes of regeneration: the recognition and rejection of error, and ultimate salvation.

> There is a limit of Opakeness and a limit of Contraction
> In every Individual Man, and the limit of Opakeness
> Is named Satan, and the limit of Contraction is named Adam.
> But when Man sleeps in Beulah, the Saviour in Mercy takes
> Contraction's Limit, and of the Limit he forms Woman, That
> Himself may in process of time be born Man to redeem.
> But there is no Limit of Expansion; there is no Limit of Translucence
> In the bosom of Man for ever from eternity to eternity.

Jerusalem 42, 29-36

At the beginning of one of his earliest prophetic works, *The Marriage of Heaven and Hell*, Blake states a principle which remains fundamental throughout the later development of his ideas. "Without Contraries is no progression. Attraction and Repulsion, Reason and Energy, Love and Hate, are necessary to Human existence." Blake realizes that progress is not possible in a static state; constant tension and ebb and flow are the essentials for arriving at truth. Nothing, therefore, is really bad except inaction and complacency; the active evils of human experience fulfil a function in that they make error apparent so that truth may be embraced. In all earthly experience, whether spiritual, intellectual, or merely material—as, for example, the alternation of night and day—we find contraries involved. It is natural that this should be so: error triumphs only when, through misguidance or for the sake of simplification, the diversities found in all phases of experience are denied and one contrary is set up by law as right at the expense of the other. This over-simplification is a refusal to recognize the essential fact that human experience is subtle and complex—yet this negation is precisely the end to which rigid systems lead. The free play of contraries—even where one has in it a preponderance of evil—will eventually give birth to liberty; denial of action by restriction enslaves both parties concerned. This idea is expressed

15

in reversed writing in the design which forms the heading for the second book of *Milton*: "Contraries are Positives. A Negation is not a Contrary."[25]

It is in the light of the above concept that we must consider Blake's views of creation and of the created world. On the one hand this is a world of strange and monstrous natural forces against which man must battle for survival. The cyclic regularity of many natural phenomena has an unbending quality akin to that of the social laws to which man has surrendered himself in an attempt to maintain himself against nature and his fellows. Caught up in the workings of a vast machine, man is forced to renounce liberty and to deny imagination. All tends to the annihilation of the essential humanity. In this aspect we live in the world of Satan.

However, as we have seen, Blake believed that in another aspect this world exists to prevent man from falling completely into the abyss where chaos rules unchecked. As such our present world—"Generation" is Blake's name for it—is the gift of God. The Fall has been great, but spiritual perception has not yet ceased and error can still be recognized and cast out.

> O holy Generation, Image of regeneration!
> O point of mutual forgiveness between Enemies!
> Birthplace of the Lamb of God incomprehensible!
> Jerusalem 7, 65-67

From this it will be seen that Blake's ideas about the creation differ widely from the conventional interpretation of the Biblical account. This is not a basically good world which man has perverted through his own wilful violation of eternal law; it is a fallen state through which man must pass in the process of regeneration after his error in renouncing the world of eternity. The satanic and the divine contraries are constantly at war within it to the end that man may ultimately recognize error and reject it. Our world is not God's original creation to bring order out of eternal chaos. The eternal order is one of unity, harmony and understanding: chaos came only with the Fall.[26] This world exists, through the grace of God, as a limit to the Fall—as a place of respite where man can redevelop the spiritual side of his nature, which in eternity he deliberately renounced, and can thus find the pathway back to salvation. Thanks to God's gift of imagination—which is never quite absent in any individual, though more developed in some than in others—man can still aspire to the divine. And God in His love for man has manifested Himself in this world in the life of Jesus so that man may learn that the way of regeneration is to be found not in unyielding rational law but in denial of the selfhood and in forgiveness of others, even as God forgives him. With this realization, man will recapture the infinite capacities of his eternal self. "Whenever any Individual Rejects Error & Embraces Truth, a Last Judgment passes upon that Individual."[27]

---

[25] Inscriptions in reversed writing occur in a number of places in *Milton* and *Jerusalem*, and have particular significance. They indicate truths that are apparent to those in the unfallen state, but are inverted by the Natural Man of this world; as seen from beyond the confines of the created world, looking in, they would appear the right way around.

[26] "Many suppose that before the Creation All was Solitude & Chaos. This is the most pernicious Idea that can enter the Mind, as it takes away all sublimity from the Bible & Limits All Existence to Creation & to Chaos. . . . Eternity Exists, and All things in Eternity, Independent of Creation which was an act of Mercy." (*Vision of the Last Judgment*, p. 648.)

[27] *ibid.*, p. 647.

We have now examined in some detail Blake's views concerning the nature of the Fallen World of our present existence and its social institutions. The life of this world is but one of the four stages of the entire "Circle of Destiny" of Blake's system. As all of these spheres of existence appear frequently in Blake's work, and as they are important for understanding his views concerning the Hell, Purgatory, and Paradise of Dante's poem, we shall proceed to examine the three remaining steps of the cycle. First it will be well to summarize them briefly, using Blake's name for each stage, terms which establish key symbols in his mythology.

First we have the world which Blake calls "Eden." This is the highest level of existence. From this mortal man has fallen and to it he will return after his recognition and rejection of error. Each of Blake's three major prophecies ends with a vision of Eden regained. The life of Eden is, however, so intense that even the soul which has not embraced error cannot remain permanently in its exalted state. Just as relaxation, refreshment, and rest are necessary to mind and body, so are they to the soul. This is found in the state of existence known as "Beulah." In this world of repose, the soul is restored for its awakening again to the pure ecstasy of Eden. In Beulah, however, error is possible. The soul may become enamoured of inaction instead of longing to return to the intense activity of Eden. When the soul thus accepts error, it sinks into a deep sleep and the Fall takes place. The third stage is "Ulro," the void and chaos of nonentity. After the Fall, souls wander aimlessly in this void until, through the mercy of God, they are reborn into consciousness in our present life. Blake's name for our world, as we have already seen, is "Generation"; its function is to give man the opportunity to recognize error through experience and, by rejecting it, to regain his immortal stature.

Before proceeding to examine these stages in more detail, it is important to realize that Blake very frequently presents his ideas from a number of different points of reference. Thus the Circle of Destiny may be regarded as embracing the entire evolution of human experience in a universal sense. Generation will then cover the course of human history from the beginning to the present as we normally think of it. However, this cycle may be applied to the individual as well and may represent the entire passage of a particular soul from its fall from Eden, through the infinite vicissitudes of physical, mental, emotional and imaginative experience in the life of this world, until the time of ultimate salvation. This duality applies to all the steps along the way. For example, the Last Judgment may be thought of as the final universal rejection of error, at which time the created world will cease to exist; however, we must remember from the quotation just given that "Whenever any Individual Rejects Error & Embraces Truth, a Last Judgment passes upon that Individual." Thus in our present life we may become, through the power of imagination, capable as individuals of comprehending events in the eternal order, where all things exist outside of the bounds of time as we know it in this world.[28]

The reader must constantly remind himself, therefore, that Blake's symbols often have several possible interpretations. Not only may the same symbol be used with different and quite divergent meanings depending upon the connotation, but each

---

[28] Hence Blake can say, as though from his own experience, concerning one of his designs: "The Last Judgment is not Fable or Allegory, but Vision . . . I have represented it as I saw it; to different People it appears differently as every thing else does." (*Ibid.*, pp. 637-638.)

of these meanings may be applicable on a number of levels: they may concern humanity in general, they may deal with individual experience, they may even be autobiographical, and they may involve any combination of these factors. Blake without doubt purposely avoided being too specific in order to test and to develop the reader's own powers of discernment. However, with familiarity there will seldom be confusion as to Blake's intention; he merely demands discrimination on our part.

It must also be remembered that Blake interprets the word "human" very widely, endowing with remarkable visionary life not only all living forms as we usually think of them, but even those which to our senses seem completely inert. "To see a World in a Grain of Sand and a Heaven in a Wild Flower"[29] is but a particularly striking statement of the insistence, which runs through all of Blake's work, that every aspect of the created universe is permeated with the immortal spirit and only awaits the time when it shall burst into joyous life. We are thus called upon to widen our understandings to take in levels of experience beyond those which readily suggest themselves to most of us. At the same time as we seek to comprehend through imagination the grandeur of the *whole*, which in its perfect unity reaches beyond time and space and the world of our sensory perceptions, we must enter too most intimately into the spiritual world of the most seemingly insignificant particle and learn to conceive of it as a separate individuality. The Circle of Destiny, as the closing lines of *Jerusalem* proclaim, is the history of the totality of spiritual experience:

> All *Human* Forms identified, even Tree, Metal, Earth & Stone: all
> Human Forms identified, living, going forth & returning wearied
> Into the Planetary lives of Years, Months, Days & Hours; reposing,
> And then Awakening into his Bosom in the Life of Immortality.
>
> Jerusalem 99, 1-4

To enlarge somewhat upon the nature of the different stages of the Circle, let us first consider Eden. Life for Blake is synonymous with energy: "Energy is Eternal Delight."[30] Hence Eden, where life is most complete, is a place of joyous and overflowing energy. Pure energy, pure imagination, and pure spirit are here one; their united radiance is that of the Spiritual Sun, which is the symbol of Eden. Above all, Eden is a world of intellectual liberty and unbounded mental activity—activity that arises not from the contemplation of truth that is already known, but from the mental joy of continual discovery. It is a world of unity, brotherhood, and oneness with God. There is no spiritual division here, no negation, no repose—but joy in unceasing energy. As such, it is an active masculine world into which the fundamental schism of differentiation of sexes can never come.[31] It is a world of pure vision in which the spiritual nature and unity of all things is triumphantly realized; time and space do not exist here, because they have no meaning for the soul and intellect that can view all things simultaneously. Forgiveness, love, knowledge, and creative energy all combine to realize in Eden the complete development of mental and spiritual liberty. It is the state of

---

[29] From the MS. poem, "Auguries of Innocence," p. 118.
[30] *The Marriage of Heaven and Hell*, p. 182.
[31] "Humanity is far above Sexual organization." (*Jerusalem* 79, 73-74.)

perfection of the universal humanity, in which the individuality is ever apparent too. Blake sums up its essential nature in the following lines:

> Our wars are wars of life, & wounds of love
> With intellectual spears, & long winged arrows of thought.
> Mutual in one another's love and wrath all renewing
> We live as One Man; for contracting our infinite senses
> We behold multitude, or expanding, we behold as one,
> As One Man all the Universal Family, and that One Man
> We call Jesus the Christ; and he in us, and we in him
> Live in perfect harmony in Eden, the land of life,
> Giving, receiving, and forgiving each other's trespasses.
>
> Jerusalem 38, 14-22

Man cannot live for ever in the realm of pure thought; he must descend for rest from the daytime of intellectual activity to a night ruled by the affections. Thus as Eden is the world of the intellect and is ruled by the sun, so Beulah is the region of the emotional life and its symbol is the moon.

As mankind—symbolized by the Universal Man, Albion—sinks into repose in Beulah, the separation of the sexes takes place. To comfort and to delight man, a feminine counterpart comes into being, called by Blake the "emanation." Every soul in Beulah is thus divided into a masculine identity and a feminine emanation.[32] At the moment of return to Eden, the division of sexes will again disappear, the soul being rejoined into perfect unity.

We have seen that the ideal of love in the sense of the love of God and of the universal brotherhood of mankind is the dominant feature of the life of Eden. In a similar sense, sexual love finds its perfect realization in Beulah. Love which forgets the selfhood through wholehearted affection for another; the joy of a physical union which can, even momentarily, lift two separate beings into a higher state of mutual adoration and spiritual harmony; earthly love in all its highest manifestations, both emotional and physical, and purged of its base ingredients—lust, jealousy, and repression: such is the sexual love of Beulah. Blake saw very clearly that, while much of the sorrow of a fallen world is bound up with a distorted conception of love, the answer does not lie in an attempt to deny its physical aspect. To do so is to stifle the vital energy that is the very core of human existence, creating far more misery than it can cure and turning much potential joy into frustration and sorrow. Physical love, one of the greatest gifts of God, has been perverted in the Fallen World because of man's lust for self-gratification and woman's passion for jealous dominion over her mate. As with everything else, the answer is developed understanding that the way to happiness is to be found in helping others to their own fulfilment rather than in seeking one's own ends at their expense. So regarded, Blake considered physical love, the most intimate of human experiences, to be the most likely means of awakening the average person to the realization of the existence of an eternal world beyond the range of normal earthly perceptions. Ideal physical love is thus a vital step in the development

---

[32] The emanation of Albion is Jerusalem: mankind to be restored to the heights of mental and spiritual self-realization requires the guidance of liberty. See note 14 above.

of the human understanding as it searches to comprehend the love of God. As such its place is in Beulah, the gateway to Eden.

While Beulah exists to restore the soul, the danger arises that the soul may be lulled into passivity by its delights and cease to aspire to the renewed mental activity of Eden, which is its proper home. Such failure on man's part to exercise to the full the capacities with which God had endowed him, Blake considered to be the fundamental error, and the cause of the Fall. Beulah is thus a transitional world: while it is the threshold of Eden, error may here be accepted and the Fall begin.

If the soul thus falls prey to error, the essential humanity is not destroyed, but sinks into a deep sleep from which it will not awaken until the Last Judgment. At this moment the selfhood divides from the soul in the form of the "spectre." It is this spectre which becomes the Fallen Man: "Man is born a Spectre or Satan & is altogether an Evil."[33]

The masculine spectre is the face which the created man presents to the world, an aspect of pure materialism and self-interest, concealing the affections and denying imagination. His feminine emanation remains to guard his sleeping identity in Beulah, speaking to man in this world through his conscience, thoughts, and dreams,[34] which in his fallen ignorance he is ashamed of and seeks to hide from his fellows.

The concept of masculine and feminine attributes in Blake's symbolism is apt to cause confusion, because he uses familiar terms in a sense different from that normally understood by them. We must remember that his imagery, as always, has both generalized and specialized meanings. Every person in this world has both masculine and feminine aspects of personality, not peculiar to the two sexes as we think of them, but mingled in each, and representing the selfhood as opposed to the conscience.

Blake believed implicitly that woman was created in Beulah to be the companion of man and that it was her true nature to be dependent upon him. Just as man may fall by turning away from the active imaginative life, so may woman through denying her dependence upon man and seeking to dominate him. Her powerful tool to this end is, of course, her physical charms, and also the wilful refusal of them. Her success, if achieved, results in man's surrender to the passive aspects of Beulah, which we have seen precipitates the Fall. Out of the desire for power over man arises jealousy, the besetting sin of womankind. When she becomes dominant, she urges man to pursue materialistic ends and to deny his imaginative self. This is what Blake means by the triumph of the "Female Will" in the Fallen World.

The reader must again be cautioned against being too literal in interpretation. Blake symbolizes two different aspects of human nature as the masculine and feminine principles: he does not, of course, imply that there are no jealous and materialistic men and no magnanimous and imaginative women. The dominance of the Female Will, which is the besetting sin of life in our world, is the pursuit of vain ends and the disregarding of visionary life. Thus Blake speaks in broad terms and cries out for the sacrifice of worldliness to the development of spiritual understanding when he

[33] *Jerusalem*, plate 52.
[34] Hence the muses of Blake's mythology are known as the "Daughters of Beulah."

proclaims: "In Eternity Woman is the Emanation of Man; she has No Will of her own. There is no such thing in Eternity as a Female Will."[35]

The complete cycle of human experience, as Blake conceives it, is thus made up of a twofold and of a fourfold alternation. Eden and Beulah are parts of both cycles. Before the individual accepts error, the soul alternates between these two stages as between night and day. The passive and feminine characteristics of Beulah are a necessary restorative for the eternal humanity after the intensity of the mental warfare of Eden. Temporarily this relaxation is desirable, but the danger is that initiative will be lost and the masculine attributes of the spirit will permanently accept the domination of the feminine. This constitutes the fundamental error. The divine humanity sinks to rest in Beulah, guarded over by the emanations—the Daughters of Beulah—and the spectre is precipitated into Ulro. Now that it has fallen into error, the soul in its passage back to salvation must complete the fourfold cycle from Beulah to Ulro, thence upward through Generation to Beulah again before the return to Eden can be made.

As Eden is characterized by creative intelligence and the divine energy which is life, so Ulro is ruled by the pure abstract rationality of moral law, ruthlessly applicable to all cases irrespective of individuality and unguided by imaginative insight. Ulro is the realm of the empty heart and of barren passivity; it is a world of coldness and emptiness in the midst of the endless sea of materialism and chaos. Its topography recalls those portions of our created world into which the transforming power of the human mind, heart, and spirit—the aspects of man which are in the image of God—has never come. Its description reminds us vividly of the Hell of Dante's *Inferno*:

> There is the Cave, the Rock, the Tree, the Lake of Udan Adan,
> The Forest and the Marsh and the Pits of bitumen deadly,
> The Rocks of solid fire, the Ice valleys, the Plains
> Of burning sand, the rivers, cataract & Lakes of Fire,
> The Islands of the fiery Lakes, the Trees of Malice, Revenge
> And black Anxiety, and the Cities of the Salamandrine men,
>
> .   .   .   .
>
> .   .   .   .
>
> The land of darkness flamed, but no light & no repose:
> The land of snows of trembling & of iron hail incessant:
> The land of earthquakes, and the land of woven labyrinths:
> The land of snares & traps & wheels & pit-falls & dire mills:
> The Voids, the Solids, & the land of clouds & regions of waters
> With their inhabitants, in the Twenty-seven Heavens beneath Beulah:
> Self-righteousness conglomerating against the Divine Vision.
>
> Jerusalem 13; 38-43, 46-52

Blake in his earlier works equates Ulro with our present world, and attributes its creation to the "Angry God of this World," or Satan, "the Jehovah of the Bible being no other than he who dwells in flaming fire."[36] However, while Blake was at first ap-

[35] *Vision of the Last Judgment*, p. 648.
[36] *The Marriage of Heaven and Hell*, p. 182. See also inscription in pencil at the top of the third Dante illustration.

palled by the hellish character of this world to the exclusion of everything else, our previous discussion of "limits" has pointed out that, as time went on, he came more and more to realize that there is still a divine principle at work giving form to chaos. Imagination, though fallen, is not annihilated even in Ulro. Personified by "Los," this imaginative power begins to rebuild a replica of Jerusalem, the eternal city of freedom,[37] in the void. This is "Golgonooza," the city of art: art being a vision of eternal truth stamped with material form. As time goes by, Los' task becomes enlarged. He forms the "Mundane Shell," a firm refuge in the void. He seeks endlessly to capture the aimless spirits who wander in the wastes of Ulro; provided with "human" forms woven for them by the Daughters of Beulah, they are reborn into the World of Generation within the confines of the Mundane Shell. Error having thus been given an established substance by imagination in a created world and in its generated forms, can now be recognized and cast out. Blake's developing ideas therefore tend increasingly to stress the divine elements of this world as opposed to the chaotic:

> . . . whatever is visible to the Generated Man
> Is a Creation of mercy & love from the Satanic Void.
>
> Jerusalem 13, 44-45

Eventually all the accumulated error of the generated world will be recognized and cast back to Ulro, while all the spiritual elements wandering in chaos will receive definite form in the World of Generation. When this is accomplished, the redemption of the Fallen World will have been achieved. Ulro, the sum total of error, will be consumed. There being no more error to be redeemed, the World of Generation will disappear too, and only the eternal life of Eden and Beulah will remain. "Error is Created. Truth is Eternal. Error, or Creation, will be Burned up, & then, & not till Then, Truth or Eternity will appear."[38]

In closing our discussion of the four stages of Blake's Circle of Destiny, we must emphasize the respects in which Ulro differs from the conventional idea of Hell. There is no place in Blake's system for a realm in which human souls who have violated the arbitrary commands of a tyrannical deity are condemned to everlasting punishment. As previously pointed out, Blake stresses that the essence of God is forgiveness. Man's error is that he voluntarily turns aside from this basic precept and, instead of forgiving his fellows as God forgives him, seeks to advance his selfhood at the expense of others. No matter how deeply the individual may sin, however, the forgiveness of God will abide with him, for God has established the limits of contraction and opacity so that no man can lose his soul in the void. However great the individual's guilt and however deep his ignorance, his error will eventually become manifest to him; he will then be able to cast aside his satanic selfhood and rejoin the great brotherhood of mankind in the universal salvation of Eden.

[37] "Jerusalem, Which now descendeth out of heaven, a City, yet a Woman." (*Four Zoas* IX, 220-221, p. 353.)

[38] *Vision of the Last Judgment*, p. 651. The final destruction of error and the triumph of truth are described in the remarkable apocalyptic vision which constitutes Night the Ninth of *The Four Zoas* (Keynes, *Poetry and Prose*, pp. 347-371).

22

The final phase of Blake's mythology with which we must deal concerns the individual personality. We have discussed the nature of the error which leads to the Fall and we have studied Blake's views concerning the created and eternal worlds. We are still faced with the problem of what predisposes man to the acceptance of error. Up to now, we have dealt with man in his relation to the universe around him and to his fellow men; at this point we must turn to an examination of the man himself.

From his very early years, Blake was absorbed by the problem of human psychology. As his ideas on the subject developed, they resolved themselves into a conviction that every personality is compounded of four basic factors: reason, imagination, emotion, and the sensory mechanism. These form four great contraries which together shape the character of the universal man, Albion, and which, in greater and lesser proportions, are blended and interwoven into the life of every individual. Being universal attributes, they are included in the category which Blake terms "states."[39] Each of these psychological characteristics has its personification in Blake's mythology. In the aggregate they are known as the "Zoas." In the earlier prophetic books the various Zoas appear sporadically and their personalities are only partially realized. Slowly the concept matured, until it reached full development in the middle of Blake's artistic career with the completion of the long epic in manuscript which bears their name, *The Four Zoas.*[40] Thereafter they remained the key figures of Blake's symbolism.

The four are named "Los," "Luvah," "Urizen," and "Tharmas," and represent the imaginative, emotional, intellectual, and sensory aspects of man in that order. As universal attributes of the eternal humanity, all exist at every level of the Circle of Destiny. Each of them, however, is particularly associated with one of these levels. Los is in the ascendant in Eden, Luvah in Beulah, and Tharmas in Ulro, while this world is ruled by Urizen, the rational principle. Pictorially, they are represented by the four beasts of Ezekiel's vision and of the Book of Revelation, the same four beasts which since early times have symbolized the four evangelists. Thus Los is portrayed in human form, Luvah as a bull, Urizen by a lion, and Tharmas by an eagle. Except in the state of Eden, each has also an emanation. The emanation of Los is named "Enitharmon;" that of Luvah, "Vala;" that of Urizen, "Ahania;" and that of Tharmas, "Enion."

Of the four, the dominant figure—particularly of the later prophecies—is Los. In

[39] "States" are phases of experience which all men either do or may enter into, and are to be distinguished from traits which are peculiar to the individual. Thus a soul may at some point of its eternal journey be in an evil state, but it is not in itself evil because it remains forever in the image of God. ("The Spiritual States of the Soul are all Eternal. Distinguish between the Man & his present State."—*Jerusalem*, plate 52. See also passage quoted at the end of the Foreword.)

[40] Further discussion of the Zoas will be found in all of the leading commentaries on Blake's symbolism as listed in the Bibliography. Of particular interest are chapters 3-6 of W. P. Witcutt, *Blake, A Psychological Study*, London, 1946. It is remarkable to how considerable an extent Blake anticipated many of the conclusions of modern psychology, creating his own symbols in the absence of a recognized scientific terminology. His contribution has been acknowledged by Carl Gustav Jung: "The English mystic, William Blake says: 'There are two classes of men: the *prolific* and the *devouring*. Religion is an endeavor to reconcile the two.' . . . These words of Blake . . . are a simple epitome of the fundamental ideas of Spitteler and my elaborations thereon." (*Psychological Types or The Psychology of Individuation*, 4th impression, New York, 1933, p. 336. Jung paraphrases *The Marriage of Heaven and Hell*, pp. 187-188.)

Eden he has another eternal name, which is "Urthona." As such he represents all the energy of the creative imaginative intellect which, as we have seen, is the essence of the eternal humanity. Such can only exist in a pure state in Eden. It is for this reason that Los is differentiated in the other worlds, since to whatever heights the divine imagination, the Poetic Genius, the spirit of prophecy may attain in lower spheres of existence, they are only an indication of the creative perfection of Eden.

The great function of Los is to keep "the Divine Vision in time of trouble."[41] In Beulah he seeks through vision to direct the aspirations of the humanity in repose toward the full life of Eden in order that he may return and not fall into error. After the Fall, Los becomes in Ulro the voice of the conscience by which man eventually becomes aware that he has not been cut off from his eternal life completely. In the World of Generation, he is the imaginative power which makes it possible for created man to commune at brief and ecstatic moments directly with God. As such he is the Zoa whose influence is paramount in forming the personalities of the prophets, poets, and artists of this world, who stand out from other men because of the power of their imaginative genius. Enitharmon, the emanation of Los, may be thought of as representing prophetic and artistic inspiration.

As is the case with all of the aspects of human personality, the imaginative gift may become distorted in this world. The selfhood of the fallen Albion may assert itself by usurping and misdirecting even the imagination. Art may be turned to worldly ends instead of seeking its true goal of keeping before man a vision of eternity; similarly, the prophetic power may degenerate into superstition, necromancy, and the like. The Natural Man usually fails to recognize that imagination is a window into eternity, and regards it purely as wayward fancy, which of course it becomes when undeveloped or misdirected through ignorance. Los, as we have seen, is known by another name in Eden; in the same manner the fallen aspects of the imagination in Ulro and Generation are symbolized by the "Spectre of Urthona," a character of Blake's myth who wrangles with Los—the unfallen imagination—throughout much of *Jerusalem*.

While Los is the dominant figure of the later prophecies, especially of *Jerusalem*, in the earlier works he plays a role secondary to Urizen. This fits in with the fact, to which we have already called attention, that in later years Blake was more concerned with the spiritual aspects of the Fallen World than with its evils. As pure reason, neither illuminated by imagination nor influenced by feeling, Urizen is the cruel figure who dominates the earlier epics, one of which is called after him.[42] Blake saw the fallacy inherent in much of the thinking of his day, as of ours, which tended to deny the existence of everything beyond the range of scientific proof and, as a corollary, which sought to prove the existence of God by material means. We have already seen how such an attitude is fundamentally opposed to the whole basis of Blake's beliefs.[43]

---

[41] *Jerusalem* 95, 20.

[42] The finest portrayal of Urizen is the well-known frontispiece of *Europe*, where he measures out the void with his compasses. See Darrell Figgis, *The Paintings of William Blake*, London, 1925, plate 1.

[43] "The desires & perceptions of man, untaught by any thing but organs of sense, must be limited to objects of sense. If it were not for the Poetic or Prophetic character the Philosophic & Experimental would soon be at the ratio of all things, & stand still, unable to do other than repeat the same dull round over again." (*There Is No Natural Religion, I,* p. 147.)

Thus Urizen, the purely rational Zoa who seeks truth solely by an attempt to correlate the data of the fallen senses, is a satanic figure. His guiding principle of "rational demonstration" is anathema to Blake, who equates his philosophy to that of Bacon, Newton and Locke—human beings in whom Blake considered that the Urizenic character dominated the other Zoas, and who appear as sinister characters of his mythology. As Urizen cannot perceive beyond the range of the senses of the "cavern'd Man," all outside their reach seems to him to be a chaos which is seeking to close in on him; he has no comprehension of the love of God or of the joy of eternity. To protect himself from this terrifying unknown, his only hope as he sees it is to set up rational laws and to command obedience at the price of death. Hence in the earlier prophetic books Urizen appears as the creator of this world, which at that time Blake considered to be a work of cruelty rather than of mercy. Throughout Blake's epics Urizen proclaims the Moral Law, which he writes in books of iron and brass. He is frequently equated with Jehovah, and the Moral Law with the Decalogue; consequently Blake always represents the Moral Law pictorially by the Mosaic tablets.

The Moral Law is, of course, the basis of all earthly systems, the evil and stultifying effects of which, in Blake's view, we have already considered. In its insistence that a system can be found which will fit every situation, Reason ties down every phase of life with restrictive laws, stifling all energy and all natural development. And so, Urizen proclaims:

> "Lo! I unfold my darkness, and on
> This rock place with strong hand the Book
> Of eternal brass, written in my solitude:
>
> Laws of peace, of love, of unity,
> Of pity, compassion, forgiveness;
> Let each chuse one habitation,
> His ancient infinite mansion,
> One command, one joy, one desire,
> One curse, one weight, one measure,
> One King, one God, one Law."
>
> Urizen, 82-91 (p. 222)

By the very fact that man is made in God's image, he requires flexibility for development; rigid law applied indiscriminately will strangle all creativeness. Under Urizen's rule, mankind forgets its greater destiny and becomes blindly bound to the Fallen World:

> Six days they shrunk up from existence,
> And on the seventh day they rested,
> And they bless'd the seventh day, in sick hope,
> And forgot their eternal life.
>
> Urizen, 493-496 (p. 233)

As with all tyrannies, the tyrant is bewildered that men are recalcitrant, but he can see no other solution than that of becoming more despotic:

He in darkness clos'd view'd all his race,
And his soul sicken'd! he curs'd
Both sons & daughters; for he saw
That no flesh nor spirit could keep
His iron laws one moment.

Urizen, 449-453 (p. 232)

One of the most powerful weapons which Urizen wields to subjugate individuals is organized religion. Instead of revealing to men the love and forgiveness of God, Urizen fashions God after his own likeness as a being who demands absolute obedience to arbitrary law. Urizen thus extends his hold over men through their fear of eternal punishment at the hand of God. Urizen is a "puritan" too. He cannot admit that pleasure is divine in origin unless misused; rather, he must banish all pleasure as potentially destructive. He, therefore, casts out his emanation, Ahania, who was created in Beulah as an embodiment of the divine pleasure which provides relaxation from the mental warfare of Eden.

Such then is Urizen, the rational principle of the human personality. Although he is the personification of the reason, we must not make the mistake of considering that Blake was anti-intellectual. Such an assumption shows a basic misunderstanding of the distinction which Blake draws between intelligence and rationalism. He is quite clear on this point, as may be seen from the following quotation from the preface to the fourth chapter of *Jerusalem*: "What is the Divine Spirit? is the Holy Ghost any other than an Intellectual Fountain? . . . What are the Treasures of Heaven which we are to lay up for ourselves, are they any other than Mental Studies & Performances? What are all the Gifts of the Gospel, are they not all Mental Gifts? . . . What is the Life of Man but Art & Science? . . . What is the Joy of Heaven but Improvement in the things of the Spirit? What are the Pains of Hell but Ignorance, Bodily Lust, Idleness & devastation of the things of the Spirit? . . . To Labour in Knowledge is to Build up Jerusalem, and to Despise Knowledge is to Despise Jerusalem & her Builders. . . . Let every Christian, as much as in him lies, engage himself openly & publicly before all the World in some Mental pursuit for the Building up of Jerusalem."

It is Blake's insistence, however, that the mind must be guided by the heart and by the imagination. If pure reason is allowed to dominate, man's potentially infinite perceptions will be bound down to this world, from which all love will disappear and with it any possibility of salvation. In the Eternal Man all the Zoas are in harmony, realizing their proper relationship and delighting in their brotherhood. It is only when one seeks to usurp the functions of one or more of the others, that the Fall comes. As long as Urthona is dominant there is no trouble, but when Albion allows his rational faculties to annihilate imagination, he can no longer sustain himself in eternity, but falls into Ulro, where imagination is dead and the heart empty. Conversely, when Albion in the Fallen World denies his selfhood, because of the love of God as revealed to him through Christ's sacrifice, the Zoas return to harmony in his bosom and Urizen—who in his fallen state is always represented as blind and aged, with long hair and beard—is restored to the beauty of eternal youth.[44]

[44] See *Jerusalem* 96, 3-97, 8. For the rejuvenation of Urizen, see *The Four Zoas* IX, 161-195 (pp. 351-352).

The two other Zoas are far less important in Blake's myth, which deals largely with the eternal warfare between the two great contraries, Los and Urizen, on all the levels of existence. The third Zoa, Luvah, represents man's emotional life. This aspect of the personality is also vitally necessary for that true development of vision which will raise man from his fallen state and permit him to regain his immortal stature. As is the case with Urizen, however, Luvah may seek to dominate and this will spell disaster. Just as man cannot yield to pure reason and survive, so he cannot follow a rule of unbridled desire. On the other hand, release from tyranny can only come when passion can no longer be controlled and rises to smite oppression. Hence Luvah has another aspect, that of revolt against law—at times necessary for salvation, but inclined also to get out of hand and itself turn to paths of injustice. In this aspect of revolt, Luvah appears in the worlds of Generation and Ulro as the fiery youth, "Orc," the rebel against authority. This figure plays a large role in some of the earlier prophecies, but later Blake came to feel that not in revolt but in forgiveness lay the way to salvation. The attainment of universal brotherhood demands sacrifice of the selfhood out of love for others. The great example of this is, of course, Jesus, who through love assumed the supreme sacrifice of His passion so that man "might have life and have it more abundantly." Thus it is that at the time of the final casting off of error, Jesus appears to Albion in "Luvah's robes of blood." Thus we have a third aspect of Luvah, that of divine love made manifest in this world: "God becomes as we are, that we may be as he is."[45]

Vala, the emanation of Luvah, is the most important of the female counterparts of the Zoas. As the feminine aspect of the emotional life, she represents the beauty of the natural world. In Beulah she fulfils her function in providing for the restoration of Albion through the tenderness of woman's love and the happiness which the spirit gains from the contemplation of beauty. She can easily become a delusion, however, and after the Fall Vala is transformed into a cruel and jealous mistress, seeking to blind man to his imaginative life and to make him her slave. She fosters sentiment and pity, desirable adjuncts of creative feeling but, because of their passive nature which has its origins in the selfhood, fatal poisons if permitted to become abstract ideals of conduct. Under her dominion, man pursues material instead of spiritual ends; she is responsible for much of the superficiality of society as it reveals itself in a desire for wordly position and outward material display. As Urizen is the king of this world, she is its queen; Urizen in the Fallen World may be likened to Satan, and Vala to Hecate.

We have already discussed Blake's views concerning the evils of the dominant Female Will. Vala is the personification of this dominance; as such she is sometimes referred to as "Vala-Rahab" and further identified as "Babylon," the harlot of the Book of Revelation. Mystery and superstition, as deliberately fostered by organized religions in order to enslave men's minds through the intoxicating power of false emotionalism, are the most sinister manifestations of Vala.

Blake was a great opponent of the tendency of his day to read moral values into the beauty of the natural world. No man had a greater appreciation of the beauty

[45] *There Is No Natural Religion, II,* p. 148.

27

of nature nor derived more joy from its study than did he, as many of his lyrics and many of the finest passages of his longer poems testify. However, as woman is the emanation of man, so nature flourishes under man's control and can become hideous and evil without it: "Where man is not, nature is barren."[46] It is the function of beauty to delight the mind and to restore the soul. If properly so regarded, it stimulates the creative powers, being a visible symbol of divine love at work in this world. Conversely, the creative powers can be destroyed if form, which is purely of this earth, is worshipped to the exclusion of content, which is of the eternal imagination. Human values cannot be found in nature, for the true humanity resides not in the outward forms of the world, but in the mind and spirit. The worship of Vala is, therefore, one to which man in a fallen natural world is much inclined, but which is a false religion that can easily prove fatal if the bounds of its true and fruitful development are overstepped.

Tharmas, the last of the Zoas, is a rather shadowy figure; he is the only one who is closely associated with the physical aspect of man. He is the latent and almost unconscious sensory power which is animated by feeling, intelligence, and spirit to complete the perfectly integrated body of the eternal man, Albion. He gives to every form its permanent identity which is never lost but is part of its eternal individuality. Just as in Dante's *Divine Comedy* the earthly form of men is not lost with the death of their bodies, so Tharmas is found on all the levels of existence. However, since the perceptive powers of man after the Fall are much less acute than in his unfallen state, the physical aspect of man grows more apparent in proportion as the spiritual becomes less so. "Man has no Body distinct from his Soul; for that call'd Body is a portion of Soul discern'd by the five Senses, the chief inlets of Soul in this age."[47] As is the case with all the Zoas, Tharmas becomes a hideously distorted version of his eternal self after the Fall takes place. From the unifying power who gives identity to the soul, he becomes the unrestrained energy of the Fallen World. He manifests himself in the brute violence of animate nature and in the irresistible natural forces of the created world. The symbol of Tharmas after the Fall is the ever-restless sea, continually changing its form, uncontrolled by mind, yet all powerful; in this "sea of time and space"—the all-conquering materialism of Ulro—man is overwhelmed, his identity lost and, but for the grace of God who in mercy puts limits to the Fall, his soul would be annihilated.

The emanation of Tharmas is Enion, the passive materiality of the Fallen World, as Tharmas is its uncontrollable energy. Enion is a strange primordial force. In common with all the eternal powers of man, she once shared equally in the full joy of the universal world; with the Fall she was thrust furthest of all away from the creative energy which is life itself down into the Hell of inert material form. Here, blind and age-bent, shut in a rocky cavern, she mourns eternally. She is that inner voice of man that at times seems a strange and intangible reminiscence of his Golden Age, rising from the depths of his being and speaking from the remotest ages of the created world with a depth of wisdom that goes back to the very foundations of human experience in the fallen state. The laments of Enion form some of the most impressive and poeti-

[46] *The Marriage of Heaven and Hell,* p. 185. [47] *Ibid.,* p. 182.

cally successful passages of the prophetic books. She is Blake's version of the Earth Mother of all mythologies.

Such are the personalities of the Four Zoas and of their emanations, Blake's symbolical figures personifying the basic contrary forces which together form the character of every individual. In the eternal state they manage to combine intense energy with complete harmony, preserving a dynamic balance in much the same way as does the atom with its nucleus and its swiftly-moving electrons. As soon, however, as man becomes inclined towards the development of his selfhood, the harmony is disrupted. Reason, desire, or the sensory aspects of man strive for dominion, upsetting the proper control which must be exercised by the divine power of vision. The Fall occurs, and eternity cannot be regained until, through experience, man once again learns to bring the Zoas into their proper relationship.

We have examined the broad outlines of the mythology which Blake found it necessary to create in order to suggest the many-sidedness of human psychology and experience as it appeared to him. There are many elaborations of the main theme which occur in his works, and his ideas naturally kept developing from the earlier works to the later ones. In addition to the characters of the myth whom we have discussed, there are many others who appear briefly and in minor roles. It is hoped, however, that what has been here set forth will indicate the main outlines of Blake's beliefs and will give a sufficient key to his individual method of expression and to the meaning of his most important symbols, so that his works may be approached with understanding. Further elaborations of his themes and further actors in his mythology will not be discussed unless the elucidation of some specific point in connection with the Dante illustrations demands it; in that case such material will be introduced in the detailed analysis of the appropriate drawing.

CHAPTER 3

BLAKE AND DANTE

~~~~~~

The worship of God is: Honouring his gifts in other men, each according to his genius, and loving the greatest men best: those who envy or calumniate great men hate God; for there is no other God.

The Marriage of Heaven and Hell, p. 191

~~~~~~

THERE is considerable circumstantial evidence which suggests that Blake was familiar with the work of Dante, at least in a general way, from his early years. The first positive indication which we have in his own production, however, dates from 1793, when Blake was thirty-six years old. In that year he first issued a small engraved "emblem-book" entitled *For Children: The Gates of Paradise*. As originally published, this little work consisted merely of a frontispiece and title page, followed by sixteen engravings, each with a brief caption below it. The twelfth of these represents Ugolino in the dungeon surrounded by his four dying sons.[1] The title reads: "Does thy God, O Priest, take such vengeance as this?"

By itself, this would not be of much significance. However, the facts of Blake's artistic background and early friendships point to a closer familiarity. As we have previously noted, Blake did not learn Italian until late in life, and the first translation of the complete *Divine Comedy* into English was not published until 1802. However, the *Inferno* appeared in its entirety in an English translation by Charles Rogers in 1782, and another version by Henry Boyd followed soon afterwards in 1785.[2] Nevertheless, it is much more likely that Blake derived his first familiarity with the poem from another source. In 1719 Jonathan Richardson had published a translation of the Ugolino incident from the thirty-third canto of the *Inferno* in his book, *A Discourse on the Dignity, Certainty, Pleasure, and Advantage, of the Science of a Connoisseur*. This continued to be a widely-read art treatise for the remainder of the century, and Blake probably came to know it during his apprenticeship. Moreover, in 1777 none other than Sir Joshua Reynolds sent a painting of Ugolino in the tower to the annual Royal Academy Exhibition, where the twenty-year-old Blake no doubt saw it.[3]

In this same year, 1777, Henry Fuseli, then in Rome, did a series of six wash drawings based on subjects from the *Inferno* and *Purgatorio*, which are now preserved in the Print Room of the British Museum. Upon Fuseli's return from Italy in 1780, he

[1] Reproduced in *Poetry and Prose*, p. 575.

[2] Paget Toynbee, "Chronological List of English Translations from Dante from Chaucer to the Present Day," *24th Annual Report of the Dante Society*, Cambridge, Massachusetts, 1905, pp. xii, xiii, xv, 7, 8.

[3] *ibid.*, p. 5. *idem*, "The Earliest English Illustrators of Dante," *Quarterly Review*, CCXI, 1909, pp. 399-409. *idem*, "Dante in English Art," *38th Annual Report of the Dante Society*, Cambridge, Massachusetts, 1919, pp. 2-3.

became a neighbor of Blake, and the two soon formed a close friendship which lasted for the remainder of their lives. Fuseli's continuing interest in Dante is attested by the fact that he exhibited paintings based upon the *Inferno* at the Royal Academy exhibitions of 1786, 1806, and 1818.[4]

Another lifelong friend of both men was John Flaxman whom Blake met at about the same time as he became acquainted with Fuseli. In 1787 Flaxman went to Italy, where he remained for seven years. Near the end of this period, Thomas Hope of Deepdene gave him a commission to do a series of designs to Dante. The one hundred and ten drawings which Flaxman produced are now preserved in an album in the Houghton Library of Harvard University. They were engraved by Piroli and published in Rome in 1793. A second Roman edition followed in 1802 and the first English edition in 1807.[5]

Blake was, of course, familiar with the Dante designs of his friends and must often have discussed the subject with them. Flaxman and Fuseli both knew Italian and could have read and explained portions of the *Divine Comedy* to Blake long before the first complete translations appeared. Thus we see that Blake in all probability was reasonably familiar with the poem thirty years or more before he undertook his own illustrations.

In addition to such evidence which points to Blake's early knowledge of the *Divine Comedy*, we have also a number of penciled notations on the drawings themselves and the record of scraps of Blake's conversation which give us an insight into his opinions concerning Dante's art and philosophy.

We have already mentioned that *Jerusalem* contains the most fully developed statement of Blake's convictions and have previously quoted an important passage from plate 52 of that work: "Every Religion that Preaches Vengeance for Sin is the Religion of the Enemy & Avenger and not of the Forgiver of Sin, and their God is Satan, Named by the Divine Name." Hence it is highly significant to find Blake again using almost the same wording in a penciled comment on one of his Dante drawings, only three of which bear notations of any length. Drawing 101 is a sketchy diagram of the circles of the *Inferno*. Among the several inscriptions on the page is the following: "Whatever Book is for Vengeance for Sin & Whatever Book is Against the Forgiveness of Sins is not of the Father, but of Satan the Accuser & Father of Hell." Obviously, therefore, Blake considered the *Inferno* to be such a book.

We have seen in the previous section that above all else Blake believed in the universal mercy of God which the Saviour has extended to every man. He sums up his conviction in another passage on the same page of *Jerusalem* from which we have just quoted: "The Glory of Christianity is To Conquer by Forgiveness." The entire fabric of Dante's poem must thus in Blake's opinion have been built upon a fundamental error. The whole theme of the *Inferno* is the terrible nature of God's punishment of sin. In the *Purgatorio* and *Paradiso* the way of salvation is hard and attainable by few. Frequently in Dante's poem the love of God seems very remote from the in-

---

[4] *idem*, "Dante in English Art," pp. 3-4, 10, 12. *idem*, "English Illustrators of Dante," pp. 409-413.

[5] *idem*, "Dante in English Art," pp. 4-8, 10. *idem*, "English Illustrators of Dante," pp. 413-415.

dividual, and not the joyous brotherhood of full forgiveness which to Blake is its essence. In the Eternal World of God, Blake was convinced that there could be no vengeance nor punishment. Fallen Man can, however, conceive of eternity only in terms of the logical and moral systems of this world. The inspired prophet and artist alone is capable of rising above such limitations to an understanding of the eternal order, but in this vital respect Dante has failed. Accordingly, in another of his notations, this time on Design 7, Blake comments: "Every thing in Dante's Comedia shews That for Tyrannical Purposes he has made This World the Foundation of All, & the Goddess Nature Mistress; Nature is his Inspirer & not the Holy Ghost."

Dante's failure to realize that vengeance stems solely from Satan and not from God is again the theme of this further notation penciled upon Design 101: "It seems as if Dante's supreme Good was something Superior to the Father or Jesus; for if he gives his rain to the Evil & the Good, & his Sun to the Just & the Unjust,[6] He could never have Built Dante's Hell, nor the Hell of the Bible neither, in the way our Parsons explain it—It must have been originally Formed by the devil Himself; & So I understand it to have been." It will be seen how clearly this fits in with Blake's views of the nature and origin of the created world as we have set them forth.

In addition to Blake's notations, we have another important source from which we can piece together some of his views concerning Dante's beliefs. This is the diary of Henry Crabb Robinson which we have had occasion to refer to before. Naturally, such a source is not nearly as reliable as Blake's jottings. Robinson wrote from memory and did not actually make notes while he was conversing with Blake. Although in each case he wrote his diary within a few hours of the interview described, it would, of course, be impossible to report conversation such as Blake's completely and accurately in such a manner. Nevertheless, Robinson's account of Blake's views as given on the two occasions when they discussed Dante, fit in well with the picture we have already formed.[7]

"I asked about the *moral* character of Dante in writing his Vision: was he pure? 'Pure,' said Blake. 'Do you think there is any purity in God's eyes? The angels in heaven are no more so than we—"he chargeth his angels with folly." ' He afterwards extended this to the Supreme Being—he is liable to error too. Did he not repent him that he had made Nineveh?"

"*Swedenborg* was spoken of . . . he said that *Swedenborg* was wrong in endeavoring to explain to the rational faculty what the reason cannot comprehend: he should have left that. As Blake mentioned *Swedenborg* and *Dante* together I wished to know whether he considered their vision of the same kind. As far as I could collect, he does. *Dante* he said was the greater poet. He had *political* objects. Yet this, though wrong, does not appear in Blake's mind to affect the truth of the vision."

Another remark of Blake's which Robinson quotes from their first meeting at dinner at the house of Charles Aders on Saturday, December 10, 1825, was: "*Dante* saw Devils where I see none. I see only good." From all these quotations it will be

---

[6] Quoted (inaccurately) from the Sermon on the Mount, Matthew v, 45.
[7] The quotations from Robinson are given as reprinted by Symons, *William Blake*, pp. 256-257, 257-258, 260, 262, 289-290.

observed that Blake considered Dante's vision partial; still, that he was a great poet and much that he wrote inspired.

On December 17, 1825, when Robinson called upon Blake at his home, "our conversation began about Dante. 'He was an "Atheist," a mere politician busied about this world as Milton was, till in his old age he returned back to God whom he had had in his childhood.' I tried to get out from Blake that he meant this charge only in a higher sense, and not using the word Atheism in its popular meaning. But he would not allow this." Here Robinson seems to have divined that Blake called Dante an atheist because he supported the dogma of a worldly organized religion, but "Blake did not want to be understood—this was one of his great failings."[8]

In summing up we cannot do better than to quote William Butler Yeats, who begins a discussion of Blake's opinions concerning Dante as follows: "As Blake sat bent over the great drawing-book in which he made his drawings to *The Divine Comedy*, he was very certain that he and Dante represented spiritual states which face one another in an eternal enmity." While this may perhaps be expressed a bit strongly, Yeats' analysis which follows is in the main true: "Dante, because a great poet, was 'inspired by the Holy Ghost'; but his inspiration was mingled with a certain philosophy, blown up out of his age, which Blake held for mortal and the enemy of immortal things, and which from the earliest times has sat in high places and ruled the world. This philosophy was the philosophy of soldiers, of men of the world, of priests busy with government, of all who, because of the absorption in active life, have been persuaded to judge and to punish. . . . Opposed to this was another philosophy, not made by men of action, drudges of time and space, but by Christ when wrapped in the divine essence, and by artists and poets, who are taught by the nature of their craft to sympathize with all living things."[9]

So far we have been concerned only with Blake's views of Dante's beliefs. As to his opinion of him as an artist, there can be no doubt that Blake considered him in the highest category. Blake always most admired works of epic proportions which deal in poetic terms with a broad view of human experience on intellectual and spiritual levels. He cannot have failed to appreciate that Dante's poem is of this class. That he should devote his last years to its illustration and should learn Italian at the age of sixty-seven in order better to comprehend it, is sufficient testimony to his admiration for the *Divine Comedy* and to his recognition of the artistic genius of its author. In recalling his meetings with Blake in his *Reminiscences* many years later, Henry Crabb Robinson states, "Dante was wrong in occupying his mind about political objects. Yet this did not appear to affect his [Blake's] estimation of Dante's genius, or his opinion of the truth of Dante's visions. Indeed, when he even declared Dante to be an Atheist, it was accompanied by expression of the highest admiration."

It will be remembered that Blake said that "Allegory addressed to the Intellectual powers, while it is altogether hidden from the Corporeal Understanding, is My Definition of the Most Sublime Poetry." In his few penciled comments and in his remarks to Henry Crabb Robinson, Blake confessed some of his doubts as to whether

[8] Keynes, *Blake Studies*, p. 90.
[9] W. B. Yeats, *Ideas of Good and Evil*, New York, 1903, pp. 197-199.

Dante did not sometimes temporize with the corporeal understanding, particularly in his adherence to orthodox religious concepts which Blake gravely mistrusted. When we come to analyze the individual drawings, we shall find that many of them are conceived in the light of his conviction that a fundamental part of the *Divine Comedy* is basically worldly. At the same time, Blake knew that Dante was a great poet and storyteller and that much of what he wrote was based upon profound spiritual conviction. We may be sure that, in spite of reservations, he realized the sublimity of the *Divine Comedy* as a whole, and rejoiced in the genius of its creator, for "Blake saw in art the great symbolical interpretation of the eternal world; and . . . he saw the vision of the artist as identical with the vision of the seer and the activity of the artist as identical with the worship of the saint."[10]

[10] Blackstone, *English Blake*, pp. 401-402. In addition to the instances given above, Blake in his writings mentions Dante on a number of occasions, although in a context not sufficiently important to call for further comment. See *Poetry and Prose*, pp. 190-191, 911. For Blake's definition of poetry, as given above, see *Poetry and Prose*, p. 869 (Letter to Thomas Butts, July 6, 1803).

CHAPTER 4
UNITY OF THEME IN THE DESIGNS

Of the Sleep of Ulro! and of the passage through
Eternal Death! and of the awaking to Eternal Life.

This theme calls me in sleep night after night, & ev'ry morn
Awakes me at sun-rise.
                                              Jerusalem 4, 1-4

BEGINNING about the year 1800, Blake sought in all of his major works to give an integrated picture of the entire cycle of spiritual experience. *The Four Zoas, Milton,* and *Jerusalem* all have this as their theme, presenting the full Circle of Destiny from the Fall, through regeneration, to final rejection of error, both in a universal sense and as it relates to the individual soul. The illustrations for the Book of Job also set forth the complete cycle and as a series are symbolically very tightly unified, each of the twenty-one designs being closely linked to the over-all scheme.[1]

In the previous section, we have pointed out that at certain points Blake was in direct conflict with Dante's beliefs. It was in the light of this conflict that Blake illustrated Dante's poem. However, while Blake's own mythological system frequently makes its appearance in individual illustrations to the *Divine Comedy*, it is not possible to trace a consistent development of that system through the entire series. Rather, the poem itself is allowed to provide the framework which relates the designs to each other. Within this general integration, each design stands for the most part on its own. Nevertheless, it is possible to divide the drawings roughly into three groups with regard to the manner in which they are related to the narrative. Some are literal illustrations of the text, some seek to find in the events and characters of the poem parallels for the incidents and personifications of Blake's own mythology, while others emphasize points in the *Divine Comedy* which Blake considered as indicating deficiency of vision on Dante's part.

It is the last of these categories, of course, which is of the greatest interest, since it is in the drawings of this type, which occur sporadically throughout the series, that we can trace what appears to be the main theme of the entire group. This resolves itself into a contrast between what Blake considered to be the basic elements of Dante's character and philosophy: inspired poetic vision on the one hand, set over against the acceptance of worldly standards on the other. Thus in the very first design Virgil appears to Dante in the guise of Christ, to give him spiritual strength and support in the passage through this world, amid the dark and threatening trees and the ferocious beasts. In the third illustration, the contrary aspect begins to assert itself and Dante hesitates to follow Virgil through the gateway of illumination, but hangs back rather than face the terrors of the Fallen World, represented by the figures in flames at

[1] Wicksteed, *Blake's Vision of the Book of Job,* pp. 33-43.

either side of the page and by the Satanic God who presides over the whole. Again and again we find this contrast: Dante seems to be on the point of perceiving truth, only to follow the path of worldly error or expediency. In the *Purgatorio*, he is borne upward in the arms of Lucia, his poetic inspiration, only to hesitate before the fire of imagination and to bow abjectly before the Female Will; in the *Paradiso*, he kneels in adoration before the Son of Man and is on the point of reuniting with his emanation and entering Eden, when he suddenly reverts to a vision of the eternal realm as a worldly empire presided over by the God of the Law and the Goddess of Materialism.

In addition to this group which may be taken to represent the contrasting elements of Dante's personality, is another, in the drawings of which Blake seeks to equate Dante's vision with his own. It was pointed out in the Foreword that Blake saw in such similarities between the creations of another poet and his own a confirmation of his faith in inspiration as an actual perception of the eternal order. In designs of this class, the incidents and characters of Dante's poem appear in such a way that they are clearly to be identified not only with the *Divine Comedy*, but with Blake's personal mythological system and beliefs as well. Thus the ninth illustration presents Blake's views on the cruelties with which human convention regulates sexual relationships, the ninety-eighth is concerned with his belief that unselfish love and art are the two avenues by which man can transcend the limitations of the physical world—and so on.

Finally, there is the third group in which Blake's own ideas do not figure to any considerable extent, the drawings illustrating Dante's text in a literal manner. In this category, Blake's interest usually lies more in the evocation of an artistic mood appropriate to that of the passage with which he is concerned, than in the rendition of details described in the poem. It is to be understood, of course, that all of the drawings are to a considerable extent dependent upon the text. There are scarcely any which cannot be connected readily with a specific passage, and comparatively few where fundamental differences from descriptions given in the poem are introduced. The drawings succeed remarkably well not only in providing literal illustration of Dante's text, but also in creating in pictorial terms a mood which is imaginatively and emotionally closely akin to that of the poem. Blake, however, is able to go still further, and in a unique manner succeeds in integrating his own symbolism with the designs in such a way that, without doing violence either literally or artistically to the text, he is able to suggest many overtones of meaning to those who are familiar with his mythological system. In the drawings in which this is most successfully achieved, the result is one of great creative richness which, with growing familiarity, continues to suggest new aspects of human experience.

When we consider the main divisions of the *Divine Comedy* separately, we find that the treatment of the *Inferno* is the most literal. There are, as we have seen, many more designs to the *Inferno* than to the other parts of the poem, sixty-nine as compared to thirty for the *Purgatorio* and *Paradiso* combined. With an average of about two illustrations to each canto, the narrative is followed quite closely and forms the co-ordinating element. Very few pictorially promising incidents are ignored, and the precise nature of Dante's descriptions affords plenty of material to provide interest. While quite a number of the illustrations involve the use of Blake's own symbolism, this generally occurs when incidents of the poem suggest comparison with similar aspects of experience which interest Blake.

In the *Purgatorio* we find that the picturesque incidents which comprise so much of the *Inferno* are less numerous and that there are long theological disquisitions, often of an involved nature and ill adapted to pictorial treatment. As a result, there is a tendency for the designs to become more symbolic and less purely illustrative. Also, as we approach the latter part of the *Purgatorio* we become increasingly aware of the disparities which Blake emphasizes between his own beliefs and those of Dante. The *Paradiso* as a poem is highly mystical, with little of the picturesqueness of setting or striking individualization of character which are found in the *Inferno* and in much of the *Purgatorio*. The artist thus faces a difficult task which demands much imaginative insight. Blake has confined himself in this section of the poem to only ten designs. These tend to illustrate passages the ideas of which either parallel or diverge radically from Blake's own, and are not at all dependent upon those portions of the text which one would normally consider to be the most pictorially suggestive. Blake is now no longer primarily illustrating the poem; rather, he seeks for incidents which recall his own mythology, and then makes drawings which present his own ideas much in the manner of the designs of his prophetic books.

To sum up, whether we consider the *Divine Comedy* as a whole or take up its major divisions individually, we find no elaborately contrived interrelationship coordinating each illustration with the entire group. Blake has not done violence to the sequence of Dante's poem in the interest of some scheme of his own. At the same time the over-all system of the *Divine Comedy* does not correspond nearly as closely as does that of the Book of Job to the main stages of Blake's mythology. Dante's progress through Hell, Purgatory, and Paradise does not altogether fit into the Circle of Destiny of Ulro, Generation, Beulah, and Eden, in spite of all that Blake could do to seek for correspondence. Thus the tight unity of the poem could not be maintained in the illustrations, at least in so far as their fitting into an integrated framework of Blake's own symbolism is concerned. In Blake's opinion, as we may reconstruct it from the designs, Dante set out upon the pathway leading from the Fall, through regeneration, to salvation, but never reached his goal. He wandered around in Ulro and Generation for a considerable time; eventually he obtained a tentative foothold in Beulah and even seemed at times about to achieve the illumination of Eden, only to slip backward. Blake doubtless found in the *Divine Comedy*, unlike the Book of Job, no final recognition and rejection of error.[2] Therefore, to him the story told by Dante is not that of the ultimate realization of the Last Judgment, but only the history of an Orc Cycle:[3] for a time regeneration seems to be imminent, but at the critical

---

[2] It was to set right what he considered to be a similar deficiency in *Paradise Lost* that Blake wrote his prophetic book *Milton*.

[3] Blake interpreted history as a series of attempts by mankind to throw off the Fallen World and regain Eden, initiated each time by Orc, the youthful spirit of revolt against tyrannical tradition. As those who overthrow tyrants by force eventually become tyrants themselves in order to maintain what they have accomplished, the cycle has always failed to overcome error and has swung back on the next round through Ulro and Generation. See Northrop Frye, *Fearful Symmetry: A Study of William Blake*, Princeton, New Jersey, 1947, pp. 207-216.

point error reasserts itself and the circle has to start over again. The series which begins with man running from the terrors of the Fallen World to find aid in the person of the Divine Humanity, ends with the Female Will enthroned on the vegetated world. The fact that, while Dante concludes on a note of triumph, Blake does not do so, is significant evidence of Blake's disagreement with Dante's vision.

CHAPTER 5
STYLISTIC CONSIDERATIONS

A Facility in Composing is the Greatest Power of
Art, & Belongs to None but the Greatest Artists.
Notation by Blake in his copy of
Sir Joshua Reynolds' *Discourses*
(Keynes, *Poetry and Prose*, p. 780).

Ideas cannot be Given but in their minutely Appropriate Words, nor Can a
Design be made without its minutely Appropriate Execution. . . . I am, like
others, Just Equal in Invention & in Execution as my works shew.

Public Address, pp. 625, 631

IN SPITE of their largely unfinished condition, we find Blake at the height of his
powers as an imaginative draughtsman in the Dante illustrations. Technically, the
Dante drawings are most unusual for their period in English art, because Blake's
emphasis—unlike that of almost all of his contemporaries—was placed principally on
the evocation of an appropriate expressive mood and not at all on realism of detail,
conventional prettiness of decorative effect, or conditioned by the formulated rules
of an academic discipline. We must always remember that for Blake drawing and
painting, like poetry, were means of expression and not ends in themselves. He was
primarily a thinker and a visionary, seeking to grasp what seemed to him to reveal
the presence of God in a fallen world and to make it permanent. His view of life
being sacramental, his emphasis in art is upon over-all unity rather than upon detail
for its own sake. He understood as few did at his time—as the quotations at the head
of this section attest—that art is fundamentally an expressive language whose basis is
composition, the framework which can give meaning to otherwise irrelevant detail.
"Shall Painting be confined to the sordid drudgery of fac-simile representations of
merely mortal and perishing substances, and not be as poetry and music are, elevated
into its own proper sphere of invention and visionary conception? No, it shall not be
so! Painting, as well as poetry and music, exists and exults in immortal thoughts."[1]

So it is that throughout his work Blake strives especially for compositional unity.
A feeling for design was natural to him, and even in his early works we notice that
he builds up composition first and only when satisfied with that does he move on to
detail. He realized that, in drawing, the use of conventional formulae and the close
copying of physical appearance could never of themselves stimulate thought and
imagination, which above all was his aim. Its realization could come only through the
selection of those elements from experience which are vital to understanding, and in
their arrangement in a clear and logical manner with inconsequentials eliminated—

[1] *A Descriptive Catalogue*, p. 607.

in short, through mastery of design which is the expressive essence of pictorial representation.

At the end of a lifetime of effort to perfect his control of drawing as an expressive vehicle, we find Blake with his creative faculties and technical resources most fully in harmony in the Dante drawings. The unfinished quality of many of them, while often to be regretted, serves to give insight into his method and to demonstrate the sureness of his understanding of his medium. The great artist is the one who can produce exactly the effect which he knows to be fundamental with the minimum of extraneous detail; his idea is thus presented quickly, clearly, and without the possibility of misunderstanding through confusion of the essential with the unimportant. It is the ability to depict in relatively simple terms the expressive essence of his subject that Blake has mastered in these later works, and even those of the Dante series which are the slightest of sketches succeed in nearly all cases in conveying their message instantly and unmistakably. Often details are barely suggested; we feel their presence, although close examination reveals them to be the merest shorthand. Just those lines are there which indicate to us what aspects of experience Blake has in mind and which supply the essential framework which we can fill in effortlessly from our familiarity with the world about us. Thus in a very few penciled strokes Drawing 100 takes us out into a barren waste and, with the two inert forms which we see there, suggests that mental and imaginative sterility leads to death both of body and soul and turns a potentially beautiful world into a desert.

Unlike most other artists of modern times in the west, Blake is essentially a linearist in his approach. It is this affinity for line which is the most striking feature of his draughtsmanship and which led to his supremacy among the engravers of his period. He continually praised line in his writings as the essential element which the artist must master, and deplored the tendency introduced by the Venetians to subordinate line to areas of tone which blend into one another without sharp edges.[2] His conceptions are nearly always worked out in linear terms to which such elements as light-and-shade, three dimensional modeling, and color may be added to achieve a particular effect, but with line remaining generally the controlling factor. This remains true of even the more finished drawings in which the very nature of the brushwork becomes part of the essential underlying design, not overpowering it but heightening its effect. Thus the frenzied circling of Rusticucci and his Companions (Drawing 29) on the fiery plain becomes real to us in terms of sure circular strokes of brilliant color and the fragile beauty of the Earthly Paradise comes alive as the celestial procession appears, moving serenely, but lightly and joyously beside the curving stream (Drawing 87).

Hence in many ways Blake explores the expressive possibilities of his medium with a freedom which contrasts greatly with the more orthodox tendencies of those of his

[2] "Such art of losing the outlines is the art of Venice and Flanders; it loses all character, and leaves what some people call expression; but this is a false notion of expression; expression cannot exist without character as its stamina; and neither character nor expression can exist without firm and determinate outline. . . . The great and golden rule of art, as well as of life, is this: That the more distinct, sharp, and wiry the bounding line, the more perfect the work of art." (*Ibid.*, p. 617.)

contemporaries who were widely acclaimed in their day, while he remained in obscurity. As in so many other fields, he anticipated trends to come and created a personal expressionism in an age marked by academic traditionalism on one hand and developing naturalism on the other. In these illustrations to Dante, his last works, the very form of the strokes, the movement of line, and the play of light suggest mood in themselves. Moving away from scientific analysis of nature and from pictorial convention, he is able to make line and tone a language of communication. It is not at the outward appearance, which is a passing phase, that he aims, but at the mental image which is permanent. Line is now not merely a means of separating an object from its background, but in its infinite and subtle variations suggests life and movement without hesitation or obvious effort. Illumination does not serve to set forth three-dimensionality so much as to emphasize the significant and, by alternation of light and dark, to suggest feeling.

Blake had developed his final manner gradually in the illustrations to the prophetic books and it reached full stature with the Book of Job engravings. The Dante drawings go a step further and introduce a new simplicity in which all but the bare essentials are eliminated. In addition, space now begins to play an important role as an expressive element as well as line and illumination. The Dante drawings are often very three-dimensional, but this is in no sense the normal use of perspective to imitate the depth of nature. Rather, space serves as does light to give form to an imaginative world; the designs are not rigidly self-contained and restricted to a flat surface; they become capable of almost limitless extension in all directions, as are mental images. Thus in the Dante drawings imaginative landscape settings are given considerable prominence and take on a new expressive importance that is not accorded them in any of Blake's earlier work. A notable example which perfectly comprehends the mood of the poem is found in the seventeenth design in which Dante and Virgil wait by the Stygian Lake as the boat of Charon approaches them through the mysterious darkness.[3]

Engraving was, of course, the art which was properly Blake's own. It was the craft to which he was trained and which he followed as his lifelong profession. In spite of his many gifts, it was the art which of all was most congenial to him, and in which he brought his creative powers to their fullest development. Working first in the sterile manner of the contemporary book-illustrators, when he came to create designs of his own he introduced important technical innovations. For the designs to his prophetic books he developed the powerfully expressive relief-etching, a process of his own invention which enabled him to combine text and decoration on the same page and which he employed with the greatest originality and beauty.[4] With the engravings for the Book of Job he developed another manner, based upon a study of Dürer, in which the monotonous formulae of cross-hatching employed by the English book-illustrators were abandoned in favor of a free use of line which varies its form to suit the character and design of each individual passage. So successful were his results

[3] See also quotation given in discussion of Drawing 40 below.
[4] For details of this process, see Ruthven Todd, "The Techniques of William Blake's Illuminated Printing," *Print* VI, 1948, pp. 53-65.

that, fine as many of the Job designs are as watercolors, the engravings in every case surpass them.

It is essentially in the manner of the Job plates that Blake engraved his seven plates to Dante. However, there are differences, although Blake again used the traditional technique of engraving with the burin, so seldom creatively employed after the development of etching. The Dante plates are among the largest which Blake ever engraved and differ principally from the Job series in that they are more purely linear in their conception and rely less upon effects of illumination. With a considerably larger area to work on, Blake chose to exploit to the full the lively quality of the thin and spring-like type of line which the graver produces and these long lines, so full of strength and character, become the basis of the composition. As an artist Blake seldom matched and never surpassed his engraving of "Paolo and Francesca." Having outdone himself in boldness of conception in the drawing (10), Blake proceeded to improve upon it in the engraving. The distinct and precise detail which is the essence of the engraver's technique adds greatly to the design; the long undulating lines gouged with the burin into the metal give shape to the swirl of forms and to the flames, filling them with life and vital movement. Starting with a masterly composition, the first expressive essence is not destroyed as the design develops, but becomes the framework for the detail which it controls and from which it derives added meaning. Blake has made Dante's poetic vision his own pictorially, has found a design that is creatively as expressive as the music of Dante's verse, and has engraved each line with the same appropriateness with which Dante chooses his words. He is able to penetrate beyond everyday appearances to the spiritual enlightenment which Dante experienced, and to give us a pictorial rendition of the *Divine Comedy* which is in keeping with the character and genius of the original. This elaborate engraving which yet remains so full of life shows in its remarkable control of detail the clarity of Blake's imagination and is testimony to the truth of his statement concerning the precise nature of the illumination which the creative artist experiences. "A Spirit and a Vision are not, as the modern philosophy supposes, a cloudy vapour, or a nothing: they are organized and minutely articulated beyond all that the mortal and perishing nature can produce."[5]

The Dante designs are, of course, not all of equal quality. This is not surprising considering how many of them there are, that they were done in the last three years of Blake's life, and that for much of this period he was in ill health. While proportionally more of the finished designs illustrate the *Inferno*, there are those which are substantially completed that have subjects drawn from both the *Purgatorio* and the *Paradiso*. The relative time of production does not, therefore, appear to have been of particular significance in establishing the degree of finish or the over-all quality of conception; besides, as we have previously seen, there is evidence that the main outline of all seems to have been formulated in a comparatively short time. For all three sections of the poem there are drawings which are undistinguished, but there are also ones which rise to heights of imaginative conception combined with mastery of expressive design of the highest order.

[5] *A Descriptive Catalogue*, p. 607.

When one considers his entire production, it becomes clear that on the whole Blake is greater as a visual artist than as a poet. In his early lyrics, such as "London" or "The Tyger," we frequently find the perfect blending of idea and form. Later, however, he was often unable to set the complexities of his thought into words with precision, and the clear waters of the lyrics become the cloudy poetry of the prophecies. In spite of many unforgettable passages of much beauty and a magnificent sense of power that is quite its own, *Jerusalem* falls far short of artistic perfection. A vast storehouse of the thought of one of the most psychologically perceptive minds that the world has produced, it is as resistant to excavation as a diamond mine. Except in rare cases, its treasures yield themselves only to a prolonged intellectual assault; it lacks completely the quality of opening profound thought directly to the human mind and heart that the greatest art possesses. There is scarcely a line or even a word in the *Divine Comedy* that is not at once appropriate and artistically beautiful, regardless of the many horrors which are described; vast tracts of *Jerusalem* remain poetically an ugly wilderness even after we have penetrated the myth sufficiently to understand its main significance.

The synthesis that Blake failed to make in poetry, he succeeded, however, in making in the pictorial arts, particularly in engraving. Perhaps he realized this, as he turned more and more to visual expression in his later years. Much of Blake's finest poetry dates from his youth, but in drawing, painting, and engraving his best works are his last. Although many of his early designs are notable for imaginative originality, he continued to conceive finer compositions, to eliminate technical deficiencies, and to find new and more expressive modes of representation throughout his life. So the Book of Job engravings and the best of the Dante illustrations have all the depth of thought and wealth of imagination of the poems, but whereas the latter suffer because the artistic structure is not sufficiently flexible for the content, the pictorial works achieve a fusion of subject matter with form which is both meaningful and artistically satisfying.

PART II
COMMENTARY ON THE INDIVIDUAL DRAWINGS

1
INFERNO

Every Religion that Preaches Vengeance for Sin
is the Religion of the Enemy & Avenger and not
of the Forgiver of Sin, and their God is Satan,
Named by the Divine Name. . . . This was the
Religion of the Pharisees who murder'd Jesus.

Jerusalem, plate 52

I could not dare to take vengeance, for all things are so constructed
And builded by the Divine hand that the sinner shall always escape,
And he who takes vengeance alone is the criminal of Providence.
If I should dare to lay my finger on a grain of sand
In way of vengeance, I punish the already punish'd. O whom
Should I pity if I pity not the sinner who is gone astray?
O Albion, if thou takest vengeance, if thou revengest thy wrongs,
Thou art for ever lost! What can I do to hinder the Sons
Of Albion from taking vengeance?

Jerusalem 31, 30-38

. . . O God, thou art Not an Avenger!

Jerusalem 46, 28

1. DANTE RUNNING FROM THE THREE BEASTS

In the midway of this our mortal life,
I found me in a gloomy wood, astray
Gone from the path direct: and e'en to tell,
It were no easy task, how savage wild
That forest, how robust and rough its growth,
Which to remember only, my dismay
Renews, in bitterness not far from death.

Inferno 1, 1-7

THIS DESIGN is illustrative of almost the entire first canto. Dante, in the middle of his life's journey, finds himself lost in a great forest. As day begins to dawn, three evil beasts appear, first a leopard, then a lion, and lastly a she-wolf. Overcome by fear, he turns backward. As he flees, he encounters a man to whom he appeals for aid. The newcomer identifies himself as Virgil and offers to lead Dante to safety. He tells Dante that, if he wishes to escape, he must abandon the course he has been pursuing and follow him along the pathway of revelation, through hell and purgatory to paradise.

On the right and left sides of the drawing, trees arch upward to meet at the top of the page. The sun is rising in the center of the design, beyond a stretch of sea which occupies the central portion of the composition on the left. As the sun's light increases, three stars at the left begin to fade. This follows very closely the description given in the poem:

> The hour was morning's prime, and on his way
> Aloft the sun ascended with those stars,
> That with him rose when Love Divine first moved
> Those its fair works.
>   Inferno I, 35-38

To the left of center, Dante, who flees with the sea behind him, gazes fearfully over his shoulder at the beasts, who approach stealthily and fiercely on the bank at the right, the leopard at the bottom, the lion in the middle, and the she-wolf near the top of the page.[1] Dante's arms are outflung as he runs. Before him, Virgil floats, looking tenderly down at Dante; he likewise extends his arms, but gently rather than violently as Dante does.

Blake must have found much in the first canto of the *Inferno* that confirmed his conviction that the vision of all creative artists is necessarily much alike, since they have developed the power of imagination which permits them, while in this world, to catch brief glimpses of the eternal order. The symbolism of Dante's poem in this passage has a great deal in common with that of Blake's own prophetic writings. Man, who has become lost in the forest of materialism, still clings desperately and stubbornly to his own way until pressed back by the evil powers of the Fallen World. Then the poet, or Divine Imagination, comes to his aid and reveals to him that through faith man can find the pathway of salvation and that with faith will come also the realization that material dangers, which seem so formidable in this life, are but passing phantoms.

Although he follows Dante's text closely, Blake yet introduces much of his own symbolism in this design. Roots and trees are constantly used by him as symbolic of the error of this world, growing as they do blindly, concealing everything, and resisting all attempts to eradicate them. Brambles too, which appear near Dante's feet, symbolize for Blake those aspects of this life which bind man down to the material world and prevent him from attaining the spiritual freedom for which his soul longs.[2]

> Till I turn from Female Love,
> And root up the Infernal Grove,
> I shall never worthy be
> To Step into Eternity.
>   Miscellaneous Poems, p. 106[3]

Dante, therefore, in this design is to be identified with the Fallen Albion, lost in the forests of this world and confronted, in the shape of the beasts, by the Threefold

---

[1] Note the similarity of the she-wolf to the wolf of the Capitoline, with which Blake was doubtless familiar from engravings.

[2] Brambles in Blake's work are connected specifically with sexual repression and frustration.
. . . binding with briars my joys & desires.
            "The Garden of Love" from Songs of Experience, p. 74.

[3] For further characteristic passages, among many which might be cited, in which Blake uses trees as symbolical of error and the Fallen World, see *Ahania* 109-125 (p. 238); *Four Zoas* I, 456-457 (p. 264); II, 389 (p. 278); *Jerusalem* 14, 8-9; 16, 3-5; 23, 24-26; 25, 3-5; 80, 1; 89, 23; and 94, 23-25.

Accusers of the Moral Law.[4] The beasts probably also symbolize the ravening selfhood which leads man to destruction (the leopard), the terrifying power of uncontrolled rationalism which to Blake was the dominant evil of this world (the lion),[5] and the Female Will, the completely materialistic aspect of the emanation (the she-wolf).[6] Beyond the Fallen World lies the sea of Ulro, separating man from the eternal worlds of Beulah and Eden.

Near at hand, however, is man's one hope of salvation from mortal terrors. It will at once be apparent that the figure which represents the Virgil of Dante's poem is undoubtedly intended by Blake to be identified with Christ. He does not touch the material world with His feet, but floats above it, making with His arms the compassionate gesture of the cross in token of love and forgiveness. The expression of this figure is similar to many of the portrayals of Christ in Blake's works. Particularly, Blake had in mind here the great design of plate 76 of *Jerusalem*, in which the Fallen Albion, at the moment of his realization of his error of selfhood and his understanding of the means of his redemption through Christ's love, stands with his back turned and his arms spread in the form of the cross, facing the figure of Christ crucified upon the Tree of Error. As the Divine Imagination, Jesus is the Eternal Poet or Poetic Genius. Behind Him in our design the sun of imagination and the stars of divine love light up the sky above the waters over which he hovers unafraid. As the spirit of imagination seeking to keep alive in the Fallen Man a knowledge of his eternal life, Virgil is to be thought of also as Los, for Blake tells us that, at the moment of salvation, "the Divine Appearance was the likeness & similitude of Los."[7]

J. H. Wicksteed, in his important study, *Blake's Vision of the Book of Job*, noted that in the Job drawings the relative positions of the right and left feet were symbolically important and very convincingly built much of his interpretation of the Job designs around this feature. According to Wicksteed, Blake conceived of the right as associated with the spiritual aspect of man and the left with the material. While this device does not appear to be used nearly as extensively in the Dante illustrations as in those to Job, it would seem to have been employed in this case. Note that the three animals each have their left feet advanced, while the human beings step forward with their right feet. Opposed to the violent forces of the Fallen World is man, created in the image of God, and with the divine spirit accompanying him as his safeguard among the terrors of his mortal life.

The composition of this drawing is well conceived to heighten the symbolical

[4] Compare the beasts as shown here with the three accusers as they appear in the design of plate 93 of *Jerusalem*.

[5] To emphasize this connection, Blake has placed a plant with berries immediately in front of the lion; it thus serves to remind us of the Tree of Mystery, which is shown bearing fruit in such designs as Drawing 89 of the Dante series and in plate 76 of *Jerusalem*. The lion is, of course, also to be associated with "The Tyger" of Blake's most widely-known poem.

[6] Empire is no more! and now the Lion & Wolf shall Cease.
Marriage of Heaven and Hell, p. 193.

[7] *Jerusalem* 96, 7. In another sense, as Damon has suggested (*William Blake: His Philosophy and Symbols*, p. 219), the sun in this design may be thought of as setting, although the text of the *Divine Comedy* speaks of the time as dawn. As Albion is about to set out upon his journey through the Fallen World, the sun of imagination goes down, giving place to darkness. Compare the first design of the Job illustrations, in which the setting sun is shown.

meaning. The general pattern follows the circular movement which sweeps upward and inward from both sides of the design. The three beasts are poised motionless at the right, their forms pointing like three accusing fingers toward the left. Behind them rise the slanting tree trunks representative of the deeply entrenched evil of the material world. By contrast to the suspended action on the right, the left side of the drawing comes alive with light movement based upon a pattern of gracefully curving lines, both in the forms and in the ground and the tree along the margin. The precipitate rush of Dante's flight is slowed and then reversed by the form of Virgil as he floats lightly back toward the center of the page. The dark threat of this world has been met and parried and this figure, bathed in light, with its gentle curve balances the menacing linear pattern of the right side of the composition. The sun, source of light and symbol of imagination and truth, is no doubt very deliberately placed in the center of the drawing as the focus around which the contrasting movements revolve.

This is one of the few drawings of the Dante series which Blake initialed; it is also one of the most highly finished.

2. DANTE AND VIRGIL PENETRATING THE FOREST

"Lead on: one only will is in us both.
Thou art my guide, my master thou, and lord."
So spake I; and when he had onward moved,
I enter'd on the deep and woody way.

Inferno II, 138-141[1]

THIS DRAWING is relatively incomplete. Some passages have been left roughly penciled; others have been worked up considerably with india ink. Few washes have been added, save in the center background; the modeling of Virgil's form alone is fairly complete. Note how by the use of sweeping lines in the tree trunks which carry up through the pattern of the branches, the eye is kept moving so that this quite simple design is anything but static. Depth too is suggested in the center where the figures, their backs turned, move away into the mysterious background of the forest.

The symbolism of the design is not involved. Los, the power of imagination, enables man in the dark confusion of the Fallen World to "keep the Divine Vision in time of trouble";[2] that is to say, even in the fallen state man still has some link with his eternal life and this is his guide in the forest of error. Here Virgil, with hands raised confidently to fend back the branches, steps right foot forward into the dark wood.[3] He represents the spiritual aspect of the Fallen Man, Albion; the latter is, of course, Dante, who here follows meekly, his left foot advanced and his hands lowered in a

---

[1] Although Blake rarely gives line references in the inscriptions on the drawings, he has done so here. In the lower right hand corner may be faintly discerned in pencil, "HELL, Canto 2, 140."

[2] *Jerusalem* 95, 20.

[3] As indicated by the leaves, the trees on the left are oaks, the symbol of Druidism in Blake's work. The poets are about to enter the dark forest of the Fallen World in which men have lost the vision of a religion of forgiveness and replaced it by one in which the Divine Humanity is sacrificed. See Frye, *Fearful Symmetry*, pp. 397-400.

Albion's Forests of Oaks cover'd the Earth from Pole to Pole.

Jerusalem 89, 23.

gesture of submission. After the terrors which he had encountered in following the selfhood, as portrayed in the first design, Dante now sets off on the pathway of faith with his Poetic Genius as his guide.[4]

[4] In symbolism this illustration is similar to the title page of *Milton* and the frontispiece of *Jerusalem*. See also the engraving by Blake on p. 4 of the edition of Edward Young's *Night Thoughts* published in London by R. Edwards in 1797.

3. THE MISSION OF VIRGIL

IN THIS DESIGN Blake departs very largely from the text of the *Divine Comedy* and relies to a great extent upon his own symbolism. Although the drawing is inscribed "HELL Canto 2," a reading of this canto will not enlighten us greatly as to what is represented; only a knowledge of Blake's ideas as set forth in his writings will enable us to understand why this subject is portrayed in this particular way.

The mission of Virgil is to guide and guard Dante on his journey through hell. Remembering that Blake identified the Fallen World of our present existence with hell, it becomes clear that this design represents Dante as he is about to enter the created world. Virgil, who is to be thought of as representing Dante's spiritual aspect, has already entered and stands upon a bank within, encouraging Dante to follow him. The latter starts back at the sight of the three beasts—representative of the evils of the natural world—which menace him from the forest of error at the left. The portal through which Dante is about to pass is composed of a layer of cloud, always used by Blake to represent the division between different spheres of existence.[1]

That we have here the gate to the Fallen World is indicated by the figure of Jehovah with arms outstretched which dominates the top of the page. Lest we should miss his significance, Blake has written lightly in pencil above him, "The Angry God of this World." In his bearded form, we can recognize the demonic Urizen as often portrayed by Blake. Although the details are not distinct here, a comparison with the drawing from the *Paradise Regained* series, "Christ's Troubled Dream," will indicate that Blake intended to show serpents—symbols of materialism—as extending across the shoulders of the figure and hanging down from his hands, probably accompanied by forks of lightning.[2] It will be noted that the right foot of the figure is human, but that the left is the cloven hoof of an animal. This figure is much akin to that of Jehovah in the eleventh illustration to the Book of Job, "With Dreams upon my bed thou scarest me & affrightest me with Visions." Job's conception of God, who hovers over him on the bed, is there shown entwined with a serpent, surrounded by jagged strokes of lightning, and with a cloven hoof in place of his left foot; in addition,

[1] This symbolism appears in many of the Job engravings, as for instance the fourteenth and fifteenth of the series.

[2] This is indicated by the fact that Blake has written very lightly in pencil near the right hand of the figure, "The Thunder," and near the left hand, "of Egypt." (For the significance of Egypt in Blake's symbolism, see discussion of Drawing 99 below.) The other penciled inscription at the top of the page is somewhat difficult to decipher, but is apparently as follows: "The Angry God of this World & [his (Porch? or Throne?) in] Purgatory."

The drawing from *Paradise Regained* referred to is reproduced in Figgis, *Paintings of William Blake*, plate 30.

he points to the tablets of the Mosaic Law behind him. The expression of the figure in the present drawing is less fierce, however, and recalls somewhat the hopelessness which we find in the features of Jehovah in the fifth design of the Job series.[3]

In Blake's view, the organized religions of this world worship a false God who operates on a basis of meting out dire punishments for violation of an arbitrary code. Ever since his early work, *The Marriage of Heaven and Hell*, Blake had identified this God with Urizen, and contrasted his nature with that of the Father described by Christ, who is all love and forgiveness. It is this false God who is portrayed here, much in the manner in which he is described in the Epilogue of *The Gates of Paradise*, which, it will be recalled, is addressed "To The Accuser who is The God of This World":

> Tho' thou art Worship'd by the Names Divine
> Of Jesus & Jehovah, thou art still
> The Son of Morn in weary Night's decline,
> The lost Traveller's Dream under the Hill.

Behind this God of Urizenic rationalism, the setting sun of divine imagination is almost eclipsed. [4]

Having set a false God before the people as a means of enhancing their power, the kings and priests of the Fallen World bow down to worship him.[5] The figure who here kneels before Urizen is young and powerful, representing the strength of the repressive forces which deprive the individual man of his liberty and compel the worship of tradition.[6] On his head is the spiked crown of empire and with his right hand he swings the smoking censer of religious mystery.[7] The Maltese Cross, *fleurs-de-lis*, and castles which form the design of his garment are alike symbols of worldly and ecclesiastical power. With his left hand, this figure points down at enslaved mankind, represented by the two figures at the lower corners of the page. One figure is hopeless and age-bent, his hands folded in resignation; the other is young and potentially revolutionary, but he is in chains.[8] Both have the bewildered

---

[3] Compare this figure also with that of plate 15 of *Milton*.

[4] The following two passages from the prophetic books suggest in a remarkable way much of the imagery of this design: *Four Zoas* viib, 17-37 (p. 323) and *Jerusalem* 66, 8-15.

> [5] . . . . . he is the Great Selfhood,
> Satan, Worship'd as God by the Mighty Ones of the Earth.
>
> *Jerusalem* 33, 17-18

[6] This figure recalls that of Satan in illustrations 2, 3, 5, 7, and 16 of the Job series. Blake has indicated its identification with military and imperial power by writing "Caesar" faintly near the censer.

[7] A similar censer appears in the drawing of the Sacrifice of Isaac in the Boston Museum of Fine Arts. Human sacrifice, both literal and figurative, signifies for Blake the extremity of perversion of which religion is capable in the Fallen World. The censer would seem to be his pictorial symbol of it as well as of religious mystery in general.

[8] "The Giants who formed this world into its sensual existence . . . now seem to live in it in chains." (*Marriage of Heaven and Hell*, p. 187) Young Orc, the revolutionary of the prophetic books, is frequently described as being bound in chains.

It should be noted that the bound figure at the left is clothed in a blue flame, that at right in a red one. From this it may be inferred that they are to be identified with the fallen spectres of

expression of inbred ignorance and are consumed by the flames of repressed desire, indicative of the stifling of the natural aspiration of the human soul toward intellectual freedom and spiritual self-expression.

These figures in flames are souls in Ulro, at the extreme nadir of the Fall. However, even here man has not completely lost all consciousness of his eternal life, and thus through God's mercy there is always hope of regeneration. This link which binds man to eternity no matter how great his fall is symbolized by Blake for each individual by his emanation, who in the aggregate are known as the Daughters of Beulah. Seated at looms, they weave bodies for the spirits who wander in Ulro, that they may be born into this mortal world of Generation and so take the first step toward salvation.

The significance of the remaining figures of this design should now be clear. We see here the gate which forms the entrance from Ulro into Generation. Having accepted the guidance of Virgil, the emissary of his emanation Beatrice, Dante is about to be rescued from Ulro and to enter the mortal world of Generation on the first stage of his journey toward salvation. Above, beneath a bower of vine leaves signifying life, Beatrice sits at her loom and spinning wheel, and from her, within the cloud which forms the gate, the Daughters of Beulah make their journeys to and from Ulro.[9]

> The daughters of Beulah follow sleepers in all their dreams,
> Creating spaces, lest they fall into Eternal Death.
> The Circle of Destiny complete, they gave to it a space
> And nam'd the space Ulro, & brooded over it in care & love.
> They said: "The Spectre is in every man insane & most
> Deform'd. Thro' the three heavens descending in fury & fire
> We meet it with our songs & loving blandishments, & give
> To it a form of vegetation."
> Four Zoas I, 95-102 (p. 254)

The lower portions of this illustration are approaching completion, but it becomes progressively more sketchy toward the top. It is initialed, in the flames near the head of the lion. S. Foster Damon, in his *William Blake*, p. 219, comments on this drawing very briefly, calling attention to much the same symbolism which we have discussed above.

Dante and Virgil. (See discussion of the following drawing, "The Inscription over Hell-Gate," for a comment on the colors of the costumes worn by the poets throughout the series.)

[9] For the Daughters of Beulah at their looms, see *Jerusalem* 59, 22-38. The four female figures were doubtless suggested to Blake by the four women mentioned in the second canto of the *Inferno* (the Virgin, St. Lucy, Rachel and Beatrice). However, their identification by Blake with the Daughters of Beulah is evident. As the emanation of Dante, Beatrice is appropriately the most prominent figure of the group.

4. THE INSCRIPTION OVER HELL–GATE[1]

THE GENERAL SUBJECT of this drawing is perhaps best given by the following lines:

[1] At the top of the design, Blake has written in pencil in Italian the inscription which Dante gives as being placed above the Gate of Hell: *"Lasciate ogni Speranza, voi ch'entrate."* Beneath he has written a very literal translation: "Leave every Hope you who in Enter." The drawing is initialed on the ground just beneath the right foot of Dante.

> . . . And when his hand he had stretch'd forth
> To mine, with pleasant looks, whence I was cheer'd,
> Into that secret place he led me on.

Inferno III, 18-20

Having stepped to the edge of the gate, Dante stands on the threshold looking in. Virgil stands a step ahead of him, looking back at him and holding him by the wrist. Both gesture toward the scene which appears beyond the gate. It will be noted that Virgil, as he bears a spiritual relationship to Dante, steps forward with his right foot and gestures with his right hand, while Dante does the opposite. Before them lies the World of Generation, with its four continents; in addition, the lost continent of Atlantis[2] is shown, sunk beneath the ocean. Blue, yellow, and red flames rise throughout the scene. A few small human figures appear upon the edges of two of the upper continents. The gateway is framed on each side by large trees with big roots and green leaves, marking the confines of the dark wood in which Virgil found Dante. It will be noted that, while the water and rising circles with fire suggest the Acheron and the circles of the Inferno beyond, the number of these and the mountain shown beneath the waves make it probable that Blake was also thinking of the created world, which he equates with hell.

In this drawing, which is the only one reproduced in color in the National Art-Collections Fund portfolio, it will be noted that Dante is dressed in red and Virgil in blue, a distinction which is maintained throughout the series, certainly with definite intent. Northrop Frye,[3] in a table of correspondences of various aspects of the Zoas, has indicated that blue is the color which Blake associates with Los and red with Luvah. We have already established in our discussion of the first drawing that Blake there identified Virgil with Los. The two Zoas which must be dominant in the creative artist are, of course, those of imagination and feeling. These two aspects of the poetic genius were doubtless associated by Blake with Virgil, the poet who already dwells in the eternal realm, and Dante, the poet in this world. Dante, therefore, wears red, Luvah's color, as symbolic of the emotional life of the poet.

[2] See *America*, lines 144-149 (p. 205).   [3] *Fearful Symmetry*, pp. 277-278.

5. THE VESTIBULE OF HELL, AND THE SOULS MUSTERING TO CROSS THE ACHERON

THIS ILLUSTRATION follows the text of the *Divine Comedy* very closely. Dante and Virgil, on a bank in the right foreground, watch the spirits mustering by the bank of the Acheron and awaiting Charon, who in a boat with oar and sail is returning from the opposite bank, on which may be seen those whom he has just deposited there, guarded by two demons. Lines 50-64 of the third canto are followed quite literally.

> And I, who straightway look'd, beheld a flag,
> Which whirling ran around so rapidly,
> That it no pause obtain'd: and following came
> Such a long train of spirits, I should ne'er
> Have thought that death so many had despoil'd.

5 4

When some of these I recognised, I saw
And knew the shade of him, who to base fear
Yielding, abjured his high estate.[1] Forthwith
I understood, for certain, this the tribe
Of those ill spirits both to God displeasing
And to His foes. These wretches, who ne'er lived,
Went on in nakedness, and sorely stung
By wasps and hornets, which bedew'd their cheeks
With blood, that, mix'd with tears, dropp'd to their feet,
And by disgustful worms was gather'd there.

It will be noted that the great line of people are shown, with the flag being carried ahead of them. They make gestures of despair as they are preyed upon by the hornets and worms. The figures, however, are clothed, although the text specifies that they were naked. Blake, as usual in such scenes, identifies various figures with those who sought and held power in this world, as indicated by the crown on one and the weapons which several carry. The woman with arms upraised near the flag recalls the Whore of Babylon as depicted by Blake in Drawing 89 of this series. The people pressing down to the dock and Charon's boat are as described in the text. The position of Dante and Virgil recalls line 49, "Speak not of them, but look, and pass them by."

In the sky above is shown the sad choir of the angels who were neither rebellious nor true to God.[2] Expelled from heaven, they are not received into hell, but wander, as portrayed here, in the vague misty spaces between. All appear to be female, save for the aged bearded figure in the center who will be recognized as the resigned and hopeless Jehovah of the fifth Job design.

Dante's description of those in hell as "the souls to misery doom'd, who intellectual good have lost"[3] would have particularly appealed to Blake, reminding him of his own query: "What are the Pains of Hell but Ignorance, Bodily Lust, Idleness & devastation of the things of the Spirit?"[4] The worms would also suggest to Blake a figure which he often employs for fallen man: "a worm of sixty winters creeping on the dusky ground."[5]

While some of the foreground figures are awkward in pose and detail, this design is notable for the handling of movement in the masses of forms; sometimes jagged, sometimes smoothly flowing, it builds up general motion in a clockwise direction. Space is well suggested too, and light is handled expressively to give the mood by means of the dark threatening sky and the stormy reflections on the water.

The drawing is signed with Blake's monogram.

[1] Pope Celestine V. He cannot be identified among the figures in the drawing, perhaps an intentional subtlety on Blake's part.
[2] *Inferno* III, 33-41.
[3] *Ibid.*, 16-18.
[4] *Jerusalem*, plate 77.
[5] *Tiriel*, line 336 (p. 160). An interesting passage in Blake's early unfinished work, *The French Revolution* (lines 131-150, pp. 172-173), recalls this drawing in a striking way. Blake may well have had it in mind when designing this illustration.

6. CHARON AND THE CONDEMNED SOULS

BLAKE has again followed the text of Dante's poem closely. The drawing is inscribed "HELL Canto 3, line 76." This obviously refers to Cary's translation, lines 76 and 77 of which are:

> . . . And lo! toward us in a bark
> Comes an old man. . . .

The design illustrates in a general way the scene described between this point and line 113.

On the right the condemned souls are gathered on the dock, gesturing and crying out as described in the text. Charon's boat is secured to the pier by a line passed through a mooring ring. It tosses on the waves to the left center of the design, its mast rising out of the top of the drawing and the rudder flapping in the stern. The after portion is shown already laden with lightly sketched forms. Behind the stern can be seen the other bank of the stream, which is piled with great rocks up which figures are climbing. Charon stands on the gunwale to the left of the mast, his arms raised as he addresses the spirits on the shore (lines 78-82). Dante and Virgil stand in the upper right center on a high bank by the edge of the river.

Certain details are quite exact as, for instance, the manner in which Charon's eyes are shown as "wheeling flames" (line 93). However, Charon carries a trident instead of an oar (line 103), probably because Blake thinks of him here as a god of the waters. Also, while the figures already in the boat seem to be naked (line 94), those on the shore are clothed.

This drawing does not contain any significant symbolism which is peculiar to Blake. It is very unfinished, being largely in pencil, with a few lines touched in with ink and a few tentative washes, mostly near the bottom of the page. The composition is effectively worked out, with two heavy masses of land rising at either side of the design; in the center the figure of Charon and the leaning mast set up a movement which is balanced by the contrary motion of the gesticulating group on the shore.

The demonic figure of Charon should be compared with one in the upper left corner of the design on plate 87 of *Jerusalem*. As lord of the waters, Charon is perhaps here to be identified with the Fallen Tharmas, whom Damon (*William Blake*, p. 474) associates with the figure in the *Jerusalem* illustration. In quite another connection, nearly thirty years previously, Blake made another illustration in which Charon appears, but he is there quite different in appearance. The design of which he forms the subject is a drawing, now in the British Museum, which illustrates the text of page 28 of "Night the Fifth" of Edward Young's *Night Thoughts*, in which Charon is mentioned.

7. HOMER, BEARING THE SWORD, AND HIS COMPANIONS

HERE AGAIN we have Blake, on the slightest of suggestions from Dante, going off into elaborate symbolism all his own. The two details of this design which can possibly have any connection with the text are the group in the upper left of Dante unconscious with Virgil bending over him (III, 123-126) and the central figure of Homer, who carries a sword (IV, 80-83). Blake has identified the latter by writing his name lightly over his head.

The key to this design is given by the long inscription in pencil on the drawing, which is as follows:

> Every thing in Dante's Comedia shews That for Tyrannical Purposes he has made This World the Foundation of All, & the Goddess Nature Mistress; Nature is his Inspirer & not the Holy Ghost. As Poor (Shakspeare?)[1] said: "Nature, thou art my Goddess."
>
> Round Purgatory is Paradise, & round Paradise is Vacuum or Limbo, so that Homer is the Center of All—I mean the Poetry of the Heathen, Stolen & Perverted from the Bible, not by Chance but by design, by the Kings of Persia & their Generals, The Greek Heroes & lastly by the Romans.
>
> Swedenborg does the same in saying that in this World is the Ultimate of Heaven. This is the most damnable Falshood of Satan & his Antichrist.

Hence Blake in the lower part of the drawing shows the natural world, with Homer, carrying an upraised sword, in the center of the page. Since Blake equates the created world with hell, the design is divided into the nine concentric circles of Dante's Inferno, with Homer in the middle. The circles are numbered, beginning with the first circle which is so labelled on the rock at the left. The ninth circle is in the center. Between the head of Homer and the sword in his hand, Blake has written the word "Satan," which is partially erased.

We now begin to see what Blake's intentions are. The group which seems to represent Dante and Virgil in the upper left, in reality shows the Fallen Albion asleep upon the rock of his eternal life, guarded over by his emanation, Jerusalem. As the sleeping form apparently has a halo and the group has very much the aspect of a Pietà, Blake probably also had in mind Jesus, who died for man's salvation, but who is not master of the created world. Homer thus becomes Urizen, holding the sword by which he enforces his iron laws for man's enslavement. In the second circle, near the rock, are seen a group of the lovers who in the *Inferno* are found in this circle; near them float a group of "Infant Joys." Love is banished to the periphery of the Fallen World,[2] while the sword rules its center. The first circle is also inscribed at the top in accordance with the description that is given of it in the fourth canto as the "Limbo of Weak Shadows."

For Blake's reasons for this conception of Homer, we must remember his antagonism to the classics, which grew in his later years. He considered that the ancients

---

[1] While "Shakspeare" is the reading given by Keynes (p. 700), close examination of the drawing will show that this is evidently incorrect. However, I have not been able to decipher Blake's handwriting at this point. The line referred to is spoken by Edmund in *King Lear*, act I, scene ii, line 1. ("Thou, nature, art my goddess.")

[2] Children of the future Age
Reading this indignant page,
Know that in a former time
Love! sweet Love! was thought a crime.
"A Little Girl Lost," Songs of Experience, p. 78

thought only in terms of this world, and were thus lacking in spiritual insight which tells us that this earth is fallen, and mortal life but a cruel mockery of that of the eternal realm. As, in Blake's eyes, the ancients were materialists, they exalted reason to supreme judge and glorified war and conquest as the ultimate arbiters of human affairs. Hence, to his mind, the appearance in Dante's poem of Homer bearing a sword has particular significance.

Blake sets forth these opinions in three main passages which, since they are vital to understanding this design, are here quoted in full.

> Sacred Truth has pronounced that Greece & Rome, as Babylon & Egypt, so far from being parents of Arts & Sciences as they pretend, were destroyers of all Art. Homer, Virgil & Ovid confirm this opinion & make us reverence The Word of God, the only light of antiquity that remains unperverted by War. Virgil in the Eneid, Book vi, line 848, says "Let others study Art: Rome has somewhat better to do, namely War & Dominion."[3]
>
> Rome & Greece swept Art into their maw & destroy'd it; a Warlike State never can produce Art. It will Rob & Plunder & accumulate into one place, & Translate & Copy & Buy & Sell & Criticise, but not Make. Grecian is Mathematic Form: Gothic is Living Form. Mathematic Form is Eternal in the Reasoning Memory: Living Form is Eternal Existence.
>
> On Virgil, p. 583

In the next two quotations, Blake expounds his belief that, since classical literature and art grew out of a rational philosophy, they must be lacking in inspiration, and that when truly creative elements do appear, they must indicate a dependence upon more inspired sources.

> The Stolen and Perverted Writings of Homer & Ovid, of Plato & Cicero, which all men ought to contemn, are set up by artifice against the Sublime of the Bible; but when the New Age is at leisure to Pronounce, all will be set right, & those Grand Works of the more ancient & consciously & professedly Inspired Men will hold their proper rank, & the Daughters of Memory shall become the Daughters of Inspiration. Shakspeare & Milton were both curb'd by the general malady & infection from the silly Greek & Latin slaves of the Sword. . . . We do not want either Greek or Roman Models if we are but just & true to our own Imaginations, those Worlds of Eternity in which we shall live for ever in JESUS OUR LORD.
>
> Milton, Preface, p. 375

> Fable or Allegory are a totally distinct & inferior kind of Poetry. Vision or Imagination is a Representation of what Eternally Exists, Really & Unchangeably.

[3] T. C. Williams' translation of the passage referred to is as follows:

> Let others melt and mould the breathing bronze
> To forms more fair, aye, out of marble bring
> Features that live; let them plead causes well;
> Or trace with pointed wand the cycled heaven,
> And hail the constellations as they rise;
> But thou, O Roman, learn with sovereign sway
> To rule the nations.

Fable or Allegory is Form'd by the daughters of Memory. Imagination is surrounded by the daughters of Inspiration who in the aggregate are call'd Jerusalem. . . . The Hebrew Bible & the Gospel of Jesus are not Allegory, but Eternal Vision or Imagination of All that Exists.

Vision of the Last Judgment, pp. 637-638

After reading these passages, the meaning of this drawing should be apparent. Dante, in Blake's opinion, has also been "curb'd by the general malady & infection from the silly Greek & Latin slaves of the Sword." This has caused him to make "This World the Foundation of All" and for this reason "Homer is the Center of All." In parts at least, the *Divine Comedy* appears to Blake to be "Fable or Allegory" instead of "Vision or Imagination."

We are now in a position to identify the remaining figures in the lower part of the design, who certainly are not the poets who accompany Homer in Dante's text. These six female figures who float toward Homer bearing the scrolls of tradition are the Daughters of Memory.[4] Their home is in the created world, while that of the Daughters of Beulah or Inspiration—whom we saw in the third design of this series—is in eternity.

Homer being the center of all, Blake has proceeded to illustrate another part of his inscription along the top and right edge of the page. "Round Purgatory is Paradise, & round Paradise is Vacuum or Limbo." In the upper right corner we see a drawing of this. A circle marked "Purgatory" is thus inscribed: "It is an Island in Limbo." Above the circle are the words "Terrestrial Paradise." From the circle radiate arcs which are labelled similarly both at the top and along the right side of the page to correspond with the spheres into which Dante divides the heaven of his *Paradiso*. From the center outward they are: "Moon, Mercury, Venus, Sun, Mars, Jupiter, Saturn, Starry Heaven," and in Blake's own characteristic phrase, "Vacuum."

The last word tells much about Blake's fundamental disagreement with Dante. In the *Divine Comedy* the scenes of the *Inferno* are extremely real, but everything becomes invisible and intangible in the *Paradiso*. This to Blake could only suggest that Dante was deficient in vision, the greatest gift of the poet, and could not visualize in terms other than those of this world. Blake felt that true vision should behold eternity more vividly than it does the Fallen World. "The Prophets describe what they saw in Vision as real and existing men, whom they saw with their imaginative and immortal organs; the Apostles the same; the clearer the organ the more distinct the object. A Spirit and a Vision are not, as the modern philosophy supposes, a cloudy vapour, or a nothing: they are organized and minutely articulated beyond all that the mortal and perishing nature can produce. He who does not imagine in stronger and better lineaments, and in stronger and better light than his perishing and mortal eye can see, does not imagine at all. The painter of this work asserts that all his imaginations appear to him infinitely more perfect and more minutely organized than any thing seen by his mortal eye. Spirits are organized men."[5]

---

[4] "The Greek Muses are daughters of Mnemosyne, or Memory, and not of Inspiration or Imagination." *A Descriptive Catalogue*, p. 595.

[5] *Ibid.*, p. 607. For a slightly different theory of the basis of this illustration, see Damon, *William Blake*, p. 219.

This drawing is a very slight pencil sketch, with only the central figure approaching completion. There are a few inked passages. Homer is clad in a red garment, and there are faint traces of blue in the three circles immediately over his head; otherwise the design is uncolored.

8. HOMER AND THE ANCIENT POETS

> . . . on the brink
> I found me of the lamentable vale,
> The dread abyss, that joins a thunderous sound
> Of plaints innumerable. Dark and deep,
> And thick with clouds o'erspread, mine eye in vain
> Explored its bottom, nor could aught discern.
>
> *Inferno* IV, 6-11

DANTE AND VIRGIL stand at the edge of a cliff at the top of the design, looking down into a chasm. A heavy cloud floats across the valley below them. The most important part of the drawing is the lower portion; this does not follow the text closely. In the poem, Dante and Virgil descend into the valley before they meet the poets, whose presence is first revealed to them in the dark forest by the light of a fire. Dante and Virgil join the group, who lead them to a castle, the seven concentric walls of which are surrounded by a stream. They enter and find themselves in a beautiful meadow. In this illustration we have in effect a combination of three scenes: Dante and Virgil looking down into the valley, the poets in the wood with the fire above them, and the verdant meadow. The castle is not shown.

The groups of figures in the lower part of the drawing call for further explanation. Dante lists but four poets; in addition to Homer, they are Horace, Ovid and Lucan. It will be noted that Blake shows five. Also, Blake has introduced a group of flying figures in the center and some other figures in the lower right without any authority for them in the text.

In seeking an explanation for these differences, we must return to the inscription on the previous illustration and to the further passages quoted in the discussion of it. The present drawing has its origin in Blake's belief that, since classical literature grew out of a rational philosophy, it must be lacking in inspiration. The classical poets, therefore, stand in a grove—Blake's symbol of error—which shuts them off from perceiving the graceful, flying forms of imagination in the center of the design.[1] Their poetry is thought of by Blake as being "Fable or Allegory" and not "Vision or Imagination." However, one of the passages previously quoted continues as follows: "Fable or Allegory is seldom without some Vision. Pilgrim's Progress is full of it, the Greek Poets the same."[2] Hence, while the trees separate the poets from the forms of fancy, the division is not a very great one. Creatures of imagination do reveal themselves in the created world and are thus shown beneath the cloudy layer. Dante and Virgil,

---

[1] A frequent theme of the marginal decorations of the prophetic books is that of emanations guiding children in spiritual flight, as shown here. See, for example, plate 2 of *Urizen*.

[2] *Vision of the Last Judgment*, p. 638.

representing as we have seen the eternal poetic attributes of feeling and creative genius, have their place outside the valley and above the clouds.

As to the presence of five poets, they represent "the five Senses, the chief inlets of Soul in this age,"[3] classical poetry being in Blake's view rationally rather than divinely inspired, and thus based primarily on the evidence of the senses.

Above the poets, a figure tends the sacred flame of Poetic Genius. The massive altar and general oriental appearance of the priest with his smoking censer remind us that these are heathen poets, whose art frequently glorified wordly power and its accompanying religions of mystery. Opposed to this less favorable aspect of classical poetry are the idyllic groups on the opposite side of the design. Blake no doubt considered the pastoral, with its emphasis on the beauty of the world and of the humble joys of life, to be the most inspired form of classical poetry, being the furthest removed from the glorification of "War and Dominion." However, the ancients failed to see that the beauties of the world are but symbols of the glories of eternity, so clouds still hover over this group; nevertheless, they are less dark and threatening than they are above the altar, and trees now reach up through them as an indication of a linking of the two worlds.

The drawing is approaching completion, although some passages are only lightly sketched. The general color effect is delicate and harmonious.

[3] *Marriage of Heaven and Hell*, p. 182.

9. MINOS

> . . . There Minos stands,
> Grinning with ghastly feature: he, of all
> Who enter, strict examining the crimes,
> Gives sentence, and dismisses them beneath,
> According as he foldeth him around:
> For when before him comes the ill-fated soul,
> It all confesses; and that judge severe
> Of sins, considering what place in Hell
> Suits the transgression, with his tail so oft
> Himself encircles, as degrees beneath
> He dooms it to descend. Before him stand
> Alway a numerous throng; and in his turn
> Each one to judgment passing, speaks, and hears
> His fate, thence downward to his dwelling hurl'd.
>
> Inferno v, 4-17

IT WILL be noted that, while Minos condemns sinners to all the various circles of hell, Blake shows only the lascivious whose place is in the second circle. Except for Dante and Virgil, none of the other figures shown are specifically mentioned. Minos girds himself with his tail as described, but he is seated on a throne instead of standing and has a spear and crown which do not figure in the text. In typical fashion, Blake has developed an elaborate treatment of his own ideas out of the briefest suggestion in the work that he is illustrating. This time his subject is sex in the Fallen World.[1]

Of all the aspects of this life which indicated to Blake that we live in a fallen world, none was more convincing than the debasement of love. The sense which, even in its most physical aspect, is capable of bringing the human being most vividly to a realization of his divine nature, he saw as the vehicle of cruel self-gratification and jealous restraint. In an unfallen world governed by love, sex could be only an expression of supreme joy. For Fallen Man it becomes too often merely sensual gratification and for Fallen Woman a means of obtaining dominion over her mate. The systems into which human beings always organize themselves attempt to solve the difficulties thus created by means of rigid moral laws; these only make matters worse by bringing in their wake secrecy, repression, and loss of individual liberty.

This illustration shows us "The Accuser who is The God of This World" sitting upon his throne and passing judgment based upon his cruel moral law. Dante may call him Minos, but to Blake he is, of course, Satan or Urizen, and has the brutal and ignorant bearded face of many representations of Urizen in the prophetic books. On his head he wears the crown of worldly power which rules through slavery of the multitude. His right hand is raised in angry condemnation and his left holds the heavy spear of cruel punishment.[2] The smoky fires of hate and wrath rise up behind him and from them peer the "angels" of convention who support his rule because of unimaginative tradition but whose faces, nevertheless, show doubt, wonder, horror and pity at the scene before them. Lightning flashes from the cloud behind them.

Virgil leads Dante up through flames in the left foreground and beckons with his right hand to attract Minos' attention. Above him a female figure plunges head downward, pointing to Minos, while a male figure, likewise plunging downward, reaches eagerly for her. This group probably represents the aspect of female love which seeks only dominion over man; the woman keeps her lover in a state of hopeless frustration by pointing to the authority of moral law. It will be noted that all the women in this illustration look at Minos, with the exception of only one who prostrates herself before him.

In the lower right of the design, another aspect of human love is shown, the cruelty of man as opposed to the jealousy of woman. A demonic man with wings and talons seeks to carry off a woman who resists him and looks to Minos for succor.

Prostrate before Minos is another couple, the man with his head in his hands in bewilderment and the woman, clothed, making a submissive gesture before him. They are doubtless to be thought of as a couple who have led a frustrated married life through ignorant and fearful interpretation of the moral law. The "marriage chain" of jealousy, wrought from "mind-forg'd manacles" lies beside them.

> . . . she who burns with youth, and knows no fixed lot, is bound
> In spells of law to one she loaths; and must she drag the chain

---

[1] *The Visions of the Daughters of Albion* is the most important of Blake's poems on this subject, although nearly all of his prophetic works treat it to some extent. For Blake's theories concerning sex, see Blackstone, *English Blake*, pp. 288-299; Damon, *William Blake*, pp. 98-104; and Percival, *Blake's "Circle of Destiny,"* pp. 107-127.

[2] So Urizen arose, & leaning on his spear explor'd his dens.
Four Zoas VI, 1 (p. 300)

Of life in weary lust? must chilling, murderous thoughts obscure
The clear heaven of her eternal spring; to bear the wintry rage
Of a harsh terror, driv'n to madness, bound to hold a rod
Over her shrinking shoulders all the day, & all the night
To turn the wheel of false desire, and longings that wake her womb
To the abhorred birth of cherubs in the human form.
                    Visions of the Daughters of Albion, 132-139 (p. 198)

Finally, in the upper right a fourth couple hover over the angry waters of annihilation, just on the point of plunging beneath the flood.[3] They are probably to be thought of as a couple who really love but who, having violated some moral law which takes no account of individualities or circumstances, are about to be destroyed. Two heads of the drowning may be seen in the waters beneath them.

Have you known the Judgment that is arisen among the
Zoas of Albion, where a Man dare hardly to embrace
His own Wife for the terrors of Chastity that they call
By the name of Morality?
                    Jerusalem 36, 43-46

Thus Blake shows how man has perverted sexual love. In his fallen state man has only one other approach to eternity—through creative art, which is vision. Hence behind the poets the bright flames of Poetic Genius arise. But the Fallen World which degrades sex despises the artist too, and Minos directs his gesture of damnation at them.

This is a finished watercolor, and is initialed. In composition it is one of the finest of the series. Note the waves of movement which sweep in at various speeds and in different planes from all sides and break against the opposing direction of Minos' gesture, an opposition reinforced by his spear and by the shape of the column of smoke behind him. The whole builds up a design of great interest and dramatic power, which perfectly unifies the elaborate symbolism and does it so successfully that even without a knowledge of its inner meaning we still have a striking picture.

[3] The sea may also have been suggested to Blake by the text. See *Inferno* v, 30-32.

10 and 10E. THE CIRCLE OF THE LUSTFUL: FRANCESCA DA RIMINI

THIS MEMORABLE DESIGN is derived from perhaps the most famous passage in Dante—*Inferno* v, 27-138.[1] Dante and Virgil find themselves in a region of hell where guilty

[1] Several preparatory sketches for this design have been noted. In W. M. Rossetti's catalogue in Gilchrist's *Life* (II, p. 234, no. 126) one is listed as belonging to "Mr. Aspland"; its present whereabouts are unknown to me. Two pencil drawings which were until recently in the collection of the late W. Graham Robertson have inscriptions by Frederick Tatham linking them with this subject. One of these has been reproduced on a number of occasions; when I had the opportunity of examining the other, through the kindness of the present owner, Geoffrey Keynes, Esq., it appeared to me that, notwithstanding Tatham's inscription, it is not a sketch for this subject, but for the nineteenth illustration of the series, "The Angel Crossing Styx." (See A. G. B. Russell, "The Graham Robertson Collection," *Burlington Magazine*, XXXVII, 1920, list iii, p. 39; Geoffrey Keynes, *Pencil Drawings by William Blake*, London, 1927, plate 79; Kerrison Preston (ed.), *The Blake Collection of W. Graham Robertson*, London, 1952, no. 83, p. 193, and no. 84,

lovers are forever tossed aimlessly about by powerful winds. Virgil points out many famous personages among them and Dante expresses a desire to speak with the lovers Paolo Malatesta and Francesca da Rimini. Francesca was the wife of Paolo's brother, Gianciotto, who slew them both when he found them together. Paolo and Francesca float by on the wind, and Francesca tells Dante of the incident which led to the awakening of their love. Dante, overcome by pity, falls unconscious to the ground.

This is one of the boldest and most original of Blake's designs and succeeds admirably in capturing the mood of eternal restlessness and longing which is so beautifully suggested by the poem. The wind sweeps the group of lovers up from the waters at the bottom of the page, tosses them in a great circle in the left center of the design, and bears them out of sight in the upper left. The river bank appears in the right half of the drawing. Virgil stands upon it looking down at Dante who lies stretched at his feet. Paolo and Francesca, who are separated from the other lovers, appear in a flame which licks upward from behind Dante toward the left. Above Virgil is a vision of the sun, in the center of which the kneeling lovers are shown at the moment of the kiss which first brought them together.

In only two respects does the illustration differ appreciably from the text. Except in a somewhat indirect manner, in lines 30-32, the poem makes no mention of a sea or river, but angry waters make up an important part of the design. The text also lists numerous lovers by name but, aside from Paolo and Francesca themselves, none can be distinguished as individuals in Blake's drawing.

In spite of the closeness with which the artist has followed the poem, and the skill with which he has developed a highly original composition in harmony not only with the literal story but also with the emotional and artistic essence of the text, we may also find here quite a number of elements which are distinctly Blake's own. In this design he shows us souls, bewildered after the Fall, just beginning to emerge into definite form from the depths of Ulro. As they are caught up in the current of love, which as indicative of God's grace fills even the Fallen World, they begin to take form and to recognize one another. The spectres and emanations draw together in the whirling circle—which represents the World of Generation—and float off in couples heavenward at the upper left. A few, however, whose attitude toward love is selfish, become lost in this life: thus we see a male figure who crashes headfirst into the shore, and a female head disappears beneath the waves just to the left of the bank.

Dante lies outstretched upon the ground. The dead world of matter lies underneath him, the whirling generated world of his mortal life is at his feet. By his head

p. 194 and reproduction; Catalogue of the Graham Robertson Sale at Messrs. Christie, London, July 22, 1949, no. 72, p. 37 and reproduction, and no. 79, p. 40.) Another sketch which has been associated with this subject, but which has little connection with the work in its final form, is in the collection of Lessing J. Rosenwald, Esq., at Jenkintown, Pennsylvania. (See the catalogue of the exhibition of Blake's work held at Philadelphia in 1939, pp. 100-101, no. 151 and reproduction.)

Anthony Blunt ("Blake's Pictorial Imagination," *Journal of the Warburg and Courtauld Institutes*, VI, 1943, pp. 201 and 211) comments on possible sources for this design. He suggests that the intertwined figures are derived from Michelangelo's "Last Judgment," a work which Blake greatly admired.

stands his Poetic Genius and from his body rises the flame of his emotional life. The flame encloses the forms of Paolo and Francesca, whose memory still lives in the created world only because of his genius. In the two groups of lovers Blake illustrates his belief that love and creative art are the two avenues of salvation which remain to man in the Fallen World. Paolo and Francesca in the flame may be thought of as the poet's spectre and emanation, the Dante and Beatrice of this world, who will become one again when the sleeping humanity of Dante awakens at the end of his mortal life and re-enters Eden. Linked to Dante through the person of Virgil, his Divine Imagination, is the sun—symbol of Eden, of Los, and of the never-failing joy of God's boundless love and endless mercy. It dominates the scene and in the very center of its disk is shown the instant when, at the moment of entry into Eden, the spectre and emanation reunite to become the Eternal Humanity.

For striking and effective creative originality, this is probably the finest design of the series and one of the masterpieces of Blake's life. This is the result, of course, of the highly unusual and yet perfectly appropriate composition which is in keeping, as no attempt at literal illustration could have been, with the lyrical and imaginative essence of the poem itself.

OF THE ILLUSTRATIONS discussed so far, this is the first which Blake engraved. As an engraving, it is by far the most effective of the Dante series; indeed only one or two of the Job plates can be considered its rivals among Blake's finest works in this medium. The engraving is even to be preferred to the drawing, the loss of color being more than compensated for by the greater precision of detail and by the added linear beauty which the technique of the graver makes possible. Blake always tended to work, as we have seen, from rough and sketchy beginnings toward very precise detail in those works which can be considered finished. The success of his best engravings resides in his ability to keep the vitality and movement of the original design in the final form. The long, flowing, wiry, and spring-like lines which are the ultimate test of the engraver's skill enhance remarkably the sweeping curves of this great composition and bring out its wonderful variety of movement, which ranges from the precipitate rush of the forms in the vortex to the gracefully floating motion of Paolo and Francesca and of the spirits leaving the page at the upper left corner.

There are few variations between the two versions, but certain features have been added in the engraving. Most notably, all of the figures of lovers in the engraving are clothed, while most of those in the drawing—with the important exception of Francesca—are naked. There are also occasional variations in the positions and action of the figures in the whirlwind, although many are the same in both. However, there are more figures in the engraving and more couples embrace. The brambles and other creeping vegetation on the ground beneath Dante—denoting the Fallen World—are also shown in considerable detail in the engraving while only barely suggested in the drawing.[2]

[2] For the partially erased inscription which appears on the engraving, see Keynes, *Bibliography*, p. 183. This is the only one of the engravings which bears any writing.

11. THE CIRCLE OF THE GLUTTONS WITH CERBERUS

In the third circle I arrive, of showers
Ceaseless, accursed, heavy and cold, unchanged
For ever, both in kind and in degree.
Large hail, discolour'd water, sleety flaw
Through the dun midnight air stream'd down amain:
Stank all the land whereon that tempest fell.
Cerberus, cruel monster, fierce and strange,
Through his wide threefold throat, barks as a dog
Over the multitude immersed beneath.

Inferno VI, 6-14

WET GROUND lies like a pool in the foreground. Beyond is a range of mountains which, in spite of the unfinished condition of the drawing, has a fine sense of massiveness and distance. In a cave at the foot of the mountain at the left, Cerberus may be seen with his three heads. Small figures appear here and there upon the sides of the mountain. In a cleft between two peaks to the right of center, the distant walls of the City of Dis are shown. Above them a circle of figures, apparently female, fall head-downward toward the watery valley.

Although but a very unfinished sketch in rough pencil, with a few inked lines and some hasty washes, this drawing achieves a striking impression of the eternal gloominess of the Third Circle. It suggests strongly a number of descriptions in the prophetic books of similar places of woe.

Void, pathless, beaten with iron sleet, & eternal hail & rain.

Four Zoas VI, 148 (p. 304)

The land of snows of trembling & of iron hail incessant.

Jerusalem 13, 47

The only puzzling feature is the group in the sky, which is not to be recognized from the text. This gloomy valley would, of course, represent to Blake the fallen material world and the gluttons who inhabit it would symbolize those who are completely materialistic without any redeeming features of spiritual aspiration. Such materialism is identified by him with the Female Will. Hence this group of female figures is shown plunging head-downward into the mire, destruction being the inevitable result of following purely worldly ends.

12. CERBERUS, first version

THE ENCOUNTER with Cerberus is described in *Inferno* VI, 12-32. Blake follows it closely, giving Cerberus hands with talons instead of paws. In each hand the monster grasps a sinner, while he opens his mouths to show his fangs. Dante stands at the upper right and near him Virgil kneels to throw earth down Cerberus' throats. The top of a cave is shown above, although Dante makes no mention of Cerberus being in a cave.

Cerberus doubtless symbolizes the Threefold Accuser, in the same manner as did the three beasts of the first and third illustrations. As such he rules over the Fallen World and is roofed off from any glimpse of eternity by the heavy rock of his cavern.

His pose suggests the brutality of human-erected systems which squeeze the life from individuals.

Blake seems always to have associated the number three with the Fall.[1] Hecate in one of his finest color-printed drawings is shown as threefold, and in plate 50 of *Jerusalem* we find a triple-headed human figure with crowns, the three heads being associated with Bacon, Newton, and Locke, the unholy triad of materialism in Blake's mythology. Hand, a mythological character emblematic of the evil selfhood who plays a sinister role in *Jerusalem*, is described in terms which recall this drawing:

> His bosom wide & shoulders huge, overspreading wondrous,
> Bear Three strong sinewy Necks & Three awful & terrible Heads,
> Three Brains, in contradictory council brooding incessantly,
> Neither daring to put in act its councils, fearing each-other,
> Therefore rejecting Ideas as nothing . . .
>
> Jerusalem 70, 3-7

Enough should now have been said to make it clear that, in addition to the sinister implications which Cerberus has traditionally, and had for Dante, he has a further dire significance for Blake as symbolizing pure rational materialism devoid of spiritual illumination. He is the Spectre, or Ravening Selfhood.

> . . . the Spectre, like a hoar frost & a Mildew, rose over Albion,
> Saying, "I am God, O Sons of Men! I am your Rational Power!
> Am I not Bacon & Newton & Locke who teach Humility to Man,
> Who teach Doubt & Experiment? & my two Wings, Voltaire, Rousseau?
> Where is that Friend of Sinners? that Rebel against my Laws
> Who teaches Belief to the Nations & an unknown Eternal Life?
> Come hither into the Desart & turn these stones to bread.
> Vain foolish Man! wilt thou believe without Experiment
> And build a World of Phantasy upon my Great Abyss,
> A World of Shapes in craving lust & devouring appetite?"
>
> Jerusalem 54, 15-24

Bernard Blackstone comments of the above passage: "It gives us the main features of *Cerberian* philosophy to which Blake objected: the exaltation of reason as the sole means of attaining truth; the teaching of humility before Nature; the experimental method, and scientific doubt; the conception of rigid law; the picture of a world of matter, colourless, soundless, and scentless, in the abyss of time and space."[2]

Here then we have Cerberus, enclosed in the cave of the world of matter in the abyss of time and space, with the eternal doleful rain pouring down upon him and his victims. But to the man of imagination and faith the material world is not as fearful as it appears outwardly. The poet throws a handful of earth contemptuously down Cerberus' throats and silences him.

The drawing is partially finished in india ink and crude red, yellow, and neutral washes. Some details, notably the figures of Dante and Virgil, are still largely in pencil.

---

[1] See Percival, *Blake's "Circle of Destiny,"* pp. 57 and 70.
[2] For the passage quoted and further comment on this topic, see *English Blake*, pp. 228-229.

13. CERBERUS, second version

THIS ILLUSTRATION is based on the same passage as the previous one, and the two are much alike. The principal difference is that Cerberus is not quite so close and the poets are more prominently shown.

Behind the figure of Dante, on the extreme right of the drawing, is seen the surface of a lake. A rocky promontory projects out into it in the distance and upon this stand two lightly-penciled figures. Perhaps Blake originally intended these to represent Dante and Virgil and later brought them closer without erasing the first group.

The monster is smaller in this version and not so convincingly fierce. The left and right heads stare vacantly and seem almost benign while the middle one quietly accepts the handful of earth which Virgil offers it. The claw-like hands each hold a victim as in the previous design. Other gluttons are shown on the ground at the left, and the heavy dirty rain is indicated as before. The head of Cerberus is set off against a curtain of flames which rise behind him. The arch of the cave is not as massive or as rocky as that in the other drawing; instead it looks somewhat like the bent trunk of a fallen tree. While many details are extremely sketchy, the figures of the monster and of the poets are approaching completion.

One can only speculate as to why Blake chose to illustrate this episode twice. The most probable explanation would seem to be that he became dissatisfied with one design when it was partially finished and decided to begin again. In view of the great importance to him of the idea of the destructive selfhood, he may have thought that the beast in this version was not sufficiently formidable and that the position of the poets, as finally determined, was so prominent as to distract attention from him. As a design, the first version is certainly the more effective, and it is probable that Blake abandoned this one in its favor.

14. PLUTUS

THIS ILLUSTRATION is based on *Inferno* VII, 1-15. Dante and Virgil, as they descend the path leading to the Fourth Circle in which are the misers and the prodigals, encounter Plutus, God of Wealth and guardian of the circle. He shouts at them, but falls to the ground when Virgil tells him to be silent and announces the divine sanction of his mission.

The design is extremely simple. Virgil and Dante approach along the top of a rock in the center, Virgil leading. Dante follows with an expression of surprise and anxiety. Plutus sits below them in the foreground. He has the spiky hair and forked beard of Urizen and is shown with swollen lips (line 7). He raises his left hand above his head as he shouts in rage. His right hand is extended across the page and rests on a sack of coins on which Blake has written lightly the word "Money."

As lord of this world, Urizen of course places his whole faith in material values, of which gold is the archetype. Pursuit of wealth as his sole aim reduces man to bestiality. Such is the obvious meaning of Dante's text and of Blake's rendition of it.

Blake refers a number of times in his works to the futility of the worship of money. Several such comments appear on the engraving of the Laocoön (Keynes, *Poetry and Prose*, p.581): "Money . . . is the Great Satan or Reason, the Root of Good & Evil In

The Accusation of Sin. . . . Where any view of Money exists, Art cannot be carried on, but War only. . . .[1] For every Pleasure Money Is Useless." This drawing also recalls one of Blake's manuscript poems which reflects upon the attitude of the artist towards worldly goods; the following two lines should be noted in particular:[2]

> The accuser of sins by my side does stand
> And he holds my money bag in his hand.

The figures of Dante and Virgil are larger and more prominent in this design than usual. The flowing lines of the garments are graceful and expressive, but as in many cases the faces of the poets are only partially finished and are very uninteresting. Probably because they appear so many times, and usually in the role of onlookers, Blake found difficulty in giving variety of expression to Dante and Virgil. This impersonality of the poets is one of the defects of the series; the same problem seems to have given trouble to most illustrators of the *Divine Comedy*.

[1] At this point Blake refers in parentheses to Matthew x, 9-10, which reads: "Provide neither gold, nor silver, nor brass in your purses, Nor scrip for your journey, neither two coats, neither shoes, nor yet staves: for the workman is worthy of his meat."

[2] *Miscellaneous Poems*, pp. 127-128.

15. THE STYGIAN LAKE, WITH THE IREFUL SINNERS FIGHTING

IN THE FIFTH CIRCLE Dante and Virgil come upon the Wrathful and the Sullen (*Inferno* VII, 110-134). Sunk in the swamp named Styx, they battle each other both on and beneath the surface, the sighs of those covered over causing the swamp to bubble.

Blake shows all of the sinners submerged. At the top of the page he has written "The Stygian Lake" in pencil.[1] Anger is the essence of original sin, for as love brings salvation so does wrath destroy. These are the people of "single vision" who have no intellectual nor spiritual perceptions whatsoever, but are motivated wholly by ignorance and bestiality, as can be seen from their facial expressions. They are in groups of threes—a number which we have seen, in our discussion of Cerberus, Blake associates with the sinister forces of the Fall and with the selfhood—and there are three groups.

At the very nadir of the Fall, these figures are in Ulro and have sunk beneath the surface of the Lake of Udan-Adan, representative of annihilation. Here they engage in warfare, the particular preoccupation of the Fallen World. They are, of course, not to be thought of as individuals, for God provides the means of salvation to all, however great their fall. Rather, these figures represent the triply-accursed "state" of anger, which must be cast to destruction before regeneration can begin.

At the bottom of the page, three forms lie dead. The final extinction of all spiritual values can lead only to death. The central figure in this group wears the cowl of a monk.[2] Dante mentions numerous ecclesiastics as being in this circle. In his writings Blake continually contrasts the false religion of worldly display, which links itself to

[1] It will be noted that the wave on the surface of the lake has the form of a serpent (compare with the serpent of page 72 of *Jerusalem*). As the instigator of the Fall, the serpent is a symbol of materialism and Blake so uses it in many of his designs. See discussion of Drawing 47 below.

[2] Blake clothes the figures in this illustration, although the text describes them as being naked.

the attainment of power over others, with the true religion of the love of God and of one's fellow man.

16.   THE GODDESS OF FORTUNE

THIS DRAWING is derived from *Inferno* VII, 22-99. In the Fourth Circle Dante and Virgil behold the Prodigals and the Misers. Their eternal punishment is to roll big weights around with their chests, butting angrily and futilely into each other, then withdrawing and beginning again. Virgil remarks that these are they who contend for worldly riches which God has put under the care of the Goddess of Fortune and, in reply to a question from Dante, goes on to describe her activities in more detail (lines 62-99).

Fortune appears at the bottom of the drawing as though standing in a pit, concealed from the sight of those whose fruitless struggle she directs.[1] On the bank above her cavern, two groups are shown rolling weights together, which meet in the center of the page. The weight on the left has been lightly inscribed in pencil "Celestial Globe" and that on the right "Terrestrial Globe." The top of the page is enclosed by heavy clouds.

As we have seen previously, clouds in Blake's designs symbolize the division between the created and the spiritual worlds. Here we are below the clouds, thus in the Fallen World. Taking his cue from the comparison of the operation of the heavenly and earthly spheres in the passage in which Dante refers to the Goddess of Fortune, Blake identifies these spheres with the weights which the sinners are pushing. The Goddess of Fortune herself Blake identifies with Vala, his personification of the Female Will as dominant in the Fallen World. As the delusive and treacherous beauty of nature, she presides over the endless and futile warfare which fallen men carry on for material gain. Their battle is seen above.[2]

In order to understand the identification of the weights with the celestial and terrestrial spheres, we must discuss Blake's peculiar theory concerning the globe. To him the concept of a globe implies bounds and indicates, therefore, deficiency of vision on the part of him who beholds it. In eternity everything must have infinite extension and hence no limits. The Fallen World is, however, very naturally created by Urizen in the form of a sphere; all beyond its periphery is thus shut out from the sight of those within, the boundary being the Starry Heavens as man perceives them. These he cannot reach and can only comprehend to a limited extent. Standing on one globe, he sees what appears to be the inner surface of another, but is ignorant of the infinite beyond which his physical senses cannot penetrate. The misers see only this earth, or the Terrestrial Globe; the prodigals speculate rationally about the skies as well. Both, however, remain in the Fallen World and are unaware of the partial

---

[1] Her position in the drawing may have been suggested by Dante's description of her as being concealed in the grass like a serpent (lines 86-87).

[2] See Frye, *Fearful Symmetry*, pp. 126-127. Blake's penciled inscription would lead one to believe that he probably intended the small circles surrounding the figure in the pit to represent bits of dung, or possibly gold thrown away by men as offerings to Fortune; of course, the connection between gold and excrement in such a context has a long tradition.

nature of their vision: "In ignorance to view a small portion & think that All, And call it Demonstration, blind to all the simple rules of life."[3] In other words, no matter how far the purely rational outlook may carry us, even to a study of the remotest regions of the Celestial Sphere, it cannot of itself perceive eternity, which is nevertheless ever-present to the imagination. The material and rational viewpoints, as represented by the two globes, are thus both delusions of a Fallen World ruled by the Goddess Nature.

As to Fortune herself, we have already, in connection with the fourteenth illustration, commented on Blake's views concerning the ultimate value of the goods of this world. Blake—although a patient and philosophical man—of course realized his exceptional gifts and suffered keenly at times from being ignored by his contemporaries while he saw all around him much lesser men being recognized. At first he voiced his disappointment moderately: "It is now Exactly Twenty years since I was upon the ocean of business, & tho' [I] laugh at Fortune, I am perswaded that She Alone is the Governor of Worldly Riches, & when it is Fit she will call on me; till then I wait with Patience, in hopes that She is busied among my Friends."[4] Later in life it became evident that Fortune would not call on him; the rewards of this earth go largely to those who pursue mundane ends. Blake kept silent before the world, but occasionally gave vent to his feelings of frustration in his manuscript notes or in such scribblings as appear in pencil upon this drawing, which was never developed beyond the stage of a mere sketch with a few hasty washes: "The hole of a Shit-house. The Goddess Fortune is the devil's servant, ready to Kiss any one's Arse."

Dante regards Fortune as merely a cosmological balancing force and as such the servant of providence. But to Blake she prostitutes herself to the oppressive tyrannies which enslave man in the Fallen World. Thus he places her in the pit of Ulro, even below the created world of material warfare.

[3] *Jerusalem* 65, 27-28. In connection with Blake's theory of the heavens, an important passage is *Milton* 31, 4-22, especially lines 15-16:
> As to that false appearance which appears to the reasoner
> As of a Globe rolling thro' Voidness, it is a delusion of Ulro.
[4] Letter to George Cumberland dated August 26, 1799 (p. 837).

17. DANTE AND VIRGIL CROSSING TOWARDS THE CITY OF DIS

My theme pursuing, I relate, that ere
We reach'd the lofty turret's base, our eyes
Its height ascended, where we mark'd uphung
Two cressets, and another saw from far
Return the signal, so remote, that scarce
The eye could catch its beam. I, turning round
To the deep source of knowledge, thus inquired:
"Say what this means; and what, that other light
In answer set: what agency doth this?"
"There on the filthy waters," he replied,
"E'en now what next awaits us mayst thou see,
If the marsh-gender'd fog conceal it not."

Never was arrow from the cord dismiss'd,
That ran its way so nimbly through the air,
As a small bark, that through the waves I spied
Towards us coming, under the sole sway
Of one that ferried it.

Inferno, VIII, 1-17

BLAKE follows this passage quite literally. Dante and Virgil stand at the edge of the Stygian Lake[1] and at the foot of the tower, from the top of which two lights are displayed. Across the lake in the far distance appears the other tower, also with a light at its summit. A small sailboat, steered by its single occupant, is approaching the shore.

Few points in this illustration call for comment. The lake is, as usual, to be thought of as Ulro, with the hills of Generation rising beyond it, the first step on the road to salvation after the Fall. The lights signify that even here God's love follows man: "God is within & without: he is even in the depths of Hell!"[2] The two lights on the nearer tower will be seen to have the shapes of crescent moons, the symbol of Beulah, and represent here the emanations of Virgil and Dante who watch over them as they make their journey through the dark valley of mortal life. "The Shadows of Beulah terminate in rocky Albion."[3] The tower is in four tiers, indicative of fourfold vision which enables man, even in this life, to catch glimpses of eternity. The lights, it will be noticed, are opposite the third tier, which would correspond to Beulah, the eternal world from which the power of love descends to fallen man.

The sense of space and of mysterious darkness is well suggested.[4] Light pervades the whole scene, gleaming from between the clouds, illuminating the shoulders of the hills, and catching upon the waves. The massiveness and remoteness of the mountains are conveyed solely by delineation; light is used, not for three dimensional modeling, but to establish mood through the suggestion of atmospheric effects. This is a fine imaginative landscape, much in the manner of Blake's woodcuts of a few years before for Dr. Thornton's edition of the *Pastorals* of Virgil. It should be remembered that this watercolor was made at a time when realistic landscape in England was still in its early years, and before the art of Chinese landscape and of the Japanese print were known in the west. Blake's artistic vocabulary is thus largely of his own devising and the relationship of such a landscape as this to oriental painting is the result of

[1] Blake has written "Stygian Lake" lightly in pencil just to the left of the sail.

[2] *Jerusalem* 12, 15.

[3] *Milton* 34, 11. For the significance of the crescent moon in Blake's symbolism, see especially the discussion of Drawing 72 below. In the present instance, however, the shape of the lights may have been suggested to Blake by the unusual word for lantern, "cresset," which Cary employs in his translation of this passage—or, it may merely have been intended to convey the idea of remoteness as in the ninth engraving for *The Gates of Paradise* (reproduced in *Poetry and Prose*, p. 573).

[4] This drawing is done in neutral wash. The figures of the poets, some details of the ship, and the moons are in pencil only. From the point of view of symbolism, it should be compared to plate 4 of *Milton*, in which the crescent moon again appears, but with a Druid arch instead of the tower.

a similarity of aim. Both seek through natural forms to express imagination and feeling, and arrive independently at similar solutions.

18. VIRGIL REPELLING FILIPPO ARGENTI FROM THE BOAT

As DANTE AND VIRGIL cross the lake in the boat of Phlegyas, they are accosted by one of the spirits doomed to live in the mire, the wrathful Florentine, Filippo Argenti. He addresses Dante, who recognizes him; Argenti thereupon attempts to grasp the gunwale of the boat, but is pushed away by Virgil. Shortly thereafter he is set upon by the other dwellers in the swamp. The episode occupies lines 30-62 of Canto VIII, of which lines 38-41 form the subject of the drawing.

> . . . Then stretch'd he forth
> Hands to the bark; whereof my teacher sage
> Aware, thrusting him back: "Away! down there
> To the other dogs!" . . .

Dante stands at the left, the sail behind him. He watches Virgil push Argenti away from the boat.[1] Phlegyas sits impassively at the tiller. Across the lake in the background appears the shore, upon which one of the towers of the previous illustration may be seen.

The shore and the boat represent the World of Generation which, while fallen, is the image of regeneration. Here, though in hell, man has the opportunity for eventual redemption through recognizing error and rejecting it. Virgil, representative of the aspect of man which is divine, thrusts the evil selfhood down into the waters of annihilation, called in Blake's terminology Ulro or the Lake of Udan-Adan.[2] Note that Phlegyas, the pilot, has the usual features of Urizen, ruler of the World of Generation: the life of this world by its nature requires the guidance of law. Each of the figures here may be logically associated with one of the Zoas, Virgil being Los, Dante Luvah, Phlegyas Urizen, and Argenti Tharmas, the purely material aspect of man who is being thrust aside into the western sea which is his proper realm. The design thus represents the process of the regeneration of the fallen soul. Mortal man should direct his life under the guidance of reason in such a way that imagination (love of God) and feeling (love of one's fellow men) are exalted and error (materialism and selfishness—attributes which breed anger instead of love) is cast out.

> Each Man is in his Spectre's power
> Until the arrival of that hour
> When his Humanity awake
> And cast his Spectre into the Lake.
> Jerusalem 41, 32-35

This drawing can, of course, be regarded as a perfectly literal rendition of the text,

[1] Argenti's features are similar to those of other representations in Blake's work of totally evil states. A good example is the expression of Behemoth—who personifies the monstrous natural forces of the Fallen World—in the fifteenth Job illustration.

[2] Considered solely from the aspect of art, this design might well illustrate *Milton* 48, 7: "To cast aside from Poetry all that is not Inspiration."

and it may appear that unnecessary difficulties are being created by attaching to it any further significance. However, it must be remembered that Blake was always seeking in the similarities of others' vision a confirmation of his own. He must almost certainly have considered that this episode of the *Divine Comedy* presented a striking parallel with much of his own symbolism.

19. THE ANGEL CROSSING STYX

> What flames are these, coming from the South? what noise, what dreadful rout
> As of a battle in the heavens? hark! heard you not the trumpet
> As of fierce battle?
>
> Four Zoas IX, 261-263 (p. 354)

DANTE AND VIRGIL come to the City of Dis, whose inhabitants refuse to open the gate for them. Presently the sound of an approaching whirlwind is heard above the Stygian Lake which girdles the city; soon an angel appears hurrying dry-shod across the water, while the ruined souls flee from him in all directions. The city and the closing of the gate is described in Canto VIII, the coming of the angel in Canto IX.

On the right of the drawing appears the crenelated wall of the city, with the barred gate in the center. Above the gate are lightly sketched the forms of the Furies, who appear again in the following design. Dante and Virgil stand upon the threshold and flames rise from within the city. At the left is the Stygian Lake with many forms partially submerged in its waters. The whirlwind sweeps in a great circle across the page with more forms visible within it. At the left, the angel strides across the lake, his wings outspread and his left hand held out before him (IX, 82). In the background may be vaguely seen some of the bridges across the circles, with human forms lightly sketched upon them in a number of places.

This illustration is quite literal and relatively free of Blake's own symbolism. As usual, the marsh is to be thought of as Ulro and the fortified city with its fires and gate as the World of Generation or the Mundane Shell. God's love, as represented by the angel, causes the souls to be caught up out of the pit of annihilation. The significance of the whirlwind is doubtless akin to that of the tenth illustration (Paolo and Francesca); the compositions of the two drawings are likewise similar. The whirling forms represent the continuously repeating Circle of Destiny which every soul must experience. It will be noted that directly opposite the angel in the circle is a figure which has fallen head down on the ground at the foot of the battlement. Fall through error and salvation through God's love are constantly recurring in this ever-circling world of nature, which is "Continually Building, Continually Decaying because of Love & Jealousy."[1]

The thirteenth illustration to the Book of Job, "Then the Lord answered Job out of the Whirlwind," has many similarities to this drawing. The spirit of God appears amid the terrors of the Fallen World and in the margin above vague forms may be seen, as here, circling in the blast. "The margin carries on the motion of the whirlwind,

---

[1] *Jerusalem*, plate 72. Blake frequently portrays figures upside down to emphasize the overturning of values in the created world, in which material things take precedence over spiritual. Note the figure in the third Job illustration and Wicksteed's comment on it (*Blake's Vision of the Book of Job*, pp. 61-62).

the time current of creation, and shows Job's vision of his own spirit swept along in the endless round of nature."[2]

Although most of this drawing has passed the pencil stage, it is still far from complete: the inking and washes are hurried and rough in character. Even in its unfinished condition, it is impressive. The murky atmosphere is effectively depicted, and the rushing movement of the figure and of the circling storm contrast well with the great static mass of the walled city.[3]

[2] Wicksteed, *op. cit.*, p. 99. Wicksteed's entire discussion of the thirteenth Job design is significant in this connection.

[3] A pencil sketch in the Victoria and Albert Museum, London, may well have served as a preliminary study for the figure of the angel in this illustration (Keynes, *Pencil Drawings*, plate 21). For another sketch which is probably a study for this drawing, see note 1 in the discussion of Drawing 10 above.

20. THE GORGON–HEAD AND THE ANGEL OPENING THE GATE OF DIS

TWO INCIDENTS of the *Divine Comedy* are combined in one illustration. From lines 34-62 of Canto IX is taken the description of the three Furies who appear above the gate of the City of Dis and threaten Dante with the Gorgon-head. On the left Dante is shown turning away while Virgil presses his hands over Dante's eyes (lines 56-62). In the center, outside the gate, the angel is shown stepping up on to the sill and commanding that the portal be opened (IX, 86-97).

While the poem is in the main treated literally, there are features here which once again make it clear that Blake was, in part at least, thinking in his own terms. The text mentions three Furies and the Gorgon-head in addition, while Blake shows only three female forms above the gate, although the center one is certainly intended to represent the Gorgon. In the text, the snake-like hair of the Furies is described. Here the heads of two snakes appear, one at each side, above the Furies; the latter hold trumpets which belch forth flames. Outside upon the ground near the poets, brambles grow, and in the lower right corner of the page are two sunflowers.

It is apparent here that the three female figures are to be identified with the Daughters of Albion—three being a number, it will be remembered, of evil import. These are representatives of the Female Will and as such have as their attributes the serpents of the Fallen World and "Sinai's trumpets,"[1] which proclaim the cruel Moral Law of Urizen.

> . . . Three Women around
> The Cross! O Albion, why didst thou a Female Will Create?
> Jerusalem 56, 42-43

It is the particular vice of the Female Will to attempt to gain control over man by hedging sex around with moral prohibitions. In the light of this, the sexual symbolism of the wall with its barred gate, surmounted by the personification of the Female

[1] In *The Everlasting Gospel* (p. 139), when the Woman Taken in Adultery is brought to Jesus, the first words with which He addresses her are "Good & Evil are no more! Sinai's trumpets, cease to roar!" The three Daughters of Albion may be seen busily dismembering the body of the Fallen Man in the design at the bottom of plate 25 of *Jerusalem*.

Will proclaiming the Moral Law, becomes obvious. However, lest because of the closeness of all of this to Dante's text the implication should be missed, Blake has introduced two additional symbols which have definite sexual implications for him: these are the brambles and the sunflowers.[2]

> I went to the Garden of Love,
> And saw what I never had seen:
> A Chapel was built in the midst,
> Where I used to play on the green.
>
> And the gates of this Chapel were shut,
> And "Thou shalt not" writ over the door;
> So I turn'd to the Garden of Love
> That so many sweet flowers bore;
>
> And I saw it was filled with graves,
> And tomb-stones where flowers should be;
> And Priests in black gowns were walking their rounds,
> And binding with *briars* my joys & desires.
> "The Garden of Love," *Songs of Experience*, p. 74

Notice that in the poem, a building has been erected in the Garden of Love, a chapel with a closed door surmounted by an inscription from the Decalogue. The details of the illustration under consideration may be different, but the symbolism is evidently the same, even to the briars which are seen here in the left foreground. And, when we come to discuss the next design, we shall find that when Dante and Virgil pass into the city they will discover that it is filled with graves. When we remember that the poem was written more than thirty years before, the similarity is even more remarkable. This coincidence doubtless indicated to Blake that vision is one and eternal and that Dante's symbolism must have the same universal meaning as his own. In the eternal world, love in all its aspects must be purest joy. Only after the Fall is it forbidden by cruel laws, which favor the dominance of the jealous Female Will and cause the innocent to suffer untold pain from repression. With but a touch of the wand (another sexual symbol), imaginative love—the messenger of God —opens the iron gate which fear and jealousy have closed. Meanwhile, the poet's imagination, as personified by Virgil, guards him against the deadly concept of the created world that sexual love is sin.

The central portion of the illustration—the figure of the angel and the gate—is quite finished, but many details at the top and bottom are still sketchy.

[2] For the sunflower as a sexual symbol in Blake, see the poem "Ah! Sunflower," in the *Songs of Experience* (p. 73).

21. FARINATA DEGLI UBERTI

WITHIN THE CITY, Dante and Virgil find the ground covered with tombs, the lids of which are raised, and from inside which emerge flames and the sound of wailing (IX, 110-120). A figure arises from one of the tombs and addresses Dante, identifying himself as Farinata degli Uberti, the Ghibelline leader who, after the battle of Montaperti,[1] saved Florence from destruction by his followers. With Virgil's encouragement, Dante converses with him (x, 23-122).

This passage is illustrated very closely. Virgil stands somewhat apart from Dante, who is between two of the graves (x, 37-38). Farinata is visible from the waist up, standing very erect (32-34). Behind him is seen Cavalcante Cavalcanti, father of Dante's friend and fellow poet, Guido Cavalcanti (51-73). As in the text, he rises only as far as his chin, and Farinata does not turn to look at him.

We have already mentioned the graves in connection with the previous illustration. Inside the city of the Fallen World men are almost entombed in materialism and consumed by the flames of false and unfulfilled desires. Farinata raises his right hand toward Dante, as symbolic of the fact that fallen man can escape at least part way from the hideous torments of mortal life through imagination. The spiritual Dante gestures with his left hand toward his fallen counterpart. The figure behind, who does not look directly at the poet, is almost completely submerged in the fiery grave. Behind the battlemented wall may be seen domes and one building with Doric columns. Blake always identifies the forms of classical architecture, or of any post-and-lintel architecture, with the Fallen World, as opposed to Gothic architecture which suggests the realm of the spirit.[2]

The conversation of Dante and Farinata, in which Farinata describes how he can view the future but not the present, must have interested Blake. However, he no doubt reversed the roles, for the poet would be able even in this world of the flaming Mundane Shell to discern eternity, which would be closed to the warrior, half buried in the earth.

This drawing, although sketchy in detail and with the washes unfinished, is brilliant in color and gives a finely dramatic effect of the burning city.

[1] September 4, 1260.

[2] "Grecian is Mathematic Form: Gothic is Living Form." (*On Virgil*, p. 583). For the two types contrasted, see the fourth and fifth engravings of the Job series and plate 32 of *Jerusalem*, among numerous other examples which might be cited.

22. THE MINOTAUR

THE ENCOUNTER with the Minotaur is described in Canto XII, lines 4-30. Blake has followed the text quite literally. At the top of the path of giant broken rocks, Virgil turns to address the monster, who rears and lunges in anger, while Dante starts to run as Virgil commands him.

This represents another encounter between the bestial violence of fallen nature and the power of spiritual faith. Notice that Virgil extends his left arm toward the monster and that the group of poets is separated from the Minotaur and from the pit of hell by two columns of clouds in the background, which as already mentioned suggest the division between the created and the eternal worlds. The facial expression of the beast recalls that of Behemoth in the fifteenth of the Job illustrations.

In the background are the walls of the City of Dis with flames rising from it.[1] The

[1] Note the structure like an altar in the center of the illustration beneath the rearing feet of the monster. Blake has printed an inscription in capital letters along its upper edge, but I have been unable to decipher it.

composition is based on a series of triangles, which are well balanced. Behind the triangle of the group of rocks in the foreground is that formed by the rearing monster on the right and the two poets on the left. Additional emphasis is given to the latter group and the general flow of movement from right to left is maintained by means of the third triangle of clouds above Dante and Virgil.

23. THE CENTAURS AND THE RIVER OF BLOOD

> . . . I beheld
> An ample foss, that in a bow was bent,
> As circling all the plain; for so my guide
> Had told. Between it and the rampart's base,
> On trail ran Centaurs, with keen arrows arm'd,
> As to the chase they on the earth were wont.
>
> .   .   .   .
> .   .   .   .   Around
> The foss these go by thousands, aiming shafts
> At whatsoever spirit dares emerge
> From out the blood, more than his guilt allows.
>
> Inferno XII, 49-54; 69-72

THROUGH A CLEFT in the rock is seen a wide view over a valley, through which the river of boiling blood winds from the foreground to disappear in the distance. Cliffs flank the river on each side and in the far distance the vista is closed by a mountain. In the river in the foreground are the tyrants with just the tops of their heads sticking out above the surface (102-112); as the river recedes into the distance, a few more forms may be seen who emerge more and more. On the banks of the river appear various groups of centaurs with bows and arrows. One in the center of the design has drawn his bow and is aiming at a form which has risen from the river.

So much of the illustration is quite literal. However, the design is framed on either side in the foreground by figures not to be associated with the text. On the left a male centaur carries a bow and on the right a centauress reclines against the cliff, her bow beside her. Dante mentions no female centaur, so Blake must have had some particular reason for introducing this figure.

"Art Degraded, Imagination Denied, War Governed the Nations."[1] Blood is, therefore, the supreme symbol of the cruelty of the fallen natural world, that world over which "The Beast & the Whore rule without control."[2] It is this Beast and Whore, representing the spectrous selfhood and the evil Female Will, which are here shown as the male and female centaur, forms in which bestiality almost conceals the human aspect. The centauress recalls representations of Vala in the manuscript of *The Four Zoas*: "Satan's Wife, The Goddess Nature, is War & Misery."[3] The centaur is another such monstrous form as the Minotaur of the previous design. As such these two figures preside appropriately over this vision of man's life in a fallen world.

[1] *Laocoön*, p. 580.
[2] Annotations to Bishop Watson's *Apology for the Bible*, p. 750.
[3] See, for example, that reproduced in Keynes, *Bibliography*, facing p. 34. The quotation is from Blake's Laocoön engraving (*Poetry and Prose*, p. 581).

The drawing is largely in pencil, but the river is crimson, the banks green, and neutral washes outline the sides of the cleft. India ink has been used to outline part of the centauress' body. The device of framing the central scenes between rock walls at each side helps to give a sense of depth. Without dependence upon light and shade, distance is very convincingly suggested by means of delineation.

24. THE WOOD OF THE SELF-MURDERERS: THE HARPIES AND THE SUICIDES

IN CANTO XIII, lines 1-111, is described the wood of the suicides and the conversation with Pier delle Vigne. Entering the second ring of the Seventh Circle, Dante and Virgil find themselves in a rough forest which is peopled with the Harpies, birds with human heads. Hearing moans and not being able to locate their source, Dante is bewildered. Virgil tells him to break off a twig, and when he does blood issues from it. A voice from the tree then accuses Dante of cruelty in willingly hurting it, and reveals to him that it is the punishment of suicides to be encased in the trunks of trees, upon the leaves of which the Harpies feed and cause the imprisoned spirits pain. The voice identifies itself as that of Pier delle Vigne, a minister of the Emperor Frederick III, who committed suicide after having lost his influence with the Emperor due to the machinations of jealous rivals.

Blake illustrates the episode closely, showing thorns on the trees, the branch dripping blood, Dante starting back, and the broken end on the ground. The form of Pier delle Vigne is visible in the tree trunk just to the right of center and several other forms may be discerned in other trees, notably a female figure upside down in the left foreground. Three Harpies are shown on the branches above, with women's heads and prominent breasts.

Pier delle Vigne, with his long beard and spiky hair, recalls certain representations of Urizen,[1] whose realm is the mortal world of "vegetative" existence. There are several descriptions in the prophetic books of dense growths of error which spring up around Urizen and close him in as he writes his cruel and inhuman laws.[2] Doubtless this is the symbolism which Blake has in mind here. We have previously discussed the significance of trees for Blake, and Urizen is associated especially with the Tree of Mystery.[3] Hence it seems clear that Blake regards these trees as symbolical of the ignorance and blindness of man in the Fallen World in which he is cut off from eternity by the limitations of his senses, and yet bases his life on laws derived from sensory evidence.

[1] As, for instance, that of plate 12 of *The Book of Urizen*.
[2] See especially *Ahania*, 103-125 (pp. 237-238).
[3] The poem "The Human Abstract" from *Songs of Experience* (*Poetry and Prose*, pp. 75-76) is of interest in connection with this design. It describes the growth of the Tree of Mystery in whose branches sits the raven, symbol of the spectre (see design to plate 37 of *Jerusalem*) as the Harpies are of the Female Will. The last verse is particularly significant:

> The Gods of the earth and sea
> Sought thro' Nature to find this Tree;
> But their search was all in vain:
> There grows one in the Human Brain.

Beyond the bounds of their own self their senses cannot penetrate:
As the tree knows not what is outside of its leaves & bark.

Four Zoas VI, 94-95 (p. 303)

In connection with the upside down form in the tree at the left, the significance of such reversed figures will be recalled from our discussion of the nineteenth design. After the Fall, which takes place head first, the Divine Humanity sinks to a point where it is scarcely more than inert matter. The three Harpies will also be recognized as the Daughters of Albion of the twentieth illustration, the evil spirits of the Female Will whose home is among the vegetative forms of materialized existence.

25. THE HELL–HOUNDS HUNTING THE DESTROYERS OF THEIR OWN GOODS

> . . . And lo! there came
> Two naked, torn with briars, in headlong flight,
> That they before them broke each fan o' th' wood.
> "Haste now," the foremost cried, "now haste thee, death!"
> The other, as seem'd, impatient of delay,
> Exclaiming, "Lano! not so bent for speed
> Thy sinews, in the lists of Toppo's field."
> And then, for that perchance no longer breath
> Sufficed him, of himself and of a bush
> One group he made. Behind them was the wood
> Full of black female mastiffs, gaunt and fleet,
> As greyhounds that have newly slipt the leash.
> On him, who squatted down, they stuck their fangs,
> And having rent him piecemeal bore away
> The tortured limbs. . . .
> Inferno XIII, 117-131

THE SCENE is shown in accurate detail. Giacomo da Sant' Andrea (lines 133-134), exhausted, has thrown himself at the foot of the tree on the extreme left which contains the unknown Florentine suicide (XIII, 131—XIV, 4). The first of the dogs has just reached him and is sinking its teeth in his flank. Two others follow swiftly behind. The other squanderer, Lano da Siena, pauses in flight and looks on horrified. From the trees two Harpies leer in pleasure at the scene.

The bestial forces of the natural world rush to destroy all that pertains to the spirit and to the Divine Humanity. The Harpies in the trees represent the feminine aspects of those below who have given themselves over to materialistic ends; for this reason there are now only two, instead of three as in the previous illustration. Now dominant, they rejoice as they see their imaginative lives destroyed. The three dogs have much the appearance of the wolf of the first design, and their number is determined by their identification, as there, with the Threefold Accuser.

This illustration recalls the drawing for page 13 of "Night the Sixth" of Young's *Night Thoughts*. In that, a huge dog attacks a prostrate man while a second man flees

80

up a tree.[1] Again the subject seems to be fallen man as victim of the violence and cruelty of the created world.

> Over them the famish'd Eagle screams on boney Wings, and around
> Them howls the Wolf of famine.
>
> Jerusalem 94, 15-16

The trees now have smooth instead of spiky trunks and the shades of the suicides are no longer visible within them. In the middle ground appears an open glade closed in by another grove of trees beyond. The sense of calm and space in the background accentuates the violent motion of the main scene as the dogs and men rush swiftly from right to left. The fleeing man, who turns backward, serves to arrest the movement somewhat and to bring the composition into balance, although the pose of the figure is exceedingly awkward.

[1] Reproduced in Keynes, *Blake's Illustrations to Young's "Night Thoughts,"* Cambridge, Massachusetts, 1927. Similar is the design on p. 70 of the published edition of the *Night Thoughts.* In that engraving, a huge hound attacks a prostrate youth while a demoniacal hunter looks on with fiendish delight.

26. THE BLASPHEMERS

DANTE AND VIRGIL stand by the edge of the third ring of the Seventh Circle of Hell, the nature of which is described in *Inferno* XIV, 9-39. It consists of a sandy plain without any natural feature, upon which flames rain down continuously, setting fire to the sand. Within it are confined three classes of sinners: the blasphemers, who lie upon their backs; the usurers, who sit; and the sodomites, who run to and fro in the fiery rain.

The three classes all appear in the drawing, so the title of "The Blasphemers" is not really sufficiently inclusive. Blake preserves the barren aspect of the place, which is without vegetation and featureless save for the small bank in the right foreground on which Dante and Virgil stand. In the upper left is a dark cloud from which the fiery flakes pour down. The blasphemers lie in the left foreground, not shown altogether literally for one figure is prone rather than on his back. Behind them at a little distance sit the usurers, gesturing in despair. In the center are seen the running forms of four of the sodomites, of which two—a woman and a man—are most prominent. Flames rise from the running figures and from the groups on the ground, to meet the other flames which pour down from above. No background is shown other than the fiery deluge.

Blake frequently associates flames with the torments and raging desires which, in a fallen world, beset those without faith. We have already seen in the third design of this series two figures swathed in flames symbolizing the frightful lot of fallen man.[1] The poets, created men who have not lost spiritual insight, here look on in pity at the dreadful torments of those whose vision is limited to this world and who are, therefore, without hope.

Most frightful of these flaming agonies of the natural world is pure physical desire

[1] After the Fall, which follows upon the proclamation of his cruel laws, Urizen finds himself in a world of raging fires. See *Urizen*, lines 96-137 (pp. 222-223).

unillumined by love. This is no doubt the significance of the central group, who gesture in despair without looking at each other as flames sweep over their genitals. The world of those who put their whole faith in a self-centered attitude towards life will eventually fall in flaming ruin.² In its symbolism, the present drawing parallels to a great extent the third engraving to the Book of Job; it is interesting to observe that the central figures here are much like the representations of Job's eldest son and of the daughter who lies stretched in the foreground of that design, which portrays the destruction of Job's children.³

Save for the two central figures and the partially finished form of Dante, most of this illustration is still in pencil.

² These figures are to be contrasted with those of Paolo and Francesca in the tenth design who, gazing at each other, are borne lightly along in the flame. It must be remembered in accordance with Blake's theory of Contraries, that the same symbol may have opposite meanings according to circumstances. Thus fire may be a symbol of purification as well as of torment: opposed to the flames of hell is the fiery sun of Eden.

³ See Wicksteed's comment on this illustration (*Blake's Vision of the Book of Job*, pp. 55-63). In the sixteenth illustration to Job, when Satan has been cast out he falls headlong swathed in a flame.

27. CAPANEUS THE BLASPHEMER

THE SETTING is the same as in the previous illustration. Capaneus, as one of the blasphemers, is shown reclining on the sand (XIV, 39-69). He was one of the seven kings who besieged Thebes; as he scaled the walls he hurled defiance at Jupiter, who smote him with a thunderbolt.¹

Dante and Virgil stand at the left, at the edge of a narrow strip which separates them from the burning sand. In the right center sits Capaneus, an imposing figure. Flames blaze up from the ground all around him, lick across his groin, and form a halo around his head. Other flames rain down from the sky, along with several jagged bolts of lightning which strike him. As described in the poem, Capaneus remains oblivious to these torments and stares steadily and proudly before him.

Satan, the limit of opacity, is shown by Blake as he rules in pride over the Fallen World. This figure should be compared with Satan as he appears in the Job designs, particularly the sixth of the series. The musculature of the figure reflects Blake's admiration of Michelangelo; in fact, this is one of the most solidly sculptural figures in all of Blake's work and shows his ability to model powerfully when the occasion required. It is fitting from the point of view of Blake's beliefs that Satan should be so powerful in aspect and that, as the personification of war and the slavery of mankind, he should have much the appearance of an antique torso.² The dying man in

¹ Rossetti, in his catalogue appended to Gilchrist's *Life* (II, p. 268), lists two uncolored drawings which he associated with this subject (numbers 131 and 132), while specifying that they are quite different from either this or the preceding illustration. He does not indicate where he saw the drawings nor who owned them and I have found no further trace of them.

² This figure is in some ways similar to that of Theseus from the Parthenon, a work with which we know Blake was familiar and which he did not altogether admire (see letter of Samuel Palmer quoted in Gilchrist's *Life*, I, pp. 345-346).

Blake's design entitled "Death of the Strong Wicked Man"—one of the series illustrating Robert Blair's poem, *The Grave*—is a similar figure; in the background his soul departs in flames.

This is a finished watercolor, signed with Blake's monogram. It is notable for a rich effect of light and shade—used, as always by Blake, not as a means of illusionistic modeling, but for dramatic effect. The whole drawing is impressive, and the figure of Capaneus, set off by a halo of flames and thunderbolts, is majestic and sinister.

28. THE SYMBOLIC FIGURE OF THE COURSE OF HUMAN HISTORY DESCRIBED BY VIRGIL

"In midst of ocean," forthwith he began,
"A desolate country lies, which Crete is named;
Under whose monarch, in old times, the world
Lived pure and chaste. A mountain rises there,
Call'd Ida, joyous once with leaves and streams,
Deserted now like a forbidden thing.

. . . .

. . . . . Within the mount, upright
An ancient form there stands, and huge, that turns
His shoulders towards Damiata; and at Rome,
As in his mirror, looks. Of finest gold
His head is shaped, pure silver are the breast
And arms, thence to the middle is of brass,
And downward all beneath well-tempered steel,
Save the right foot of potter's clay, on which
Than on the other more erect he stands.
Each part, except the gold, is rent throughout;
And from the fissure tears distil, which join'd
Penetrate to that cave. They in their course,
Thus far precipitated down the rock,
Form Acheron, and Styx, and Phlegethon;
Then by this straiten'd channel passing hence
Beneath, e'en to the lowest depth of all,
Form there Cocytus." . . .
                    Inferno XIV, 89-94; 98-114

THE CENTER of Blake's design is entirely taken up by the majestic symbolic figure. Behind him appears the bulk of Mt. Ida, reaching almost to the top of the page and having large clumps of vegetation on its slopes. On the shoulders of the mountain recline two figures sketched in pencil, a man on the left and a woman on the right.

Dante adopted as the source of his symbolic figure the image seen by Nebuchadnezzar in his dream, and extended its symbolism to cover the whole course of human history from the Golden Age to the present.[1] Blake has followed his description closely in

[1] Nebuchadnezzar's dream is described in the second chapter of Daniel. For an extended discussion of Blake's presentation of the course of human history, together with some parallels of his symbolism with that of the Book of Daniel and of Dante, see Frye, *Fearful Symmetry*, pp. 128-134, 252, 275-276, and 291-292.

some particulars, but not in others. The weight of the figure rests principally upon the right foot; the different metals of which the figure is made are, however, not shown, nor is the cleft. Tears roll from the eyes, down the cheeks and body; some flow along the legs, while others form a stream which is seen pouring down behind. In Dante these waters represent all the sins of the world which flow together to form the rivers of hell. Blake doubtless saw in them a perversion of his own four rivers of Paradise, which symbolize the four senses of the unfallen Albion.[2] The principal details which Blake has introduced prominently which are not described in the poem are the crown, the orb and the scepter which the figure holds, and the scaly genitals. All of these are, however, symbols which Blake frequently employs.

Here as in the previous illustration, Satan appears as Lord of the Fallen World. Its mountainous form appears behind him, covered with the groves of error and surmounted by personifications of the Selfhood—who holds a sword—and of the Female Will. As Jerusalem represents for Blake the ideal of human liberty, so does Babylon stand for the tyrannical human systems which destroy the freedom of the individual in the Fallen World. This drawing shows us "Babylon, represented by a King crowned, Grasping his Sword and his Sceptre."[3]

The marks of kingship—scepter,[4] orb and crown—indicate that Blake intends to represent another vision of the Satanic material powers which dominate this world. It will be recalled that the third illustration of this series shows Satan, as the personification of War and Dominion, doing obeisance before the aged and enfeebled false God of Natural Religion. Here again we have Satan with kingly attributes; and now his genitals are covered with scales to indicate that, as tyranny and war originated with the Fall, so did physical love degenerate to lust and cruelty.

Power, however, never brings happiness for long, and even while bearing the symbols of his glory, Satan's face shows bewilderment and pain, and the tears of human woe run down his cheeks. He is the epitome of that mortal error of selfhood which mankind must reject before redemption.[5]

[2] Frye, *op. cit.*, pp. 274-275 and 363.

[3] *Vision of the Last Judgment*, pp. 641-642. For similar descriptions of the satanic spectre, see *Four Zoas* VI, 297-311 (p. 308) and *Jerusalem* 83, 77-78. Among Blake's designs we can find quite a number of parallels for this figure. Examples are plate 5 of *Europe* and the drawing, "Satan in his Original Glory." (Figgis, *Paintings of William Blake*, plate 8.)

[4] There are numerous examples in Blake's work of scepters of trefoil shape as shown here. The sinister significance of the number three for Blake has been commented on. Other examples of scepters similar to this will be found in the drawing "Moloch" (Figgis, *op. cit.*, plate 37), the engraving of "The Counseller, King, Warrior, Mother & Child, in the Tomb" from Blair's *Grave*, the design to plate 11 of *Europe*, and the drawing "Christ Interceding for the Magdalen." Compare also the shape of the throne of Vala as shown in plate 53 of *Jerusalem*.

[5] Anthony Blunt, *Journal of the Warburg and Courtauld Institutes*, VI, 1943, p. 198, has suggested that Blake derived his conception of this figure from some antique statue of Helios.

29. JACOPO RUSTICUCCI AND HIS COMRADES

THE FIRST EIGHTY-NINE LINES of Canto XVI of the *Inferno* tell of Dante's meeting with his three fellow-townsmen, who comprise the second group with whom he converses in the portion of the Seventh Circle given over to the punishment of the sodomites.

Led by Jacopo Rusticucci, the trio also includes Guido Guerra and Tegghiaio Aldo-brandi; all were thirteenth-century political figures in Florence. Blake's illustration follows closely lines 20-27:

> And, soon as they had reach'd us, all the three
> Whirl'd round together in one restless wheel.
> As naked champions, smear'd with slippery oil,
> Are wont, intent, to watch their place of hold
> And vantage, ere in closer strife they meet;
> Thus each one, as he wheel'd, his countenance
> At me directed, so that opposite
> The neck moved ever to the twinkling feet.

Dante and Virgil stand on a low bank at the left, Dante raising his hands in pity and dismay at the scene before him. At the right, the three sinners run in a circle through the flames. All look at Dante, as described, and the nearest seems to speak to him. They are handsome naked figures and do not show the wounds mentioned in the poem (line 10). As is the case with the other illustrations showing scenes from this circle, there is no background.

The poets, who through the divine power of imagination have preserved their link with eternity, stand looking in horror at the fiery torments of those who are caught up in the cruel toils of the Fallen World, and are swept past in the never-ceasing round of natural forces and of man-made moral systems.

In both conception and composition, this design is much like the great thirteenth illustration to the Book of Job, "Then the Lord answered Job out of the Whirlwind." The circling motion is remarkably suggested by blending the running figures into the pattern of the whirling flames. An area of intense action is set up by means of brightly colored brush strokes, and this contrasts strikingly with the repose of the group at the left. The figures of the running men are in themselves much akin to ones found in the Job engravings. Thus the one at the lower right parallels almost exactly—except for being reversed—that of the messenger in the fourth Job illustration, while the other two figures recall the representations of Satan in the second and fifth designs.

30. THE USURERS

DANTE IS SHOWN conversing with a group of usurers who, according to the terms of their punishment, sit upon the hot sand under the rain of fire. The drawing follows closely the episode as described in *Inferno* XVII, lines 41-74. Dante, having been sent ahead by Virgil, stands all alone at the left, looking down at the usurers. Four are shown, of whom the three in the center may be taken to be the three who are specifi-cally mentioned in the text. The fourth, who sits near the right edge of the design, has his back turned and looks at Dante over his shoulder. The other three face Dante; they have big purses around their necks with escutcheons on them, as described. Blake has indicated the markings on the purses, but only that in the center is suffi-ciently distinct to be recognizable. This shows a goose and identifies its wearer as a member of the Ubbriachi family of Florence. The figure nearest Dante addresses him and also sticks out his tongue (lines 70-71); by this he may be identified as Rinaldo degli Scrovigni of Padua, whose purse was white and decorated with a blue pregnant sow. The third figure, that with the beard, would thus be the member of the Gianfigliazzi family of Florence, whose coat-of-arms was a blue lion on a gold background. All gesture with their hands as they endeavor to ward off the fiery flakes which continually fall on them. A few lines in the background indicate the rain of flames, but no other setting is shown.

Blake follows all of this quite literally with but one exception: the three most prominent usurers all wear crowns, and the one nearest Dante also has a cross on a chain around his neck. While all three belonged to noble families, there is no indication in the text of their wearing coronets. Blake again calls attention here to the materialism of church and state, which acquire a preponderance of wealth through vested interests. It is his constant theme that the power and wealth of a fallen world come not from hard work and merit, but as a result of selfishness and subtlety. Human systems, in his opinion, are all erected to exploit the poor to the advantage of the wealthy and powerful; hence, those who have worldly position, either political or ecclesiastical, are mostly usurers.

The illustration is largely in pencil, and is very sketchy. A few lines are inked; the only color is the red mouth of the sinner nearest to Dante.

31. GERYON CONVEYING DANTE AND VIRGIL DOWNWARD

IN INFERNO XVII, lines 1-28, Dante and Virgil see Geryon coming toward them. Later in the canto, lines 75-132, they climb on his back and are conveyed downward to Malebolge.

Blake has followed the description of Geryon and of the descent closely. The monster's face is human and quite young in expression; his body is that of a serpent, and he has paws covered with hair. At the end of his tail is a spur like that of a scorpion; he propels himself through the air with his paws and by swishing his tail under him up to his breast. Dante and Virgil ride upon his shoulders, Virgil behind with his arms around Dante. Below them fires appear (line 118). Blake has shown more detail in the background than is actually described. The edge of the abyss rises like a mountain peak behind and in the lower left may be seen a curtain of flames; beyond these appear several of the rock ridges with the figures of sinners fleeing along them. A large cloud floats behind the monster's head.

A great serpent, or dragon, has of course always been symbolic of the forces of chaos.[1] As such it appears arising out of the sea in the form of Leviathan in the fifteenth illustration to the Book of Job. We see it again in the magnificent serpent which forms the title page of *Europe*,[2] and in that of the title page of "Night the Third" of Young's *Night Thoughts*. This dragon-like human figure well suggests

[1] See Frye, *Fearful Symmetry*, pp. 138-140.
[2] The loop of Geryon's tail here recalls the coils of the design in *Europe*.

the bestiality of materialism following upon the Fall and giving rise to fraud, the vice punished in the Eighth Circle into which Geryon conveys Dante and Virgil.

The illustration is symmetrically composed with considerable skill so that it seems neither static nor artificial. The head of the monster is balanced by the mountain peak in the upper right, and the coiled tail by the cloud which also sets off Geryon's head. Note that the opening in the cloud reflects the shape of the tail, as the summit of the mountain does that of the sloping shoulders on which Dante and Virgil sit.

32. THE SEDUCERS CHASED BY DEVILS

THE GENERAL DESCRIPTION of the first trench of the Eighth Circle is given in Canto XVIII, lines 1-39. In this trench are the panders and the seducers, who circle in opposite directions while horned demons continuously beat them with lashes.

Blake, while showing the figures pursued by demons, has introduced variations into this design which cannot be explained solely on the basis of the text. In the first place, there is no mention in the poem of water in this trench, but here the bottom of the ditch contains a lake crossed by two arching bridges. Some of the sinners clamber up the edge of the trench in the foreground while others flee along the bridges behind. The text would indicate that the demons with lashes are on foot, but they are shown flying and some have serpents' tails instead of feet. Dante and Virgil stand upon a bank at the left watching.

The most remarkable feature of this illustration is in the center of the foreground and has no parallel in the poem. A corpse-like figure in armor lies flat upon its back, its left hand grasping a sword on the ground beside it. Crouched over this figure is a winged demon who bends vampire-like as though to suck the blood from its throat. Behind this group is a fragment of masonry wall to the left of which, near Dante and Virgil, may be seen what appear to be large cogged wheels with chains.

Here again we have a picture of the Fallen World in Blake's own terms. The water is the Lake of Udan-Adan, symbol of the spiritual annihilation of Ulro. From its shores the created spirits take their first steps upward on the solid ground of the World of Generation, pursued by demons who personify the corporeal and material desires which beset humanity. The body of the sleeping giant, Albion, lies upon the ground in the trance from which he will not arise until the day of his salvation through the casting off of error. His hideous Spectre has separated from him, and now preys upon the recumbent form.

> . . . till these terrors planted round the Gates of Eternal life
> Are driven away & annihilated, we never can repass the Gates.
> Thou knowest that the Spectre is in Every Man insane, brutish,
> Deform'd, that I am thus a ravening devouring lust continually
> Craving and devouring. . . .

Four Zoas VIIa, 302-306 (p. 317)

In addition to the Spectre, other symbols of the Fallen World are the rocky battlement, the cog wheels and the chain of jealousy.[1] All can be recognized from other

[1] The wall, the wheels, and the chains are, of course, suggested by the description in the first

designs and from various passages of the prophetic books. The chain we have already seen in the ninth design, that representing Minos. Another remarkable illustration, which shows the whole of the Fallen World encircled by the chain and suspended by it from the heavens, is the unpublished drawing to page 12 of "Night the First" of Young's *Night Thoughts*. The handsome frontispiece of *America* shows the Spectre brooding in a gap in a broken masonry wall much like this one, while a woman and child beside him are shut out from any glimpse of eternity. One of the finest pages of *Jerusalem* from the standpoint of decoration (plate 37) shows at the top of the page the falling Albion being caught in the arms of the Saviour and at the bottom a bat-like Spectre hovering over a sleeping form, much as here. The cog wheel too occurs in Blake's work as a symbol of the mechanistic materialism of this world, which grinds on oblivious of the suffering of individuals. Plate 22 of *Jerusalem* has a design showing giant cog wheels with weeping angels hovering above them.

Finally, the following lines from *The Everlasting Gospel* (p. 141) should be re-called in connection with this drawing:

> Then Roll'd the shadowy Man away
> From the Limbs of Jesus, to make them his prey,
> An Ever devouring appetite
> Glittering with festering venoms bright.
>
> . . . .
>
> But, when Jesus was Crucified,
> Then was perfected his glitt'ring pride:
> In three Nights he devour'd his prey,
> And still he devours the Body of Clay;
> But dust & Clay is the Serpent's meat,
> Which never was made for Man to Eat.

Blake probably introduced this group of the sleeping Man and the Spectre into this scene, in which the seducers are punished in the Circle of the Fraudulent, to remind us that sex, which can be one of the two gateways to eternity, when perverted to lust in Ulro becomes a scourge. The man of vision has now sunk into sleep and in his fallen state becomes a prey to the lustful demon who feeds upon him.

---

nineteen lines of the canto, in which the Eighth Circle is compared to a fortress which is sur-rounded by a series of moats crossed by bridges. However, it is certain from the non-representa-tional character of these details in the drawing that Blake identified them with his own symbols and did not regard them merely as features necessary to a literal illustration of the text.

33. THE FLATTERERS

The ditch of the flatterers is described in Canto XVIII, lines 98-133. Blake in this case follows the description of the *Divine Comedy* closely. Dante and Virgil have climbed to the top of the arch and look down into the ditch, holding their noses against the stench which arises from below. Clouds of the noxious steaming vapour hang above the trench, and in the trough itself are to be seen the people immersed in excrement. Two of them protrude somewhat from the filth and are thus more prominent than the others; they are the two who are mentioned by name in the poem. The man, Alessio Interminei of Lucca, shouts at Dante and beats upon his head. The woman is Thaïs, shown crouching as described. High up upon the left appears another of the bridges. Along it flees one of the seducers from the previous trench, pursued by a flying demon with a whip. Note, however, that the demon is now female and has no wings.

By contrast with the preceding illustration, this one is quite literal and without overt symbolism, except for Blake's undoubted conception of this scene as showing man in the foul mire of Ulro which shuts him off from any view of his spiritual self. Fallen Woman is, of course, the Female Will who seeks dominion over man chiefly by sexual attraction and flattery, the vice of this trench. For this reason Thaïs is not made as disgusting as the description of her in the text. This same cruel pursuit and domination of man by the Female Will explains the substitution in the group at the upper left of the figure of a woman for the male demons with wings as seen in the previous illustration.

This is a finished watercolor and especially rich in color effects. It is signed with Blake's monogram.

34. THE DEVILS UNDER THE BRIDGE

> . . . that other sank,
> And forthwith writhing to the surface rose;
> But those dark demons, shrouded by the bridge,
> Cried, "Here the hallow'd visage saves not: here
> Is other swimming than in Serchio's wave:
> Wherefore, if thou desire we rend thee not,
> Take heed thou mount not o'er the pitch." This said,
> They grappled him with more than hundred hooks,
> And shouted: "Cover'd thou must sport thee here;
> So, if thou canst, in secret mayst thou filch."
> E'en thus the cook bestirs him, with his grooms,
> To thrust the flesh into the caldron down
> With flesh-hooks, that it float not on the top.
>
> Inferno XXI, 44-56

ALTHOUGH BLAKE has inscribed this drawing "HELL Canto 18," there is nothing in that canto resembling this subject. Properly, this illustration should come after Drawing 37; the Lucchese magistrate having been hurled into the boiling pitch is here tormented by the devils on the bank. Some flames rise from the surface of the lake. In the distance, beyond the pool, the edge of the trench is shown and also one of the rock bridges. Along this flee groups of the seducers, pursued by flying demons with whips.[1] The lightly drawn forms of Dante and Virgil may be seen near the left edge of the page at the far side of the pool.

[1] As the incident of the seducers belongs to Canto XVIII, it is possible that Blake originally intended to use this page for a scene from that ditch, and then decided to adapt it to this subject

The most interesting feature of the design is the rock bridge in the foreground in which Blake has shown various monstrous portions of human anatomy petrified into the form of an arch. Similar figures are to be found in Drawings 58 and 65. As in Eden man is all divine energy and unity, so at the nadir of the Fall he becomes inert and divided. Blake frequently describes fallen man as frozen solid or petrified and depicts him in a rocky cavern or dismembered. Here we see "the scatter'd portions of his immortal body"[2] turned to stone; the only faint link which still remains with his eternal life is his emanation, which probably explains the faint sketch of what apparently is a small female figure, walled in but sitting up alertly at the upper left of the rocky bridge.

> Coldness, darkness, obstruction, a Solid
> Without fluctuation, hard as adamant,
> Black as marble of Egypt, impenetrable,
> Bound in the fierce raging Immortal;
> And the seperated fires froze in:
> A vast solid without fluctuation
> Bound in his expanding clear senses.
>
> The Immortal stood frozen amidst
> The vast rock of eternity times
> And times, a night of vast durance,
> Impatient, stifled, stiffen'd, hard'ned.
>
> Book of Los, 53-63 (p. 243)[3]

Love is, of course, the dominant power of Eden and likewise cruelty is the epitome of Ulro. Thus this scene of a human being tortured by fiends[4] takes place appropriately beneath the rock bridge in which imagination is petrified and all vision of man's divinity is lost.

> And Los was roof'd in from Eternity in Albion's Cliffs.
> Which stand upon the ends of Beulah, and withoutside all
> Appear'd a rocky form against the Divine Humanity.
>
> Jerusalem 19, 33-35

The design shows many varying degrees of completion. Most of the figures are still in pencil, but a few passages have been inked. The devil with the hook, the figure in the pitch, and the pier of the bridge are nearly finished. Washes have been applied throughout most of the design, but are still in an early stage. The composition is well devised, with an area of movement in the center balanced by the foreground bridge

---

instead. Otherwise it is hard to account for the inaccuracy of the inscription. In any case, it is puzzling that the wrong inscription should have been inked, as Blake usually wrote tentative inscriptions in pencil first.

[2] *Four Zoas* VIII, 557 (p. 346).

[3] The title page of *The Book of Los* is an illustration of this passage.

[4] Notice that one demon has scaly genitals (compare Drawing 28) and that the middle figure of the group of three is apparently a woman. Blake is again reminding us that the perverted attitude of the Fallen World towards sex is the cause of much human suffering.

and by the static group at the right. A sense of great depth has been achieved and dense murky atmosphere is well suggested.

35. THE SIMONIAC POPE

THIS INCIDENT occupies all of Canto XIX. The punishment of the simoniacs, who are in the third trench of the Eighth Circle, is to be placed head-down in wells filled with fire, with only their legs protruding and flames licking across the soles of their feet. Dante and Virgil look down into the trench from the summit of one of the bridges and Dante expresses a wish to try to speak with one of the sinners who writhes more than the rest. Virgil then picks Dante up and carries him down into the ditch until they are beside the hole in which the sinner is enclosed. He proves to be Pope Nicholas III (Gian Gaetani degli Orsini), notorious for the simony and nepotism which he practiced during his pontificate (1277-1280). On hearing Dante address him, Nicholas mistakes him for Boniface VIII (1294-1303) whose arrival he is anticipating. On realizing his error, he explains to Dante that earlier simoniac popes lie beneath his head, crushed in fissures in the rock and that when Boniface comes, he will himself sink into the well and Boniface will take his place. He also goes on to predict that Boniface's feet will not cook for very long, for his place will be taken by Clement V (1305-1314). Dante then upbraids him for his wickedness and tells him that his punishment is richly deserved. As Nicholas kicks with wrath and remorse, Virgil again picks Dante up and carries him back out of the trench.

Blake shows all of this quite literally. In the background Virgil is seen carrying Dante toward the hole, in which the Pope is immersed head first. The sides of the well are transparent, as though of glass, so that the entire naked figure of the Pope may be seen. In one respect, however, the illustration differs from the setting as described. The whole scene takes place within a cave, instead of on the open floor of the trench. Through the mouth of the cave at the rear the trench filled with flames is visible. In the foreground and on both sides is to be seen the rough and rocky interior of the cavern.

We have already discussed in connection with the nineteenth and twenty-fourth designs Blake's frequent portrayal of the Fall by a figure in an upside down position.[1] We have also seen examples in the third, twenty-sixth, and twenty-seventh illustrations of figures in flames. In this description in the *Inferno* of a figure tortured in flames in an inverted position, Blake would again have found a close parallel to his own symbolism of the horrors of the fallen state of man in the created world of our present existence. With these, he has combined another of the symbols by which he often refers to the limited powers of the human senses. "If the doors of perception were cleansed every thing would appear to man as it is, infinite. For man has closed himself up, till he sees all things thro' narrow chinks of his *cavern*. . . ."[2] Hence the rocky cave with its narrow opening into the world of greater perception beyond—

[1] On this subject see Percival, *Blake's "Circle of Destiny,"* pp. 181-182.
[2] *Marriage of Heaven and Hell,* p. 187. "The cavern'd Man" (*Europe,* line 1) is depicted in the third design to *The Gates of Paradise* (reproduced in *Poetry and Prose,* p. 570).

that world from which the poets approach and with which they provide the Natural Man's only link.

This is a finished design and is notable among the series, and indeed among all of Blake's work, for brilliant and dramatic use of color. The rocks at the bottom are of intense hues of blue, red and orange. A fine effect is given of the heat and light coming from the mouth of the hole; the flames issuing from the well are orange, while brilliant red ones rise from the soles of the feet. The drawing is signed with Blake's monogram.

36. THE NECROMANCERS AND AUGURS

IN THE TWENTIETH CANTO, Virgil and Dante look down from the summit of a bridge into the fourth trench of the Eighth Circle in which Necromancers and Augurs are punished. Their heads have been completely reversed, so that they face behind them and are compelled to walk backwards, which they can do only slowly. The appropriateness of their punishment is described by Virgil in speaking of one of them (lines 34-37):

> . . . Lo! how he makes
> The breast his shoulders; and who once too far
> Before him wish'd to see, now backward looks,
> And treads reverse his path.

Dante is so overcome by pity at their deformity that he weeps bitterly; Virgil thereupon chides him for letting his feelings judge divine decrees. He then begins to point out various figures whom they see and to tell Dante something about each of them.

Blake has treated the subject literally. Dante and Virgil sit on the rock bridge, and Dante leans his head on his hand as though weeping. Below them four figures with their heads reversed are to be seen walking backward. Three of them are bearded men and the fourth a woman. Dante mentions seven men by name in this canto, and it is impossible to tell which of this group Blake intended to represent. The woman must be Manto, after whom Virgil's native city of Mantua was named, as she is the only woman identified in the text.

The rock bridge here suggests the cloudy layers which serve, as in the Job designs, to depict the division between the created and eternal worlds. Walled in by their rocky cave, the people of single vision do not realize the partial and warped nature of their point of view—fallen man being unaware of the limitations imposed upon him by the imperfect nature of his senses.

> In ignorance to view a small portion & think that All.
> Jerusalem 65, 27

This drawing is in an early stage. The figures below have been worked up partially with washes, but Dante and Virgil are still largely in pencil and alternative positions for their figures have not yet been erased. The bridge is very sketchily indicated and all the coloring is hasty. No setting is indicated behind the figures.

37. THE DEVIL CARRYING THE LUCCHESE MAGISTRATE TO THE BOILING PITCH-POOL OF CORRUPT OFFICIALS

IN THE FIFTH TRENCH of the Eighth Circle, Dante and Virgil view the punishment inflicted on corrupt politicians—to be cast into boiling pitch and to be harried by devils with sharp hooks whenever they attempt to rise above the surface. The episode illustrated here is related in *Inferno* XXI, 22-44. As Dante and Virgil watch, a demon arrives carrying one of the Elders of Lucca on his shoulders. Calling to the other demons, he hurls the magistrate into the pitch and then runs off to look for further prey.

The treatment of this scene is quite literal. On top of the rocky edge of the pool stands the demon with wings outstretched (lines 31-32), the sinner on his back; he is leaning forward on the point of throwing his burden into the pitch, which may be seen in the foreground. The shape of the wings of this demon and of all the others in the series is bat-like and they are leathery in texture as compared to the graceful feathered wings of the angels in the illustrations, such as that in the twentieth design. In the upper left on the bank Virgil and Dante stand looking on. At the lower right two leering devils sit by the pool; one is tusked and carries a hook. Some more hooks lightly sketched behind indicate that Blake originally intended to portray a larger group of demons.

This drawing is interesting chiefly as showing clearly the various stages by which Blake proceeded from the first sketch to a finished work. The figures of Dante, Virgil and the Elder are mainly in pencil with occasional lines inked. The demons in the foreground have been carried a little nearer completion. The principal figure, that of the demon on the rock, is modeled to a considerable extent, but only around the right eye has it been substantially completed. In only a few places have colored washes already been applied. In spite of the unfinished quality of the drawing, the sense of form and substance of the rocks is admirable for its solidity, an effect obtained with the utmost economy of means.

38. VIRGIL ABASHING THE DEVILS

THE INCIDENT illustrated here will be found in *Inferno* XXI, lines 57-88. Telling Dante to crouch down behind a rock in order to conceal himself, Virgil steps forward to speak to the devils. They rush upon him, but stop when Virgil demands that one of them advance to confer with him. Malacoda comes forward and, when Virgil explains that the Divine Will has directed him to show another the road through hell, he commands the other demons not to molest them.

The treatment is quite literal, although Malacoda is shown seated on a rock in the center while the text infers that he was standing. Another rock rises behind the devil and to the left of it Dante crouches. Malacoda has horns and his wings are raised; scales cover his genitals. He gestures upward with his right hand. His hook lies on the ground in front of him where he has dropped it in accordance with lines 83-84. Virgil stands next to him to the right of center, his right hand before his face and his left hand held above him as he gestures heavenward. Two more winged demons, one with a hook, stand quietly behind Virgil at the right of the page. In the left foreground the edge of the pool of boiling pitch may be seen.

The Man of Vision confronts the Natural Man and renders him powerless. The gesture of Virgil should be compared with that of Eliphaz in the ninth Job engraving as he points toward his vision of the deity.

This drawing is almost entirely in pencil; only a few lines have been inked and washes appear only at the left, above and below Dante. The figure of Malacoda is more developed in detail than are the others.

39. THE DEVILS SETTING OUT WITH DANTE AND VIRGIL

In Canto xxi, lines 95-133, Malacoda appoints ten of his demons to guide Dante and Virgil along the bank of the lake of boiling pitch as far as the bridge that will carry them over to the next trench. All the while Dante is alarmed by the threatening aspect of the devils.

Dante and Virgil are in the center of the design, facing toward the right. Beside them stands Barbariccia, whom Malacoda has appointed to be leader of the group. An impressive figure with horns and raised pointed wings, he looks back over his shoulder and with his right hand summons the other devils to follow as he strides off toward the right. In his left hand is a hook and he has a barbed tail. Behind him may be seen the pool of pitch; flames rise from its surface and mount to the top of the page. Four fiends stand behind Dante and Virgil, the one immediately to their left being Ciriatto, recognizable by his tusks (line 120). At the extreme left stands a demon with his back turned; he too has a tail and his bat-like wings are folded on his back. Only five of the ten demons who were ordered to join the group are shown.[1]

An expressive contrast is formed by the agitation of the two groups of fiends as opposed to the quiet forms of the poets in the center. The compactly massed devils on the left are balanced by the single figure at the right who spreads his wings and gestures violently. The flames rising behind him fill out the corner of the design in the same manner as do the hooks grouped at the left. Three of the demons have their forms modeled to a considerable degree, but the rest of the drawing is sketchy.

[1] A very faint trace of a small portion of the figure of a sixth demon may be seen in pencil at the extreme left edge of the page.

40. THE DEVILS, WITH DANTE AND VIRGIL, BY THE SIDE OF THE POOL

This design does not show any particular incident, but rather gives the general impression of the Trench of the Corrupt Politicians in the Circle of the Fraudulent. The shore is in the foreground and behind it the lake of boiling pitch stretches into the far distance. One bridge frames the page in the manner of a theater proscenium and three others arch across the lake in the distance. Between the second and third bridges at the left and under the farthest arch flames arise from the surface of the pool. Dante and Virgil with their escort of devils walk along the bank at the left. Barbariccia, the leader of the demons, turns to urge the others on. A group of the sinners who lie on the bank partially submerged like frogs (XXII, 26-29) may be seen in the right foreground.

Blake does not seem to have intended any particular symbolism here. Rather, his interest appears to have been in creating a sense of spaciousness and grandeur. In relatively small compass the drawing conveys a feeling of vastness; light is handled masterfully to enhance the mysterious and gloomy effect. The whole would make a simple and yet impressive stage setting. It was such a design as this that caused a recent critic to remark of the Dante series, "Their chief quality is . . . elemental. . . . In these drawings Blake has developed an interpretative expression of landscape, unique at that date. Superb as some of the figures are, the grandest of his illustrations are those in which the mood of sky or sea or mountain landscape predominates."[1]

While the setting is carried almost to completion, all of the figures are very lightly drawn, those in the pitch being barely discernible. The group of the poets and their demonic guides is much like that of the previous illustration, although on a somewhat smaller scale; it is so sketchy that it is impossible to say exactly how many fiends are represented, probably four or five.

[1] C. H. Collins Baker, "William Blake, Painter," *Huntington Library Bulletin*, x, 1936, pp. 146-147.

41 and 41E. CIAMPOLO TORMENTED BY THE DEVILS

THE SUBJECT of this illustration is drawn from Canto XXII, lines 31-123. As the devils proceed along the shore of the lake of boiling pitch with Dante and Virgil, they surprise one of the sinners on the surface close to them and one of the demons with his hook pulls him up by the hair onto the bank. As the devils threaten him with their hooks and claws, Virgil questions him. He identifies himself as a retainer who practiced graft at the court of King Thibaut II of Navarre; although he does not mention his name he has been associated with a Navarrese courtier called Ciampolo. Still menaced by the demons, and twice wounded, he goes on to tell Virgil of a number of the other sinners in the pitch. Finally he offers to try to tempt some more of them onto the bank. As the demons confer upon this plan, their attention is distracted and Ciampolo escapes by diving back into the pitch. The episode illustrated here occurs after Ciampolo has confessed his fear of the demons to Virgil and expressed a wish that he were safe beneath the surface of the lake. This arouses one of the devils to tear him with his hook (lines 69-71):

> "Too long we suffer," Libicocco cried;
> Then, darting forth a prong, seized on his arm,
> And mangled bore away the sinewy part.

Ciampolo stands naked and alone at the left, looking down in anguish at his arm as the hook tears it. Three winged demons sit on a rock at the right, the middle one wielding the hook. The lightly penciled head of a fourth—"Ciriatto, from whose mouth a tusk issued on either side, as from a boar" (54-55)—appears behind them in the upper right corner. Another rock is in the extreme left foreground and behind may be seen the lake of pitch from which flames and waves of heat are rising. There is no other background.[1] Dante and Virgil are not shown.

There are no details here which require a knowledge of Blake's symbolism to explain them. We can only conjecture that Blake perhaps thought of this incident as signifying that the road of escape from the violence and suffering of this world does not lie in self-destruction, for new terrors lie beneath the surface of the Lake of Ulro. Salvation cannot come through running away from the evils of the world, but only through spiritual regeneration.

The figures of Ciampolo and of two of the devils are substantially complete. The third demon, that in the foreground, is approaching completion although his hands and feet and the hook which he holds have only been sketched in. The rest of the drawing is quite unfinished.

THIS IS THE SECOND of the illustrations which Blake engraved. The engraving is far more finished and it is of interest that Blake worked on his plate from such an incomplete preparatory drawing. This is particularly evident in the case of the tusked Ciriatto; barely sketched in the drawing, he appears as a fine demoniacal figure in the engraving. The other three devils are similar in both versions, but their facial expressions are more effective in the engraving. The demon in the foreground points toward Ciampolo with his left hand, a detail that is scarcely indicated in the drawing. All of the demons in the engraving are shown with hooks. The figure and expression of Ciampolo is much the same in both, but the hook as shown in the engraved version is smaller and less curved and does not seem to tear quite as much flesh. The details of the setting are also more precise in the engraving. Vegetation covers part of the ground and also grows upon the rocks. There are more flames rising from the surface of the lake and a black cloud of smoke hangs behind Ciampolo's head.

In spite of its being far more complete than the drawing, however, and although parts have been fully worked up, the plate itself is in an unfinished condition. The modeling of the upper portions of Ciampolo's body has only been begun and details along the right margin have merely been outlined.

[1] Properly speaking, Ciampolo should be shown clasped in the arms of the leader of the group of devils, Barbariccia, who was holding him at this point (lines 57-58). However, the composition is made more effective by the omission of this detail and by placing Ciampolo alone as he is preyed upon by the violent forces of the infernal regions.

42 and 42E. BAFFLED DEVILS FIGHTING

CIAMPOLO having dived back into the lake of pitch, following the episode of the previous illustration, two of the demons fly out over the lake in pursuit. Unable to find their victim, they vent their wrath upon each other and in their struggle both fall into the boiling pool. They can no longer fly with their wings stuck with tar, and have to be pulled out by their comrades. While the rescue is going on, Dante and Virgil depart (Canto XXII, lines 124-148).

The boiling lake from which flames rise is shown in the foreground. In the center above it the two flying demons fight with clawed hands raised. In the background the shores of the lake slope up to hills behind. A path curves up the center and near the point where it disappears over a crest may be seen two lightly sketched figures which evidently represent Dante and Virgil making their escape. Standing and seated on the bank at the right by the shore are ten more figures of demons who gesture with eagerness and excitement as they watch the fight. Above the mountain peaks behind them flames mount into the sky.

The illustration follows the text closely and is apparently without symbolism. However, the scene recalls the warfare between the Zoas which in numerous passages in Blake's longer prophecies is the signal for the fall into Ulro.[1] The demons, or Natural Men, on the bank give their whole attention to violence and turn their backs on the poets.[2]

The foreground portion of the drawing is quite finished, especially the forms of the flying demons. The background, however, is incomplete, the group of devils being but faintly indicated.

THIS DESIGN also was engraved. By exception, the engraving in this case is less finished than the drawing and the effect produced by the latter is better, more spacious and dramatic.

In particular, the faces of the fighting devils have been somewhat modified in the engraving and their bodies are less muscular. The hands of the devil to the left and the position of his left leg are very tentatively indicated, as though Blake had not quite made up his mind as to how he wished them to be. New lines have been engraved and the plate printed before the old ones were completely erased. The wings also are not as well worked out as in the drawing. The group of demons in the background is also very sketchy, some being slightly more finished and others somewhat less so than in the drawing; however, in general their poses and gestures are much the same in both versions, as are the details of the background and of the lake. The only passage which is considerably nearer completion in the plate than in the drawing is that showing the two figures of Dante and Virgil; however, they are still unfinished.

In a letter written to John Linnell on April 25, 1827, less than four months before his death, Blake mentions that he is just beginning work on this engraving: "I have Proved the Six Plates, & reduced the Fighting devils ready for the Copper."[3] It is thus apparent that Blake was working on this plate during his last illness. This accounts for its unfinished character, as a result of which it is the least satisfactory engraving of the series.

[1] See, for example, *Four Zoas* i, 468-541 (pp. 264-266).
[2] Blake has mistakenly shown ten devils in the group, the number which originally set out (XXI, 118). As two are fighting over the lake, there should only be eight on the shore. In the engraving, while traces of the two devils in the right background may be seen, it appears that Blake may have been in the process of eliminating them, to reconcile the number shown with the text.
[3] *Poetry and Prose*, p. 928.

43. DANTE AND VIRGIL ESCAPING FROM THE DEVILS

THIS ILLUSTRATION is based upon *Inferno* XXIII, 1-57. Having left the devils busy rescuing their comrades from the lake of pitch, Dante and Virgil continue on their way. Presently they become aware that the demons, made even more wrathful by Ciampolo's escape and its sequel, are pursuing them. Virgil seizes Dante in his arms and, holding him, slides down the rocky wall from the fifth trench into the sixth. Immediately the demons appear on the bank above them, but as Dante and Virgil have escaped into the next trench the devils no longer have the power to follow them.

A rock bridge arches across the page near the top. Above it the flying demons, waving their hooks, halt in frustration, looking down at the poets below.[1] Virgil, having slid down the wall, is shown running along a narrow path by the cliff, holding Dante in his arms. Behind is seen a glimpse of the floor of the sixth trench with a group of the hypocrites in their cowls filing through it (XXIII, 58-67). A low hill rises behind them and above that, but beneath the arch, is a layer of clouds.

Imagination can freely cross boundaries that are closed to the natural senses. Hence the rock bridge and the cloud that repeats its shape are not barriers to the poets although the demons cannot pass them. It will be noted that seven cowled figures are shown and also seven demons. This may well be intended to suggest that in all of the seven ages into which Blake divides the history of man from the Fall to the present,[2] created man has been blind and has been bowed down under the stultifying rule of organized religion. As a result, in each age his spiritual life has been possessed by demons who above all attack men of vision, as being the greatest threat to the rule of law and its supporters.

The position of Dante and Virgil make it hard to visualize how they have slid down the rocky wall. Virgil is now shown running swiftly along the ledge. The outflung right legs of the two poets serve admirably to convey a sense of speed and repeat the pattern of the cloud, the bridge, and the group of devils in the sky. Except for this feature, the composition would be out of balance. In the group of demons, movement which is at the same time on the point of being arrested is finely suggested.

The figures of Dante and Virgil and of the foremost fiend are quite complete, but the rest is unfinished in detail. Of the seven demons, the heads of four are merely sketched in pencil.

[1] The figure of the principal demon in this design, with his scaly genitals, is much like that of Satan in the fifth Job illustration.

[2] Percival, *Blake's "Circle of Destiny,"* pp. 242-250; Frye, *Fearful Symmetry*, pp. 128-134.

44. THE HYPOCRITES WITH CAIAPHAS

DANTE AND VIRGIL now find themselves in the sixth trench of the Eighth Circle in which hypocrites are punished (XXIII, 58-129). It is their lot to wear heavy habits like those of monks, with cowls which hang down before their eyes. Although gilded on the outside so that they shine with dazzling brightness, the cloaks are in reality made of thick lead, and those encased in them can move only slowly and with great difficulty. Thus clad they must file endlessly around their trench. Two of them speak to Dante, identifying themselves as Bolognese friars who served jointly in the office of Podestà in Florence and became—in spite of their being in holy orders—notorious for peculation. As Dante talks with them he notices a figure lying crosswise in the trench and fastened to the ground in the shape of a cross by means of three stakes. One of the friars identifies him as Caiaphas, the high priest who counselled that Christ should be put to death on the grounds that "it is expedient for us, that one man should die for the people, and that the whole nation perish not."[1] Each of the hypocrites must step upon him every time that he passes, the friar explains, and goes on to inform Dante that Annas, the father-in-law of Caiaphas, and other members of the Jewish council whom Caiaphas persuaded suffer like punishment in other parts of the trench.

In the illustration, Caiaphas lies nailed to a wooden cross in the center. Near him, in the right foreground, Dante and Virgil stand watching. The floor of the trench is seen behind with hills closing it in in the distance. One of the rock bridges arches in the middle. The procession of cowled figures approaches from the left, making a number of turns on the way. The figure who has just reached Caiaphas places a foot on his chest as he prepares to step across him. Others who have already passed the recumbent figure file off behind a low bank in the left foreground. In the sky above the arch appear five of the frustrated demons from the previous trench, all armed with hooks.

Caiaphas is mentioned several times in Blake's writings. As the priest who invoked the law to take the life of an innocent man, he serves as the archetype of Natural Religion, Blake's name for that organized religion which sets up laws of punishment for sin, instead of proclaiming forgiveness through love.

> I stood among my valleys of the south
> And saw a flame of fire, even as a Wheel
> Of fire surrounding all the heavens: it went
> From west to east, against the current of
> Creation, and devour'd all things in its loud
> Fury & thundering course round heaven & earth.
>
> .   .   .   .
>
> And I asked a Watcher & a Holy-One
> Its Name; he answered: "It is the Wheel of Religion."
> I wept & said: "Is this the law of Jesus,
> This terrible devouring sword turning every way?"
> He answer'd: "Jesus died because he strove
> Against the current of this Wheel; its Name
> Is *Caiaphas*, the dark preacher of Death,
> Of sin, of sorrow & of punishment:
> Opposing Nature! It is Natural Religion;
> But Jesus is the bright Preacher of Life
> Creating Nature from this fiery Law
> By self-denial & forgiveness of Sin."

Jerusalem, plate 77

[1] John xi, 50.

Hence, Caiaphas is for Blake the epitome of the Natural Man as opposed to Jesus, the man of Vision and Imagination. As such he is bound down to this world without hope of redemption and becomes inevitably a victim of its cruel tortures.[2] He is thus to be identified with the Spectre, or Selfhood, and is here shown with the likeness and long beard of Urizen, the tyrant of the Moral Law. Caiaphas is also associated with the Threefold Accuser, as in the design at the top of page 93 of *Jerusalem*, the caption of which is: "Anytus, Melitus & Lycon thought Socrates a Very Pernicious Man; so *Caiaphas* thought Jesus."[3]

The drawing is unfinished in certain details; for example the figures of Dante and Virgil are still in pencil. The entire effect, however, is spacious and fine. The slow file of hypocrites is skilfully balanced by the group of demons flying swiftly in the reverse direction and by the quiet forms of the poets near the edge of the page.[4] Keynes has pointed out the similarity of the cowled figures in this design to one of the watercolor illustrations for Young's *Night Thoughts*.[5] This is an interesting example of the persistence of certain artistic motifs in Blake's work, as thirty years separate the two drawings.

[2] We must, of course, bear in mind that Caiaphas was regarded by Blake as a "state" rather than as an individual. States may be eternally evil, but each individual has the capacity to recognize and reject error and thus attain salvation. It will be recalled that Blake's chief reservation concerning the *Divine Comedy* was that it dwells so much upon the justness of God's punishments, whereas Blake held that "The Glory of Christianity is To Conquer by Forgiveness." (*Jerusalem*, plate 52.)

[3] Compare also: "Natural Religion . . . was the Religion of the Pharisees who murder'd Jesus." (*Jerusalem, loc. cit.*) Quite a number of sinister references are made to Caiaphas in *The Everlasting Gospel*, pp. 131-143.

[4] Anthony Blunt (*Journal of the Warburg and Courtauld Institutes*, VI, 1943, p. 211) considers that this design is very similar to that by Flaxman of the same subject; however, the relationship of the two does not seem to be any closer than would naturally ensue from the fact that both artists were following the same text quite closely. Even if there is a connection, we can certainly agree with C. H. Collins Baker (*Huntington Library Quarterly*, IV, 1940-1941, p. 366) that "it is interesting . . . to see how immeasurably, in adapting, Blake surpassed Flaxman."

[5] Keynes, *Blake's Illustrations to Young's "Night Thoughts,"* introductory note to plate 30.

45. THE LABORIOUS PASSAGE ALONG THE ROCKS, first version

AT THE END of the twenty-third canto, one of the hypocrites informs Virgil that near at hand lies a rock bridge in ruins, by means of which he and Dante can climb out of the sixth trench. Lines 19-44 of Canto XXIV tell of their finding the broken arch and of their climbing with difficulty up the huge boulders, Dante going first and Virgil pushing him from behind.

The design is a very simple one, but conveys a sense of vastness. The huge pile of rocks is shown at the left, their hardness and three-dimensionality remarkably suggested by means of a few pencil lines and faint washes. Two-thirds of the way up the pile the lightly penciled forms of Dante and Virgil may be seen, Dante going ahead and testing the firmness of the rocks and Virgil following as described in the poem. A column of cloud which repeats the shape of the rock pile rises in the void at the right.

The composition of this illustration recalls that for page 41 of "Night the Fifth" in the series of drawings for Young's *Night Thoughts*. Blake used the idea again in much more finished form in Drawing 74 of the present series, one of the designs to the *Purgatorio*. The climbing group as shown here might, if it had been finished, been much like that in the drawing "The Brothers Plucking Grapes" from the series of designs to Milton's *Comus*. These are further instances of the revival by Blake of pictorial ideas first conceived many years before.[1]

This drawing is one of two versions of the same subject. Possibly Blake wished to obtain a greater sense of vastness and wanted the rock pile to appear more formidable than it does in the next design, and so made this sketch later, achieving a more spacious effect.[2]

[1] The drawings for Young were made in 1796-1797; those for *Comus*, about 1810. See reproduction in Keynes, *Illustrations to Young's "Night Thoughts,"* and Figgis, *Paintings of William Blake*, plate 97.

[2] If the drawing is turned sideways so that what is now the upper right corner becomes the lower right, "Hell canto 16" may be discerned faintly in pencil along what then becomes the lower edge in the right corner. Blake apparently originally intended to use this sheet for a horizontal design from the sixteenth canto, later deciding to employ it for the present vertical drawing. The number "87" can also be seen in the upper right, arranged in accordance with the present orientation of the page. For this there seems no apparent explanation, unless Blake also intended to use it at one time for another in the series of vertical designs for the *Purgatorio* which form an unbroken sequence from number 79 to number 86 inclusive. As this drawing is largely unfinished, it is not surprising that earlier inscriptions were not erased.

46. THE LABORIOUS PASSAGE ALONG THE ROCKS, second version

THIS DRAWING illustrates exactly the same passage of text as the previous one.

The present version is less spacious and more like a conventional stage set. The ruins of the broken arch lie at the right. Dante stands on a ledge, making an inexpressive gesture, as Virgil scrambles up behind. On the left may be seen the half of the arch which has not fallen. Near the point where it is broken off in the middle of the page, two heads are visible close to the top. These figures were probably at first intended to represent some of the demons from the fifth trench still watching their escaping prey; later it was decided to eliminate them and now all but the heads have been covered by the wash which forms the sky in the upper left. In the background beneath the arch is a low mountain above which clouds rise through the gap of the broken bridge to the top of the page.

The fallen arch does not seem to present nearly as formidable an obstacle as in the previous illustration; in fact, it is quite short and would not appear sufficient to cause Dante's exhaustion as described in the text. While the other version is more effective, this design has considerable grandeur expressed in the simplest of terms.

47. THE THIEVES AND SERPENTS

We from the bridge's head descended, where
To the eighth mound it joins; and then, the chasm
Opening to view, I saw a crowd within

> Of serpents terrible, so strange of shape
> And hideous, that remembrance in my veins
> Yet shrinks the vital current. . . .
>
> .   .   .   .
>
> Amid this dread exuberance of woe
> Ran naked spirits wing'd with horrid fear,
> Nor hope had they of crevice where to hide,
> Or heliotrope to charm them out of view.
> With serpents were their hands behind them bound,
> Which through their reins infix'd the tail and head,
> Twisted in folds before.   Inferno xxiv, 77-82; 89-95

THE TRENCH is shown filled with roaring flames which rise to the top of the page. On the right is a cliff from the top of which a demon with a club hurls a sinner into the valley below.[1] Five of the thieves in the grip of snakes occupy the foreground. On the ground at the left a woman lies with the coil of a serpent bound around her body just below the breasts. Next is a male figure with back turned and his arms bound behind him by smaller snakes. Then comes a male figure squatting on the ground,[2] a standing female figure, and a man in profile running toward the others. All have their arms pinned behind them, but the reptiles are not shown thrusting their heads and tails between the crotches of the sinners as described. In the rear at the left, three more serpents are seen who have not yet fastened themselves upon the thieves. Two glide along the ground and one rises on its tail amid flames. The nearest and largest has a woman's breast, small wings, and a diabolic half-human head.

The serpent, as the instigator of the Fall, and with its coils suggesting the endless cyclic quality of nature, symbolizes for Blake the material world in which humanity is preyed upon by savage forces. Having counselled man to submit to the feminine side of his nature and persuaded him to accept material temptation, it is the symbol of the evil of the created world, blind to reason or the spirit, an utterly fierce personification of the selfhood. As such it appears frequently in Blake's poetry and designs.

The following passage, which is the account of the Fall as given in *Europe*, lines 137-150 (p. 216), is significant in connection with the present illustration.

> . . . When the five senses whelm'd
> In deluge o'er the earth-born man; then turn'd the fluxile eyes
> Into two stationary orbs, concentrating all things:
> The ever-varying spiral ascents to the heavens of heavens
> Were bended downward, and the nostrils' golden gates shut,
> Turn'd outward, barr'd and petrify'd against the infinite.
> Thought chang'd the infinite to a serpent, that which pitieth
> To a devouring flame; and man fled from its face and hid

[1] This detail is so unlike Blake in its execution as to suggest that it was probably added later by another hand. There is also no logical explanation for it, either in the text or in terms of symbolic intent.

[2] Blake adapted this figure from his drawing, "The Stoning of Achan." (Figgis, *Paintings of William Blake*, plate 81.) It occurs also in a fine pencil drawing of an unidentified subject in the possession of Geoffrey Keynes, Esq. (Keynes, *Pencil Drawings*, plate 26).

In forests of night: then all the eternal forests were divided
Into earths rolling in circles of space, that like an ocean rush'd
And overwhelmed all except this finite wall of flesh.
Then was the serpent temple form'd, image of infinite
Shut up in finite revolutions, and man became an Angel,
Heaven a mighty circle turning, God a tyrant crown'd.

It would seem apparent, therefore, that Blake saw in this subject from Dante an allegory of the Fallen World in which "Thought [has] changed the infinite to a serpent, that which pitieth to a devouring flame."[3] As all this came about when "the five senses whelm'd in deluge o'er the earth-born man," five human figures are seen in the grip of the serpent forces of the created world. Through this Fallen World, in which man is bound down by materialism, closed in by the limitations of his senses, and preyed upon by the flames of fierce and unquenchable desires, glides the serpent of that false physical love which is pure lust and self-gratification and which comes always to wound and to bring suffering.[4]

This design thus represented for Blake a pictorial rendition of the terrors of mortal life when mental and spiritual illumination are lost. It has a very close counterpart in the fine drawing in the Boston Museum of Fine Arts, "The Brazen Serpent," which dates from about 1810. There "The Serpent Bulk of Nature's dross"[5] is raised aloft and all around it are shown figures in the grip of serpents: some of the figures are wholly in the serpents' power, others have triumphed over the material through the power of the spirit and the serpents hang dead about them, others being innocent are untouched.[6]

In many other designs by Blake serpents are a prominent feature. Drawing 102 of the Dante series is a striking example; as will be brought out in the analysis of it, it cannot be specifically connected with any canto, but appears to be an allegory of Woman in a Fallen World as suggested by the *Inferno*. Another important occurrence of this symbolism will be found in the watercolor on the reverse of the title page to "Night the Third" in the series of drawings to Young's *Night Thoughts* in the British Museum. The globe of the created world is formed of a giant serpent with its tail in its mouth; within it is imprisoned an agonized human figure bound in chains and entwined by roots.[7]

---

[3] Flames are not mentioned in the text, but Blake has made them a prominent feature of his design.

[4] There are a number of other examples of serpents with female heads in Blake's work, as plate 75 of *Jerusalem* and the drawings on pp. 4r, 7r and 7v of the MS of *The Four Zoas* in the British Museum. Page 49v of the same MS has an interesting drawing of a cobra within whose hood is a bewildered male face. The devil in the well-known drawing in the Fogg Museum of Harvard University, "Michael Subduing Satan," (Figgis, *op. cit.*, plate 10) has a man's head on a serpent's body.

[5] *The Everlasting Gospel*, p. 135. See also *Jerusalem* 29, 78-80.

[6] The symbolism of this drawing is discussed by Anthony Blunt in *Journal of the Warburg and Courtauld Institutes*, VI, 1943, pp. 225-227.

[7] There are many other striking designs involving serpents in the illustrations to Young's *Night Thoughts*: e.g. among the published engravings, the title page to "Night the Third" and the design on p. 12, and among the drawings reproduced in the volume edited by Keynes, the illus-

The drawing shows many different stages of completion, from slight passages in pencil to the fully modeled form of the standing woman. The general effect is quite unfinished. The wall of roaring flames is finely conceived.

---

trations on p. 8 of "Night the Fifth" and on pp. 3 and 23 of "Night the Eighth." The fine serpent of the title page of *Europe* has already been mentioned in the discussion of the thirty-first Dante illustration. For other examples, among many that occur, see the eleventh and fifteenth Job engravings and the drawings reproduced in Figgis, *op. cit.*, plates 11, 12, 13, 20, 24, 30, 67, and 90.

48. THE SERPENT ATTACKING VANNI FUCCI

> . . . And lo! on one
> Near to our side, darted an adder up,
> And, where the neck is on the shoulders tied,
> Transpierced him.
> Inferno xxiv, 95-98

AS THE SERPENT bites the sinner at the nape of the neck, the latter catches fire and burns wholly to ashes; immediately the man springs up again in the manner of the Phoenix and appears stunned and bewildered like one coming out of an epileptic fit. Virgil asks him his name and he identifies himself as Vanni Fucci of Pistoia, a violent partisan of the Neri in the blood-feud which raged in that city and one of those who in 1293 had plundered the treasury of San Jacopo in the church of San Zeno. In order to give pain to Dante because he has heard his confession, Fucci then prophesies the imminent expulsion of the Bianchi, Dante's party, from Pistoia (xxiv, 98-150).

Fucci runs toward the left in a crouching position. He looks fearfully over his left shoulder at the snake who is biting him on the neck. Flames spring up from the ground and to right and left several more serpents are seen upon the floor of the trench. In the background are three mountains; above the peak of the middle one floats a cloud behind which may be seen the rays of the setting sun.

The symbolism of the serpents is the same here as in the previous illustration. A prey to material error, man cannot see the spiritual sun hidden behind the clouds which shut off his perception of eternity.

The entire drawing is very sketchy; only Fucci's figure has gone beyond the first stage of development and it is far from finished.[1]

[1] "Canto 24 Hell" may be discerned very faintly in pencil along the right margin of the drawing in the upper corner. This suggests that Blake originally intended this to be a vertical drawing, and later changed to the present orientation.

49. FUCCI "MAKING THE FIGS" AGAINST GOD

> When he had spoke, the sinner raised his hands
> Pointed in mockery, and cried: "Take them, God!
> I level them at thee." From that day forth
> The serpents were my friends; for round his neck
> One of them rolling twisted, as it said,

"Be silent, tongue!" Another, to his arms
Upgliding, tied them, riveting itself
So close, it took from them the power to move.
Pistoia! ah, Pistoia! why dost doubt
To turn thee into ashes, cumbering earth
No longer, since in evil act so far
Thou has outdone thy seed? I did not mark,
Through all the gloomy circles of the abyss,
Spirit, that swell'd so proudly 'gainst his God;
Not him, who headlong fell from Thebes.

Inferno xxv, 1-15

VANNI FUCCI stands in the center of the design, his hands raised above his head as he makes the insulting gesture of the "figs" by placing his thumbs between his first and second fingers. One of the serpents has already coiled itself about his neck and two others are leaping to seize his arms. Dante and Virgil watch with deploring gestures at the right, near the foot of a rock bridge which arches across the scene behind Fucci. Under the bridges are flames in front of which several more serpents glide along the ground, one in the act of swallowing another.[1] A bluff rises behind Dante and Virgil. The top of the design is closed in by a dark cloud from which flames and lightning rain down upon the arrogant blasphemer.

The Natural Man in the very pit of error is not only blind to spirit, but actively hostile to it and to the things of the spirit. The victim of the terrors of the material world, he stubbornly curses that power inherent within himself that alone can deliver him from his fearful state. Fucci here represents Satan, that "limit of opacity" which is so monstrous that it serves eventually to reveal to all men the nature of error and thus save them from it. "We do not find any where that Satan is Accused of Sin; he is only accused of Unbelief. . . . Satan thinks that Sin is displeasing to God; he ought to know that Nothing is displeasing to God but Unbelief."[2]

This is a splendid composition, one of the most effective and dramatic of the series. The upward rush of movement suggested by Fucci's raised hands, the leaping serpents, and the rising flames, is parried by the lightnings and flames which hurtle down from above. The greater movement at the lower left of the design tends to balance the static figures of Dante and Virgil at the right and to prevent them from drawing attention from Fucci. The bluff behind the poets at the same time provides a background for them and also separates them from the main center of interest.

[1] To those whose whole philosophy is materialistic, all others of their kind are rivals to be hated and destroyed.

[2] *Vision of the Last Judgment*, p. 649.

50. CACUS

. . . He[1] fled,
Nor utter'd more; and after him there came
A Centaur full of fury, shouting, "Where,

[1] Refers to Vanni Fucci, the subject of the two previous illustrations.

Where is the caitiff?" On Maremma's marsh
Swarm not the serpent tribe, as on his haunch
They swarm'd, to where the human face begins.
Behind his head, upon the shoulders, lay
With open wings a dragon, breathing fire
On whomsoe'er he met. To me my guide:
"Cacus is this, who underneath the rock
Of Aventine spread oft a lake of blood.
He, from his brethren parted, here must tread
A different journey, for his fraudful theft
Of the great herd that near him stall'd; whence found
His felon deeds their end, beneath the mace
Of stout Alcides, that perchance laid on
A hundred blows, and not the tenth was felt."

Inferno xxv, 15-31

THE CENTAUR, who is moving from right to left, takes up nearly the entire drawing; no other figure is shown. His hind feet are on the ground and he has just raised his forefeet as if about to rear. The many snakes on his rump are only very sketchily drawn and would not be recognizable as such were it not for the text. The figure is bearded and his arms are outstretched across the design. In his left hand he holds a club with a large head. The description of the dragon is very closely followed. It squats with opened wings upon the nape of Cacus' neck and breathes out flames. Behind, the floor of the trench is very lightly shown. Some snakes are seen on the ground and in the distance a rock bridge.

Fucci having defied God in the previous design, we see here the bestial God of vengeance as the Natural Man conceives him. He is bearded and has the usual countenance of Urizen. In his left hand he holds the scepter of imperial authority to indicate that the forces of assumed power are often marshalled by fraud and exercised with stupidity and brutality. With arms outspread, Urizen proclaims himself as God of the Moral Law.

Lo I am God, the terrible destroyer, & not the Saviour.

Four Zoas I, 330 (p. 260)

Similar representations of Satanic figures occur in a number of Blake's other designs. Perhaps closest to this is the drawing after *Paradise Regained*, "Christ's Troubled Dream," in which Urizen appears bearded and with wings and arms outstretched, as here. Draped across his shoulders and hanging down from his arms are fire-breathing snakes which correspond to the dragon of the present illustration. A similar figure ruling over a world of people in torment, as are the inhabitants of this trench of the Inferno, is shown in the color-printed drawing, "The Lazar House."[2]

[2] Figgis, *Paintings of William Blake*, plates 30 and 73. Though different in pose, the figure of Jehovah in the eleventh Job design represents a similar concept.

51 and 51E. THE SIX-FOOTED SERPENT ATTACKING AGNOLO BRUNELLESCHI

THE SUBJECT of this illustration, and of the next as well, is drawn from *Inferno* xxv, lines 33-70. After Cacus has left, Dante and Virgil observe three spirits standing in the trench below them. They are subsequently identified as Agnolo Brunelleschi, Puccio Sciancato, and Buoso Donati, all notorious Florentine robbers. As they question each other as to the whereabouts of another of their number, Cianfa Donati, he appears suddenly in the guise of a six-footed serpent. He flings himself tightly upon Agnolo Brunelleschi and gradually the two forms of serpent and man blend together and become indistinguishable; the new monstrous form then moves slowly away.

Blake has followed the description closely. The beast grasps the unfortunate man's thighs with two of its feet, his paunch with two, and his arms with two, and sinks its teeth into both his cheeks; it thrusts its tail through his crotch and wraps it around one of his legs. Dante and Virgil stand on a low bank at the left, watching rather placidly. Puccio and Buoso look on in terror at the right; they are nude figures, one shown from the front and the other from the rear. The figure facing has long hair and, although on close examination it is seen to be male, it is very effeminate in appearance. The hair of the other figure stands on end with fright, as does that of the man who is being attacked. Numerous evil-looking serpents glide along the floor of the trench; two of them just below the poets watch intently as the attack takes place close to them. The background is formed by the shoulders of two mountains, between which may be seen large flames. The whole makes a tremendously effective illustration of one of the most horrifying episodes among all of the terrors described in the *Inferno*.

The symbolism of the serpents is as previously described. Brunelleschi is here to be thought of as "Man in his Spectre's power,"[1] that is, wholly overwhelmed by the material aspect of his dual nature. The imaginative or spiritual aspect of man—Los—and his emanation look on in terror as they behold the creation of the monstrous Spectre. This fact explains why, although two men are mentioned in the text, one of them here appears at first glance to be a woman.

> For as his Emanation divided, his Spectre also divided.
> *Jerusalem* 6, 3

It is significant to note that we have here, in the guise of characters of Dante's poem, the same group which appears in the design to plate 8 of *Milton*, in which Los and Enitharmon watch as a male figure representing the Spectre is consumed by flames.[2]

---

[1] See reversed inscription on plate 41 of *Jerusalem*.

[2] The following passage, describing the endless labors of Los, suggests the present illustration:

> Yet ceas'd he not from labouring at the roarings of his Forge,
>
> .   .   .   .
>
> Striving with Systems to deliver Individuals from those Systems,
> That whenever any Spectre began to devour the Dead,
> He might feel the pain as if a man gnaw'd his own tender nerves.
> *Jerusalem* 10, 62; 11, 5-7

THIS IS THE FOURTH of the drawings of which Blake made an engraving. As usual, the engraving is more finished in detail than is the drawing; there are, however, incomplete passages in the plate, notably in the upper left corner. The greater detail is especially noticeable in the case of the vegetation on the rock on which Dante and Virgil stand, and in the flames shown on the floor of the trench, whereas there are none in the drawing. The small serpents, whose number and location is the same in both versions, are shown in a more detailed manner in the engraving and the two in the right foreground also have feet, as they do not in the drawing. The scales of the serpent which attacks Brunelleschi are very clearly shown in the engraved version. The two figures at the right are taller in the engraving, their heads being higher than the back of the six-footed serpent and reaching nearly to the crest of the hill behind them; this results in a considerable improvement in the scale. The heads of Dante and Virgil are also not so close to the top of the design. The figure which appears rather effeminate in the drawing now has distinctly male genitals and the hair on its head stands up with terror as does that of the other figure.[3]

[3] In the Huntington Library there is a pencil sketch of this drawing which is substantially complete; it does not introduce the slight variations which occur in the engraving (C. H. Collins Baker, *Catalogue of William Blake's Drawings and Paintings in the Huntington Library*, San Marino, California, 1938, p. 32 and plate 23). This is perhaps the same drawing as that listed in W. M. Rossetti's catalogue in Gilchrist's *Life*, II, p. 264, no. 86. On p. 276 of the same volume a pencil sketch that may have been of this subject is listed as having been sold at the George Smith sale at Christie's in July 1880. This must in all probability have been the same drawing as that lent by George Smith to the 1876 exhibition at the Burlington Fine Arts Club, in the catalogue of which it is entitled (no. 242) "The Transformation of the Thieves in 'Dante.'" The title is not sufficiently specific to indicate whether this was the particular scene represented or whether it corresponded to one of the other drawings in the series from number 47-54 inclusive; however, the different dimensions given in the catalogue prove that it was not the sketch now in the Huntington Library.

Archibald G. B. Russell, in *The Engravings of William Blake*, London, 1912, p. 117n, notes that a pencil study of the two figures of Brunelleschi and the serpent was sold at the Richard Johnson sale on April 25, 1912.

52. BRUNELLESCHI HALF TRANSFORMED BY THE SERPENT

The Spectre is in every man insane & most Deform'd.
Four Zoas I, 99-100 (p. 254)

THE RESULT of the attack of the serpent upon Agnolo Brunelleschi—the subject of the previous illustration—is shown here, as the blending of the natures of the man and the reptile proceeds.[1] The monstrous character of the hybrid creature, as described in the text, is well suggested. Wings and a forked tail have sprouted from the figure and scales cover most of his body and the upper half of his face. His toes have turned to claws. Close beneath the monster, a huge snake lies watching the transformation eagerly. In the background are two intersecting rock bridges, beneath which amid flames three more serpents look on. Above the left bridge is a cloud from

[1] W. M. Rossetti in his catalogue of Blake's works in Gilchrist's *Life*, II, p. 264, no. 87, lists a sketch for this design, but without any mention of its location or the source of his knowledge of it. Nothing further concerning it has been published.

which issue lightning and flames. None of the other robbers are shown; neither are Dante and Virgil.

The serpent of nature watches in triumph the hideous bestialization of the human being in a fallen state of narrowed perceptions. The scales, wings and forked tail all indicate the Satanic nature of the figure which represents that "limit of opacity" which is the quintessence of the material aspect of man in a fallen world.

> . . . The Prester Serpent runs
> Along the ranks, crying, "Listen to the Priest of God, ye warriors;
> This Cowl upon my head he plac'd in times of Everlasting,
> And said, 'Go forth & guide my battles; like the jointed spine
> Of man I made thee when I blotted Man from life & light.' "
>
> Four Zoas viib, 111-115 (pp. 325-326)

> Hid in his caves the Bard of Albion felt the enormous plagues,
> And a cowl of flesh grew o'er his head, & scales on his back & ribs.
>
> America, lines 230-231 (p. 207)

This monstrous figure recalls that of the famous tempera, "The Ghost of a Flea";[2] the symbolism of both is no doubt similar. Another design showing a human figure largely turned into that of a serpent is the illustration on page 23 of "Night the Ninth" of Young's *Night Thoughts*.[3]

[2] Figgis, *Paintings of William Blake*, plate 68.
[3] Reproduced in Keynes, *Blake's Illustrations to Young's "Night Thoughts."*

53 and 53E. THE SERPENT ATTACKING BUOSO DONATI

> . . . toward the entrails of the other two
> Approaching seemed an adder all on fire,
> As the dark pepper-grain livid and swart.
> In that part, whence our life is nourish'd first,
> One he transpierced; then down before him fell
> Stretch'd out. The pierced spirit look'd on him,
> But spake not; yea, stood motionless and yawn'd,
> As if by sleep or feverous fit assail'd.
> He eyed the serpent, and the serpent him;
> One from the wound, the other from the mouth
> Breathed a thick smoke, whose vapoury columns join'd.
>
> Inferno xxv, 74-84

THE MOMENT shown is just after the serpent has bitten Buoso Donati and before his transformation has begun. Buoso looks bewildered and yawns; he and the snake gaze at each other. Smoke issues as described from the snake's mouth and mingles with that which comes from the man's navel where he has been bitten. The instant of suspense before the metamorphosis commences is well suggested.

Dante and Virgil stand at the extreme left looking on. Near them is Puccio Sciancato; he watches in terror, his body half turned on its axis. The pose of this figure is awkward and is an unfortunate feature of an otherwise effective and dramatic illustration. A few small flames are seen near the foreground and behind the figure of Puccio a single additional snake glides along the floor of the trench. A curtain of flames rises in the background toward heavy clouds from which other flames rain down.

Materialism takes possession of all of us as we are born into the created world; hence the serpent bites the man in the navel. His expression shows a realization of the terrors of the fallen state at the instant before his human form begins to take on a monstrous likeness.

This is a completed watercolor save for a few incidental details. The color effects are very sumptuous. The ground shades from yellow at the left to red at the right, the clouds and flames from blue and green at the left to red with touches of blue at the right.

THIS DRAWING is the fifth of the series which was engraved. The engraving is almost identical with the drawing, although as usual more precise in detail. Fewer flames are shown in the background. The chief differences are that the serpent has feet and Buoso's genitals have already become scaly. Suspense is rather more effectively conveyed by the drawing. Of all the engravings, this is the most finished.

54. DONATI TRANSFORMED INTO A SERPENT: GUERCIO CAVALCANTI RETRANSFORMED FROM A SERPENT TO A MAN

AFTER the small serpent has bitten Buoso Donati, as shown in the previous illustration, lines 85-131 of Canto xxv tell of the transformation of Donati into a serpent and of the serpent into a man, who is identified as Francesco Guercio de'Cavalcanti.

Blake has not chosen a dramatic moment of the episode for his illustration and this is the least effective of the series of designs dealing with the thieves and serpents.[1] Although the text goes into considerable detail concerning the process of transformation and describes both figures as they appeared at various stages of the change, Blake shows the metamorphosis complete. Cavalcanti stands at the left, his hands raised. The snake lies on the ground behind him, and one or two other serpents are also lightly sketched on the floor of the trench. The background is formed by the intersection of two rock bridges, above and below which rise flames. A cloud closes in the top of the design.

This drawing is in its very first stages in most passages; only the figure of Cavalcanti approaches completion.[2]

[1] For a much better treatment of a similar theme, see the design for page 23 of "Night the Eighth" of Young's *Night Thoughts*, as reproduced in Keynes, *Blake's Illustrations to Young*.

[2] In the upper left, the number "95" may be seen written sideways. This may possibly refer to line 95 of Canto xxv which forms part of the passage in which the transformation is described. Another explanation might be that Blake originally intended to use this page for a vertical drawing near the end of the series. It will be recalled that the number "87" appears similarly on Drawing 45.

55. ULYSSES AND DIOMED SWATHED IN THE SAME FLAME

DANTE AND VIRGIL proceed along the arch which crosses the eighth trench of the

Eighth Circle. Dante sees myriads of fires gleaming brightly in the valley below him and Virgil tells him that they are the spirits of fraudulent counselors who are punished by being enclosed each within a separate flame. Dante notices that one of the flames rises to two points and is informed by Virgil that within it are two spirits, those of Ulysses and Diomed who were associated in many acts of fraud, such as the stratagem of the Trojan horse, the theft of the Palladium, and the winning of Achilles away from Deidamia. When the flame comes close to them, Virgil questions it as to the manner in which Ulysses met his death. In reply, Ulysses tells of his journey beyond Gibraltar into the Atlantic which ended with his shipwreck upon the mountain of Purgatory. This episode occupies all but the first thirteen lines of the twenty-sixth canto.

A rock bridge arches across the page. Beneath it on the floor of the trench are numerous single flames[1] stretching off into the distance where, above the crest of a low rise, may be seen a dark cloud. The right side of the horizon is light, but the sky is darkening above it. Dante and Virgil kneel near the summit of the rock bridge looking down. Near them, and directly in front of the arch of the bridge, floats the double-pointed flame. In it may be vaguely seen the forms of Ulysses and Diomed. Ulysses, who kneels in an upright position and appears to be speaking to Virgil, is an elderly bearded figure. To the left of him, Diomed, who is younger, is shown as though falling head-downward.

We have seen in a number of previous illustrations in this series that figures consumed by flames suggest to Blake man in the fallen state preyed upon by the desires of the selfhood. We find this same symbolism even in such early works as *The Gates of Paradise* (1793), in which the selfhood is shown as a naked figure with scaly genitals, carrying a spear and shield amid flames.[2] Dante's description of each soul wholly clothed in its own particular flame must have been especially suggestive to Blake.

It is only, however, in the case of the double flame that Blake injects his own beliefs into this design in unmistakable fashion. It will be remembered that the Fallen World is ruled by pure reason which distrusts vision and imagination: in Blake's terminology Los, who as Urthona rules in Eden, is after the Fall displaced by Urizen. The flame in which Ulysses and Diomed are swathed here represents the Fallen World, or Mundane Shell,[3] and the enveloping flame shuts off their perception of eternity. The rock bridge likewise symbolizes the boundary between worlds, which does not restrain the poets but is an impassable barrier to the fallen senses. Within the Fallen World Urizen rules, and hence Ulysses is shown erect with the aged, cruel, and bearded countenance of Urizen; the youthful Los, who has been displaced, appears in an upside down position.

In connection with the flames which envelop the false counselors as they are described in the *Divine Comedy*, it is of interest to note that Blake compares the false

[1] Within the front flames there are slight indications that Blake intended to show the enclosed spirits, though to have done so would have been contrary to the text (lines 41-43).
[2] Reproduced in *Poetry and Prose*, p. 571.
[3] For a schematic portrayal of the Mundane Shell enclosing a world of flames—in certain respects comparable to this illustration—see plate 36 of *Milton* (reproduced in *Poetry and Prose*, p. 421). Compare also with this design the account of the building of the Mundane Shell as given in *Urizen*, lines 119-137 and 143-147 (p. 223).

tongue of the Fallen Tharmas to a "wat'ry flame revolving every way."[4] In addition to their identification with Urizen and Los, the figures of Ulysses and Diomed in this design may well have been intended by Blake to symbolize the two aspects of the fallen senses in the created world. The youthful figure falling headlong would then represent Tharmas as the "human pathetic," the pitiably contracted senses of man in his fallen state, while the fierce form of Ulysses becomes his angry spectre, the uncontrollable violence of physical nature.[5]

[4] See *Jerusalem* 14, 2-9, and comment in Frye, *Fearful Symmetry*, pp. 281-282.

[5] See the discussion of Drawing 62 below, especially footnote 5. It is interesting to compare also the appearance of Ulysses here with that of the figure in the upper left of the design of plate 87 of *Jerusalem*, which Damon (*William Blake*, p. 474) has associated with Tharmas.

56. THE SCHISMATICS AND SOWERS OF DISCORD

> . . . A rundlet, that hath lost
> Its middle or side stave, gapes not so wide
> As one I mark'd torn from the chin throughout
> Down to the hinder passage: 'twixt the legs
> Dangling his entrails hung, the midriff lay
> Open to view, and wretched ventricle,
> That turns the englutted aliment to dross,
> Whilst eagerly I fix on him my gaze,
> He eyed me, with his hands laid his breast bare,
> And cried, "Now mark how I do rip me: lo!
> How is Mohammed mangled: before me
> Walks Ali weeping, from the chin his face
> Cleft to the forelock; and the others all,
> Whom here thou seest, while they lived, did sow
> Scandal and schism, and therefore thus are rent.
> A fiend is here behind, who with his sword
> Hacks us thus cruelly, slivering again
> Each of this ream, when we have compast round
> The dismal way; for first our gashes close
> Ere we repass before him."   *Inferno* XXVIII, 21-40

ALI STANDS at the left, his face gashed by the sword. Next to him is Mohammed spreading open his breast with his hands so that Dante can see how his entire trunk is split open. Dante stands in the center, staring in horror; Virgil is behind him. To the right and a little to the rear the demon is seen upon a low mound. He is a handsome, impassive figure who stands with wings and sword arm raised as he goes methodically about his work. A group of three sinners crouch before him in terror and make imploring gestures as he is about to strike them. Behind Mohammed and Ali three others who have just been freshly wounded may be seen dragging themselves painfully away; one of them has had his hands cut off. In the background two arches intersect and flames rise beneath and above them. Down the nearest one, that on the left, walks the decapitated form of Bertrand de Born (lines 107-138), carrying his head in his hand.

Blake probably interpreted this incident from the *Inferno* as an allegory of the Moral Law: justice which rules by fear and punishment rigorously applied in all cases, rather than by love, individual understanding and forgiveness. This is the law proclaimed by Natural Religion which, as we have seen in the passage from plate 77 of *Jerusalem* quoted in connection with our discussion of the forty-fourth illustration, Blake described as a "terrible devouring sword turning every way."

The fiend who wields the sword is not represented here in the same guise as those who in the fifth trench guard the sinners in the pitch, but is a young, handsome figure with fair hair. While his wings are of the type which Blake associates with devils, they are elongated and raised majestically above his head.[1] These features combine to suggest the dual nature of the "angel" who, in the name of law, order, and justice metes out all sorts of cruelties without pity.[2] The poets look on in dismay and horror at the wounds which the sword inflicts—regardless of age and circumstances, laying bare the cruelties and terrors which lie so close to the surface of the life of the created world. In this world the "Natural Sword" of punishment and vengeance must always reign supreme. Man's only hope of release lies in developing his spiritual perceptions for triumph in the "Mental Warfare" of Eden. "He never can be a Friend to the Human Race who is the Preacher of Natural Morality or Natural Religion; he is a flatterer who means to betray, to perpetuate Tyrant Pride & the Laws of that Babylon which he foresees shall shortly be destroyed, with the Spiritual and not the Natural Sword."[3]

In spite of its spacious effect and excellent grouping, this drawing suffers from a number of figures which are unfortunate in their conception. Dante's face reveals rather more feeling than usual, and the result is not happy. The three sinners before the angel are all very awkward in pose and the two nearest Dante are ridiculous in expression as well. As for many years Blake never worked from models, his faces tend to follow a number of set types, and attempts to show more intense emotion often, as here, resulted in failure. Except for the flames above the right arch, this is a finished watercolor. It bears Blake's monogram.

[1] The demoniacal angel of this design is much akin to Satan the destroyer as represented in the third Job illustration: the wings are similar and both have haloes of light.

[2] Even when wounded by worldly systems, the attitude of the spiritual aspect of man is that of forgiveness. Hence Ali, who may be likened to Los, makes a gesture of blessing, while Mohammed —who has the bearded countenance of Urizen and represents the Natural Man—displays his wound as though demanding vengeance. For Mohammed as the false God in Blake's work, see *The Song of Los*, line 29 (p. 247).

[3] *Jerusalem*, plate 52.

57. THE SCHISMATICS AND SOWERS OF DISCORD: MOSCA DE'LAMBERTI AND BERTRAND DE BORN

IN CANTO XXVIII, lines 98-138, are described the encounters between the poets and two more of the sinners among the sowers of discord who are punished in the ninth trench of the Eighth Circle. The first, whose hands have been severed, is Mosca de'Lamberti, who urged a murder as a result of which the Guelf and Ghibelline factions came into being in Florence. He is to be seen at the right of the drawing, striding off with the stumps of his arms raised above his head. Dante and Virgil have turned from him and are now intent upon Bertrand de Born, a famous troubador and Viscount of Haute-fort, near Périgueux, who stirred up strife between Henry II of England and his son, which resulted in the death of the latter. For separating those who by relationship were so closely linked, Bertrand's punishment is to have his head severed and to carry it around with him.

The drawing follows closely the description given in the poem. Bertrand de Born is shown just at the foot of one of the bridges, holding out his head to Dante so that the latter can better hear its words. The sinner holds the head in his left hand and points toward it with the index finger of his right; the head is speaking and gives off rays of light like a lantern. The headless body is dressed in a thin garment which hangs down behind it. In the middle of the design, to the rear of the foreground figures, the devil with the sword is seen, standing upon a low mound. His pose is the same as in the previous illustration, except that his weight is on the other foot; however, he is now shown from behind. Beyond him more sinners file past, those to the left lamenting as they await the blow of the sword and those on the right dragging them-selves off in pain. There are ten figures in this group and two of them are women, although all those specifically mentioned in the poem are men.[1] Two more arches intersect in the background, and flames rise throughout the design.

The divided body is frequently used by Blake as a symbol of the Fall. The partition of the body of the Fallen Albion is illustrated in the design of plate 25 of *Jerusalem*: "Now the Starry Heavens are fled from the mighty limbs of Albion."[2] Similarly the division of Urizen leads to the fall of Ahania and the division of Urthona is followed immediately by his fall.[3]

On the other hand, Regeneration is also a process of reuniting. All the divided por-tions of the body of the Eternal Man, as they exist in this world awaiting salvation, will ultimately be brought together to reform the giant body of Albion, which will become one with Christ.

> So Man looks out in tree & herb & fish & Bird & beast
> Collecting up the scatter'd portions of his immortal body
> Into the Elemental forms of every thing that grows.
>
> . . . .
>
> . . . . wherever a grass grows
> Or a leaf buds, The Eternal Man is seen, is heard, is felt,
> And all his sorrows, till he reassumes his ancient bliss.
> Four Zoas VIII, 556-558; 576-578 (pp. 345-346)

[1] Only the two center figures of the group of sinners appear in finished form; the others are merely sketched. It is brought out later in the discussion that these two figures in all probability had special significance for Blake, and he probably chose this device to give them emphasis. Aside from the unfinished figures in this group, this is a completed watercolor; it is signed with Blake's monogram.

[2] *Jerusalem* 75, 27.

[3] *Ahania* 26-43 (pp. 235-236); *Four Zoas* I, 511-526 (p. 266).

All Human Forms identified, .even Tree, Metal, Earth & Stone: all
Human Forms identified, living, going forth & returning wearied
Into the Planetary lives of Years, Months, Days & Hours; reposing
And then Awaking into his Bosom in the Life of Immortality.

Jerusalem 99, 1-4

Here in the depths of the hell of the Fallen World, we see the ultimate degradation in the severing of the human head from its body. The poet, Dante, looks in horror at this most terrible symbol of the fallen state of man. All of man's functions suffer under the cruel law of the created world. Thus in the background Vala and Urizen, the Goddess of Nature and the Angry God of This World, also wait in terror as the sword is about to fall upon them.[4] Nevertheless they uphold the Natural Law because, being devoid of spiritual insight, they can see no other solution to the evil of man's state.

[4] Vala is shown much as here in the design on plate 57 of *Jerusalem*.

58 and 58e. THE PIT OF DISEASE: THE FALSIFIERS

IN THE tenth and last ditch of the Eighth Circle are confined the falsifiers who are punished by being inflicted with loathsome diseases. This illustration follows quite literally the description of the trench as given in Canto XXIX, lines 35-138, particularly the following passages:

More rueful was it not methinks to see
The nation in Aegina droop,   .   .   .

.   .   .   .

.   .   .   .   .   than was here to see
The spirits, that languish'd through the murky vale,
Up-piled on many a stack. Confused they lay,
One o'er the belly, o'er the shoulders one
Roll'd of another; sideling crawl'd a third
Along the dismal pathway .   .   .   .

.   .   .   .

.   .   .   .   Then two I mark'd, that sat
Propt 'gainst each other, as two brazen pans
Set to retain the heat. From head to foot,
A tetter bark'd them round. Nor saw I e'er
Groom currying so fast, for whom his lord
Impatient waited, or himself perchance
Tired with long watching, as of these each one
Plied quickly his keen nails, through furiousness
Of ne'er abated pruriency.

Inferno XXIX, 57-58; 63-68; 71-79

Dante and Virgil have descended the rock bridge shown in the right foreground and stand together on a ledge near its foot, looking at the heaps of the diseased in the trench below them. In lines 42-43 is described how Dante put his hands over his ears to keep from hearing the cries of the sufferers; Blake, however, shows both him and Virgil holding their noses against the stench which rises from the diseased (lines 49-50). Two groups of sinners are shown. At the left, at the foot of the bridge made of petrified human forms, are three figures, of whom two lie on their backs and one crawls painfully along on his stomach. At the right, just beneath Dante and Virgil, is a pile of forms, all quite inert except for a dimly conscious head looking up from the rear and for the two who sit on the top of the heap, leaning back to back and scratching themselves furiously. From the text these two last can be recognized as Griffolino of Arezzo and Capocchio of Florence, notorious forgers.

In the center of the background, two more rock bridges are shown which overlap, and in the distance at the extreme right another portion of a bridge is seen beneath that on which Dante and Virgil stand. In the upper left is a dark cloud on the lower edge of which appear flickering flames. More flames and smoke are suggested very faintly in pencil behind Dante and Virgil.

"The Seven Diseases of Man" or "the seven diseases of the Soul" is the collective name given by Blake to the seven cardinal virtues of the Moral Law.[1] The rottenness, corruption, and misery of life in a fallen world become for him identified with the plague.

> The disease of Shame covers me from head to feet. I have no hope.
> Every boil upon my body is a separate & deadly Sin.
>
> Jerusalem 21, 3-4

Many of the figures and the general theme of this drawing recall very vividly the watercolor "Plague" in the Boston Museum of Fine Arts. In the background of that design may be seen a heavy column of smoke with flames licking around its edge, similar to the black cloud edged with flames in the present illustration. The original tempera version of "Satan Smiting Job with Sore Boils," in the Tate Gallery,[2] has a corresponding dark cloud with flames, although the flames are omitted in the later engraved version; the symbolism of Job's disease is, of course, comparable to that of this design.[3] For the rock bridge of petrified forms as a symbol of fallen humanity, see the discussion of the thirty-fourth illustration above.

Disease and insanity—as in the group at the left—is thus for Blake another frequently employed emblem of man's fallen state. The poets, men of imagination and spiritual insight, here look down with loathing into the pit in which Natural Men are confined on account of their own blindness to the inner light.

THE DRAWING is brilliantly colored and close to completion. It is among those which Blake initialed. It is also the sixth of the series which were engraved. The engraving follows the general scheme of the watercolor closely, but is much more elaborate in detail. The group at the right in the engraving contains more figures, and all are clearly shown as they are not in the drawing. The two sinners who

---

[1] *Four Zoas* VIIb, 116 (p. 326); *Jerusalem* 19, 26. See D. J. Sloss and J. P. R. Wallis, *The Prophetic Writings of William Blake*, Oxford, 1926, I, p. 330n.

[2] Figgis, *Paintings of William Blake*, plates 64 and 61.

[3] Wicksteed, *Blake's Vision of the Book of Job*, p. 74.

scratch themselves wear loincloths, although they are naked in the drawing. The petrified forms of which the bridge at the left is composed are much more clearly shown in the engraving and shadowy forms may also be seen in the rocks at the right, where there are none in the drawing.[4] The engraving also has several additional figures which lie on the floor of the trench under the rock bridge in the center background. In addition, flames lick along the floor and rise under the arches; the flames in the sky are shown in much greater detail. Some spiky vegetation appears on the rock to the right of Dante and Virgil. In spite of all these added features, the engraving is not quite finished; this is particularly noticeable in the upper part of the rock bridge at the left.

[4] Note in the engraving that directly beneath Dante and Virgil is the form of the sleeping humanity shown exactly as it appears in the design to plate 41 of *Jerusalem*. Also, at the base of the bridge at the right, Urizen may be seen writing in his book.

59. THE PIT OF DISEASE: GIANNI SCHICCHI AND MYRRHA

> . . . ne'er the Furies, or of Thebes, or Troy,
> With such fell cruelty were seen, their goads
> Infixing in the limbs of man or beast,
> As now two pale and naked ghosts I saw,
> That gnarling wildly scamper'd, like the swine
> Excluded from his stye. One reach'd Capocchio,
> And in the neck-joint sticking deep his fangs,
> Dragg'd him, that, o'er the solid pavement rubb'd
> His belly stretch'd out prone. The other shape,
> He of Arezzo, there left trembling, spake:
> "That sprite of air is Schicchi; in like mood
> Of random mischief vents he still his spite."
> To whom I answering: "Oh! as thou dost hope
> The other may not flesh its jaws on thee,
> Be patient to inform us, who it is,
> Ere it speed hence."—"That is the ancient soul
> Of wretched Myrrha," he replied, "who burn'd
> With most unholy flame for her own sire,
> And a false shape assuming, so perform'd
> The deed of sin; e'en as the other there,
> That onward passes, dared to counterfeit
> Donati's features, to feign'd testament
> The seal affixing."
> Inferno xxx, 23-45

A PORTION of one of the rock bridges found so frequently in these designs serves to divide the page in two. Upon this Gianni Schicchi and Myrrha,[1] with dog-like heads,

[1] Myrrha was the daughter of Cinyras, King of Cyprus, whom she tricked into fathering her son, Adonis. Upon the death of Buoso Donati (Drawing 53), Gianni Schicchi de'Cavalcanti impersonated him on the deathbed and dictated a will in his own favor.

fangs, and claws, run enveloped by flames.[2] Myrrha, at left, appears almost as if flying; just to the right of center Gianni Schicchi has bitten Capocchio in the back of the neck, and drags him along with his belly scraping the ground.

In front of the rock bridge, on a low mound and seen from behind, Dante and Virgil stand watching the attack on Capocchio. Behind them are a number of figures who are not specifically described in the text, although they clearly represent some of the diseased who are punished in this trench. Three squatting forms are shown at the left underneath the arch of the bridge; behind Dante and Virgil another lies on his back, looking up at the underside of the bridge—which is just above him—and crying out and gesturing as he writhes in torment. In front of the arch at the left, another sinner falls headlong to join those who are already below.[3] Flames rise from the floor of the trench in the left foreground and a dark cloud, as of smoke, fills the upper right of the page.

We have already discussed in a number of places the symbolism of figures in flames and of those shown falling headlong. The inclusion of these two features, neither of which comes directly from the text, in this illustration indicates that Blake is again thinking in terms of his own mythology. The rock bridge serves, as in other instances, to separate two different levels of existence, much in the manner of the cloud layers of the Job designs. In the World of Generation above, material desires and ambitions, shown as violent bestial forces, seize upon the soul and overwhelm it. As a result man falls into Ulro to join the group of those of "single vision" who are already there. Including the falling form, five figures are shown in the bottom group, representing the five senses of Fallen Man. As usual, man in this state is shown surrounded by flames and shut up in a cave.[4] Only the poets, types of those who have cultivated the power of spiritual perception to a point where they can dissociate themselves from the Fallen World, are able to view both levels of material existence, as though from a neutral vantage point. They symbolize the love of God which never deserts man no matter how great his fall into error.

> When Thought is clos'd in Caves Then love shall shew its root in deepest Hell.
>
> Four Zoas v, 241 (p. 300)

The form lying on its back under the arch is very reminiscent of the principal figure in one of Blake's illustrations to Robert Blair's poem, *The Grave*, that entitled "Death of the Strong Wicked Man," and its expression and gesture much like that of the soul flying out of the window in that design. The symbolism is certainly the same.

This drawing is only partially finished. Many passages are still in pencil and in

[2] W. M. Rossetti, in his catalogue of the Dante designs in Gilchrist's *Life*, II, p. 231, very rightly pointed out that the animal heads of Gianni and Myrrha are "a point of Blake's own invention, though probably suggested by a simile introduced by Dante into this passage." In lines 13-22, just before the incident illustrated, Dante speaks of Hecuba who, after her children had been killed, went mad and barked like a dog.

[3] Rossetti, *loc. cit.*, also remarked of this figure: "perhaps a soul newly arrived to its doom, which is a vivid and important point of invention."

[4] As, for instance, in the engravings from *The Gates of Paradise* reproduced in *Poetry and Prose*, pp. 570-571. See also discussions of Drawings 34 and 35 above, and of 61 below.

others pencil can be seen through the thin washes. The composition is effective, the rapid motion of the two dog-headed figures being very convincing. The violence of the action is balanced by the falling figure and by the static forms of the poets and of Capocchio, which keep the lines of movement, swift as they are, within the bounds of the design.

60.   PRIMEVAL GIANTS SUNK IN THE SOIL

THIS DRAWING illustrates *Inferno* XXXI, lines 16-40. Dante and Virgil are drawing near to the Ninth and innermost Circle of the infernal regions, which takes the form of a deep pit set down below the level of the rest. It is guarded by giants who stand in the well with only the upper parts of their bodies towering above the edge.

Huge rocks rise up on either side of the design. Through the gap between them five forms of giants are seen, as though from the rear. What seem to be dead growths of foliage lie on the ground and cover the rock at the left; rain and snow pour down. From a dark cloud, which completely covers the top of the page, forks of lightning hurtle down upon the giants, a detail suggested by lines 39-40 of the text. Dante and Virgil, sketched lightly in pencil, appear as two tiny figures looking on from the foreground. Their small scale contrasted with the rocks which frame the page and the giant forms behind serves to convey a sense of vastness and impressive foreboding, which is increased by the slanting lines of rain and the jagged strokes of lightning.

Before the Fall, Albion was a Giant Man in terms of his intellectual and spiritual capacities as compared to those of man in this world. Man, however, when he lost his power of vision and with it the ability to see all things in their true unity, was swallowed up in the great bulk of nature, the huge forms of which became objects of terror. "His world teem'd vast enormities."[1] In the Fallen World, Giants are blind and brutal forces, struggling vainly and without comprehension to destroy the material bonds that by the very nature of mortality hold them prisoner.

> Come & mourn over Albion, the White Cliff of the Atlantic,
> The Mountain of Giants: all the Giants of Albion are become
> Weak, wither'd, darken'd, & Jerusalem is cast forth from Albion.
> They deny that they ever knew Jerusalem, or ever dwelt in Shiloh.
> The Gigantic roots & twigs of the vegetating Sons of Albion,
> Fill'd with the little-ones, are consumed in the Fires of their Altars.
> The vegetating Cities are burned & consumed from the Earth,
> And the Bodies in which all Animals & Vegetation, the Earth & Heaven
> Were contain'd in the All Glorious Imagination, are wither'd & darken'd.
>
> Jerusalem 49, 6-14

Blake has shown five giants in this illustration, in order to represent "the Five

[1] *Urizen*, line 429 (p. 231). It is interesting to observe in this connection that Blake's drawing of David and Goliath in the Boston Museum of Fine Arts (Figgis, *Paintings of William Blake*, plate 67) is undoubtedly intended as an allegory of the victory of the child of imagination over the giant of materialism. Note that on Goliath's shield—carried for him by a retainer—is represented a serpent with a human head in the likeness of Urizen.

Senses, half buried in the storm of Materialism."[2] Guarding the center of hell, they are frozen into an inert and almost lifeless existence. The senses, which in eternity are infinite, in the Fallen World are but "Giant beauty and perfection fallen into dust."[3]

[2] Damon, *William Blake*, p. 219. For further discussion of giants in Blake's symbolism, see Frye, *Fearful Symmetry*, pp. 128-129, 361, 366-367, and 374-375.
[3] *Jerusalem* 19, 8 and 38, 17. Compare also *Milton* 17, 36-40.

61. NIMROD

As DANTE AND VIRGIL approach the well where the giants are confined, they hear a horn blown loudly (XXXI, 9-11). After a time they come upon the one who had blown it. This turns out to be the giant Nimrod, like the others visible only from the waist up. Seeing the poets approaching, he starts to jabber at them, at which Virgil tells him to vent his wrath by means of the horn which hangs around his neck on a cord. Virgil then tells Dante that this is Nimrod who built the Tower of Babel and that his speech is as incomprehensible to all as that of others is to him.[1] The encounter with the giant is described in Canto XXXI, lines 41-74.

Nimrod squats at the right with his legs drawn up under him. His jabbering mouth is open, and he looks over his right shoulder at Dante and Virgil, small figures in the left foreground. A large horn hangs about his neck on a chain and he grasps it with his left hand. His face is bearded and on his head he wears a crown of large spikes. His right arm hangs at his side and the wrist is fettered; the chain may be seen beside him, passing around his waist and hanging down onto the ground.[2]

Behind the giant, a wall of solid masonry rises to the middle of the page and stretches part way across it. To the left of the wall and behind the small figures of the poets appears an unfinished masonry tower. In a niche at the base of this is a winged figure seated on a throne, holding an orb and scepter and wearing a spiked crown. The top of the design is closed in by a great arch of jagged rocks, like the mouth of an enormous cave.

A glance at this drawing is sufficient to show that Blake has introduced numerous features which are not literally in accord with the text and which, therefore, probably have some explanation based upon his own mythology. Since Nimrod's connection with Babel is mentioned in the poem, it is, of course, logical that a portion of the tower should be shown in the illustration. But why the crowned figure in the niche at its foot, and why the rocky mouth of the cave?

[1] The link between Nimrod and the Tower of Babel can be inferred only indirectly from the Bible, and the identification of him as a giant is even more remote (see Genesis vi, 4; x, 8-10; xi, 2-9). However, as early as the end of the fourth century, St. Augustine made the connection, whence Dante probably derived it. In *Paradise Lost* XII, 24-62, Nimrod and his followers build Babel, the city of tyranny, with its tower. Blake was, of course, familiar with this passage and has introduced both the city wall and the tower into this drawing.
[2] Notice the low mound between the giant and the poets. It seems to pass across the lower part of Nimrod's body and yet it is possible to see his legs through it. For this feature and also for Blake's reason for showing him seated, which is contrary to the text, see the discussion of the following illustration.

The Eternal Man, who was a giant in intellectual capacity and spiritual strength, has now fallen and become a monstrous form, vast in strength and cruelty but utterly without spiritual enlightenment, mental illumination, or human feeling. Nimrod in this design is to be identified with the Fallen Tharmas, personification of the blind and brutal physical violence of the Fallen World.[3] Glorious in their eternal state, after the Fall "The Giants who formed this world into its sensual existence . . . seem to live in it in chains."[4] Hence manacles are shown in this and in the following illustration.

It will be recalled that the sublime occupation of Eden is "Intellectual Warfare." "Our wars are wars of life, & wounds of love With intellectual spears, & long winged arrows of thought." With the Fall, however, "the two Sources of Life in Eternity, Hunting and War, Are become the Sources of dark & bitter Death & of corroding Hell."[5] In the Fallen World Nimrod, "a mighty hunter before the Lord,"[6] becomes a symbol of that violence against life which expresses itself in hunting and war. He is thus appropriately shown here with the crown of the despot and the horn of the hunter.

Since he represents the epitome of the ignorance and brutality of Natural Men, the hostility of Nimrod is directed especially against men of vision. Nimrod appears a number of times in Blake's writings and is always associated with the hunting down and destroying of imagination by those in power on earth. As such he is shown here, glaring furiously but helplessly at the poets.

> I send you the Riposo.[7] . . . It represents the Holy Family in Egypt, Guarded in their Repose from those Fiends, the Egyptian Gods . . . I have given, in the background, a building, which may be supposed the ruin of a Part of *Nimrod's tower*, which I conjecture to have spread over many Countries; for he ought to be reckon'd of the Giant brood.
>
> From a letter to Thomas Butts, dated
> from Felpham, July 6, 1803 (p. 867)

The daughters of Albion girded around their garments of Needlework,

. . . .

They go forth & return to Albion on his rocky couch:

. . . .

[3] Nimrod's crown, and that of Satan, are like that of The Symbolic Figure of the Course of Human History in the twenty-eighth design. The facial expression of the giant recalls that of many of Blake's figures which suggest the insane brutishness of the Natural World. Compare the features of Ulysses in the fifty-fifth illustration, for instance, and those of Behemoth in the fifteenth Job engraving. However, the most interesting and significant comparison in this connection is with the visionary head inscribed by Blake as "The Man who built the Pyramids." (Reproduced in Keynes, *Pencil Sketches*, plate 41; note the architectural sketch which accompanies the portrait.)

[4] *Marriage of Heaven and Hell*, p. 187. The chained giant figure of the third Dante illustration, "The Mission of Virgil," will also be recalled.

[5] *Jerusalem* 38, 14-15; 43, 31-32.

[6] Genesis x, 9.

[7] The well-known watercolor of this subject now in the Metropolitan Museum, New York, is a later version, being dated 1806. The pyramids and the city in the background are not a prominent feature, but are doubtless what Blake refers to; perhaps they were more conspicuous in the earlier drawing, the present location of which is unknown to me.

Binding Jerusalem's Children in the dungeons of Babylon;
They play before the Armies, before the hounds of *Nimrod*.

Four Zoas II, 57; 60; 63-64 (p. 269)

Great is the cry of the Hounds of *Nimrod* along the Valley
Of Vision, they scent the odor of War in the Valley of Vision.
All Love is lost! terror succeeds, & Hatred instead of Love,
And stern demands of Right & Duty instead of Liberty.

Jerusalem 22, 8-11

Thus we are now safe in identifying the buildings shown here as the Tower of Babel on the left and, behind the giant, the dungeons of Babylon. Northrop Frye has pointed out that ruins are all that remain of the successive failures of man's attempts to build the City of God, or life of the imagination, in this Fallen World. "As the chill of old age comes over the historical cycle, its life dries up in huge tumorous cities, Nineveh, Babylon, Rome, Tyre, which thereupon become the symbols of the tyranny denounced by the prophet. . . . All these relics except the pyramids are ruins, and a ruin is a pile of stones. Now stones are as near as we can get to existence without life; they are at the limit of opacity, the reduction to the inorganic which in Blake's symbolism is both death and Satan."[8] It is to make this symbolism clear to us that Blake has shown Satan walled up in a blind niche in the Tower of Babel, wearing the panoply of earthly power. And as the Giant Man, once one with God, is now brutish and in chains, so he too has entered into the Satanic state. Thus Nimrod is shown with the cave of this world closing down on him from above.[9]

[8] *Fearful Symmetry*, p. 224. Ancient ruins, particularly of Druid type, appear frequently in Blake's designs as representative of the early giant phase of the Fallen World. Particularly fine examples are the huge Stonehenge-like arches of plate 4 of *Milton* and of plate 70 of *Jerusalem*.

[9] See footnote 4 to Drawing 59 above. Anthony Blunt ("Blake's Pictorial Imagination," *Journal of the Warburg and Courtauld Institutes*, VI, 1943, p. 205) has suggested that this figure of Nimrod may have been derived by Blake from engravings of Persian art.

62. EPHIALTES AND TWO OTHER TITANS

Then to the leftward turning sped we forth,
And at a sling's throw found another shade
Far fiercer and more huge. I cannot say
What master hand had girt him; but he held
Behind the right arm fetter'd, and before,
The other, with a chain, that fasten'd him
From the neck down; and five times round his form
Apparent met the wreathed links. "This proud one
Would of his strength against almighty Jove
Make trial," said my guide: "whence he is thus
Requited: Ephialtes him they call.
Great was his prowess, when the giants brought
Fear on the gods: those arms, which then he plied,
Now moves he never."

Inferno XXXI, 75-88

122

EPHIALTES was a son of Neptune who made war on the gods. He was slain by Apollo while attempting to pile Pelion on Ossa. Blake shows him here much as described, his left arm before him and his right behind, with a chain bound around him from the neck down.[1]

The illustration has, however, many features which the poem does not explain. First, at the point where it crosses Ephialtes' body, the bank which covers him from the waist down is not opaque and through it can be dimly seen the lower part of his form. He does not stand in the well, as the text indicates for all the giants, but squats on the ground with his legs bent under him in the manner of Nimrod in the previous design.[2] The lower part of his left arm can also be seen, bound by a manacle and chains. Beside him are two more giants; they cannot be associated with any of those mentioned in the *Divine Comedy*, none of whom were near Ephialtes. That on the left is bearded, and the one on the right is a young figure seen from behind. Both are buried from the waist down. From clouds above the giants slant rain and what is probably intended to represent snow and hail.[3] Dante and Virgil, diminutive figures in the left foreground, stand looking on.

The key to this design seems to be given by a well-known passage in *A Descriptive Catalogue* which refers to the lost painting of "The Ancient Britons" which Blake included in his exhibition of 1809. "In the last Battle of King Arthur, only Three Britons escaped; these were the Strongest Man, the Beautifullest Man, and the Ugliest Man. . . . The Strong Man represents the human sublime. The Beautiful Man represents the human pathetic, which was in the wars of Eden divided into male and female. The Ugly Man represents the human reason. They were originally one man, who was four-fold; he was self-divided, and his real humanity slain on the stems of generation, and the form of the fourth was like the Son of God."[4]

From the above, it should be clear that Blake intends to show here the fallen forms of the Zoas. Ephialtes, the strong man in chains, is Orc who as the passionate spirit of revolt is an aspect of Luvah after the Fall. In many passages of the prophetic books Orc is described as being bound in chains, which of course represent the restrictive laws of rational systems which deprive man of his liberty. The aged bearded figure— the Ugly Man—is, of course, Urizen, who is always depicted much in this manner. The other giant is the "shadowy" Tharmas,[5] the Zoa who is associated with man's

[1] Blake undoubtedly associated the five circles of chain in which Ephialtes is bound with the five senses. In the drawing only three of the bands of chain appear above the level of the ground; the others may be dimly discerned beneath it.

[2] Inasmuch as Blake drew both this figure and that of Nimrod as squatting—a point in direct contradiction to the text—and then only partially covered them over, it is evident that he wished this pose to be apparent in order to indicate their fallen nature. Fallen Man is always described by Blake as sinking down or outstretched, never as erect (e.g. *Jerusalem* 23, 24-26).

[3] It is shown in a very similar manner in the sixtieth illustration.

[4] *Poetry and Prose*, pp. 608-609. The three may also be seen falling through space in the design to plate 6 of *Urizen*.

[5] As "the human pathetic," Tharmas is shown in the less sinister of his fallen manifestations; the other, in which he represents the senseless physical violence of the created world, is portrayed by Nimrod in the previous design. These two aspects of the Fallen Tharmas appear side by side as Ulysses and Diomed in Drawing 55.

physical aspect. The fourth, who "was like the Son of God," is Los.[6] Since this drawing illustrates the nadir of the Fall, when all the powers of man are half-buried in the earth and almost overwhelmed by the storm of materialism, Los is no longer a giant form. He is represented by Dante and Virgil, the poet and his inspiration: through prophetic vision alone can the salvation of Fallen Man be achieved. As the Son of God who appeared walking with the three children of Israel in the midst of the burning fiery furnace,[7] Los by the power of the purging fire of imagination will eventually bring about the reuniting of Albion's divided self.

[6] And the Divine Appearance was the likeness & similitude of Los.

Jerusalem 96, 7

[7] Daniel iii, 19-25. For this analogy and for a comment on the passage quoted above concerning "The Ancient Britons," see Frye, *Fearful Symmetry*, p. 272. I do not agree with Frye's identification of Orc as the Beautiful Man and Tharmas as the Strong Man.

63. ANTAEUS SETTING DOWN DANTE AND VIRGIL

THE SUBJECT of this illustration is taken from *Inferno* XXXI, 91-136. Virgil and Dante approach the giant Antaeus who, unlike the other giants whom they have so far seen, is neither bound nor incapable of speech. Virgil appeals to him to pick them up and set them down in Cocytus, the Ninth Circle of Hell, which is at the bottom of the well in which the giants stand. As an inducement, Virgil mentions that Dante, being still alive, will return to earth and can there renew Antaeus' fame. Antaeus, without replying, picks them up and, bending down, sets them lightly on the floor of the Ninth Circle. He then immediately straightens up again.

This is an audacious and splendid design, in most respects treated literally. Antaeus' feet are planted on a ledge of a cliff near the middle of the right margin of the page, and some distance above the floor of the Ninth Circle (XXXII, 16-18). He has picked Dante and Virgil up and is bending over backwards, steadying himself as he does so with his left hand, which grasps an outcropping of rock near the top of the page. His right arm is outstretched toward the bottom of the well. Virgil has already climbed out of his hand and is standing on the ground helping Dante, who lowers himself from Antaeus' hand with his arm linked around the giant's thumb. Surrounding Antaeus' head is a semi-circular roll of cloud and just above him a flurry of hail bursts from the cloud, which also gives off flames. The head of the giant is outlined against a dark sky within the ring of cloud. He looks at Dante and Virgil as he sets them down, but they take no notice of him.

Antaeus is handsome and youthful. His muscular body is modeled boldly, with grace and a good sense of rhythm, and without seeming heavy or lumpy. This figure is one of Blake's best nudes and shows the influence of Michelangelo upon him. The powerful modeling, the unusual pose, and the great contrast in scale between the giant and the poets all tend to make this an impressive design.[1] The giant is not in this case particularly Satanic in appearance, having neither scaly genitals, wings, nor other

[1] For a discussion of the contrast between Blake's treatment of this subject and that of Flaxman, see Blunt, "Blake's Pictorial Imagination," *Journal of the Warburg and Courtauld Institutes*, VI, 1943, p. 211. The figure of Antaeus should also be compared with that of Capaneus as discussed in Drawing 27 above.

such attributes. Rather, he recalls the figure of Tharmas in the previous drawing, although his facial expression is more stern. He represents the physical aspect of Fallen Man—strong, beautiful, but wedded to matter and unconscious of thought, feeling, and imagination. The roll of cloud serves again as in the Job illustrations to separate the material world of man's physical nature from the eternal world in which his imagination—here personified by the poets—has its home.[2]

This is a completed watercolor. It is finely reproduced in color as frontispiece to the recently issued catalogue of the National Gallery of Victoria.

[2] The arm of Antaeus here reaches through a cloud into another sphere of existence in much the same manner as does that of Eliphaz in the ninth Job engraving; however, Antaeus reaches down while Eliphaz points upward. Compare also the gesture of the Lord in the fifteenth Job design.

64. THE CIRCLE OF TRAITORS: THE ALBERTI BROTHERS

ONCE at the bottom of the well, Dante and Virgil find themselves standing on a frozen lake. Immersed in ice to the faces, which they keep turned downward, are the traitors. Their teeth chatter and their cheeks are covered with frozen tears. A voice cries out to Dante and Virgil to look where they are going and not to step on the heads. Looking down, Dante sees the Alberti brothers breast to breast and so close that their intertwined hair is frozen together. Raising their heads for a moment to look at Dante, the frozen tears are shaken loose; fresh tears gush out and immediately freeze. Overcome by fury, the brothers then butt each other viciously. One of the other shades, Camicion de'Pazzi, a Florentine who had treacherously slain a kinsman, speaks up and identifies the brothers as Alessandro and Napoleone degli Alberti who had killed each other in a quarrel over their inheritance. This episode is related in Canto XXXII, lines 16-68.

Blake has not followed the text very closely. Most of the figures protrude much further from the ice than described and all look ahead or upward instead of down. The poets are at the left, Virgil standing stiff and indignant, while Dante makes a gesture of wonder as he looks down at the sinners. Eleven traitors are shown in all, of whom one lies on his back between Virgil and the left margin, another is almost completely submerged in the immediate center foreground, and the others are in a group to the right of the poets. All of these last but two are erect and stare straight ahead of them. The Alberti brothers are, with the exception of one other figure, at the extreme right. They protrude further from the ice than the others, and sit upon it with only their legs beneath the surface. Their hair is intertwined as described; however, they are shown shoulder to shoulder instead of breast to breast. A lowering sky to the right serves to balance the figures of Dante and Virgil at the left, who are placed against a light background.

Although Camicion de'Pazzi names a number of the others in the ice in addition to the Alberti brothers, it is not possible to identify any of them or even to recognize the speaker. Blake has introduced a characteristic feature of his own, in that he has shown some of the sinners as kings, warriors, and priests. A figure close to Dante wears a helmet and holds the hilt of a large sword which lies on the ice. Between this figure and the brothers are two heads with crowns and in the center one wearing a monk's cowl.[1] Treachery is, of course, usually undertaken in order to win material rewards and, therefore, is to be associated particularly with those in positions of worldly power. We have seen how frequently Blake bestows the trappings of political or ecclesiastical authority or of warfare upon those in Hell. Those who have material ambitions are, in his opinion, most surely to be considered blind to spirit and hence are most truly in the fallen state.[2]

Just as does Dante, Blake in his writings frequently symbolizes the Fallen World as frozen. As heat, light, and the sun suggest freedom, energy, imagination, intellectual activity, and spiritual joy, so does an extreme of darkness and cold imply the opposite pole of inaction and death. While Los is portrayed tending a furnace and shaping red-hot metal on an anvil,[3] Urizen is associated with storms of snow and ice.

> Urizen slept in a stoned stupor in the nether Abyss,
> A dreamful, horrible state in tossings on his icy bed
> Freezing to solid all beneath .   .   .   .   .   .
>
> .   .   .   .
>
> For Urizen fix'd in envy sat brooding & cover'd with snow;
> His book of iron on his knees, he trac'd the dreadful letters
> While his snows fell & his storms beat to cool the flames of Orc.
> Four Zoas IV, 170-172 (p. 290); VIIa, 28-30 (p. 310)

Thus in this illustration we see the fallen "in fetters of ice shrinking, disorganiz'd, rent from Eternity."[4]

Although washes have been begun, this design is quite incomplete in detail. Nevertheless, the atmosphere of eternal cold and the mood of hopeless despair are well conveyed. The background has a very effective bleak arctic landscape, with formations which suggest pack-ice covered with snow. The names of Dante and Virgil have been written lightly in pencil near their heads.

[1] Compare the helmet worn by the warrior with that of the illustration to Blair's *Grave* entitled "The Counseller, King, Warrior, Mother & Child, in the Tomb," and also with those of the guardians of the Sphere of Mars in Drawing 97 below. The monk's cowl is similar to that worn by one of the figures in Drawing 15 above.

[2] Dante, of course, frequently describes individual kings and ecclesiastics as being in Hell; however, the marks of worldly power are with him usually honorific in themselves. On the other hand, for Blake they nearly always have a sinister connotation.

[3] O Lovely terrible Los, wonder of Eternity, O Los, my defence & guide,
Thy works are all my joy & in thy fires my soul delights.
Four Zoas VIIa, 445-446 (p. 321)

[4] *Four Zoas* IV, 212 (p. 291).

65 and 65E. THE CIRCLE OF TRAITORS: DANTE STRIKING AGAINST BOCCA DEGLI ABATI

As DANTE AND VIRGIL walk across the ice in which are the frozen forms of the traitors, Dante stumbles over one of them, giving him a violent blow in the face. The sinner cries out to ask why he has been smitten. Dante asks him his name, telling him that as he is alive he can carry news of him back to the world. The traitor replies that he wishes only oblivion and bids Dante begone. Because in crying out he has mentioned the name of Montaperti, Dante has a suspicion of his identity. To make him talk, Dante seizes him by the hair and starts to pull it out, but the sinner still refuses to tell him who he is. Another of the traitors then speaks up and identifies him as Bocca degli Abati who, while ostensibly on the side of the Guelfs at the Battle of Montaperti, had at a critical moment cut off the hand of the Guelf standard bearer, causing such confusion and rout that the Ghibellines gained the victory. His name having been disclosed, Bocca then proceeds to tell Dante the identity of several of the other traitors, including the one who had given him away.[1]

Dante stands near the left margin of the drawing facing toward the center, with Virgil beside him and on his left. Submerged in the ice near Dante's feet is Bocca degli Abati, his body visible as far as his chest. He gazes furiously over his shoulder at Dante as he expostulates with him.[2] Between Dante and the left edge of the page is a low rock-like mound in which a head appears as if petrified in an upside down position. To the right of the poets are sketchily shown heads and other parts of the bodies of a number of figures which protrude slightly from the ice; all are in reclining positions. At the upper right in the background is the foot of one of the rock bridges, here shown much in the manner of the side of an iceberg. As though frozen into it, several forms may be discerned, two in upside down positions. The wintry sky behind grows dark in the vicinity of the icy cliff.

For the symbolism of forms frozen in ice, see the discussion of the previous illustration; and for the bridge of petrified forms, the comments on the thirty-fourth and fifty-eighth designs. We have also previously come across a number of instances of figures shown head downward as indicative of the Fall. One of the forms here has its arms stretched above its head as if crucified upside down; it recalls very closely the upside down figure in the lower right corner of the third engraving of the Job series.[3] Damon says of this drawing: "On the right of the picture we see the 'Crucifixion Upside Down'; or Man with his lowest instincts dominating both heart and brain."[4]

THIS ILLUSTRATION is the seventh and last of those engraved. The engraving is much more finished than the drawing and is another example of a detailed plate being based upon an incomplete sketch. In this case, however, Blake changed many incidentals in the process, so that there is less correspondence between the two versions than is true of the other illustrations which were engraved.

The most important variation is in the positions of the figures frozen in the surface

---

[1] Canto XXXII, 68-120.

[2] In the drawing Dante appears to kick Bocca in the back of the head, which is contrary to the text.

[3] "The Modern Church Crucifies Christ with the Head Downwards." (*Vision of the Last Judgment*, p. 650) That is, it sees in Him a deity who punishes sin rather than forgiving it. As brought out in the discussion of the engraving from this design, this figure is to be identified with Los. See also Wicksteed, *Blake's Vision of The Book of Job*, pp. 61-62.

[4] *William Blake*, p. 219.

of the lake to the right of Dante and Virgil. All now face toward the poets, whereas in the drawing some face in the other direction. Also, in accordance with the previous illustration, several of the figures have emblems of authority which do not appear in the drawing. One grasps a scepter and one a sword; three wear crowns, in one instance combined with a laurel wreath. All the facial expressions in the engraving are distinct, whereas in the drawing many are the merest indications. In the engraving another head appears in the ice in the extreme left foreground where there is none in the drawing; however, the rock near the left margin is now much smaller and encloses no petrified head. The figures in the arch at the right are, however, much more clearly visible. There are four, two sitting in an upright position, and the two between them upside down. The heads of the latter are now shown beneath the surface of the frozen lake, while in the drawing they are above it. Inasmuch as there are four figures, they are probably intended to represent the Zoas of the Fallen Albion. The bearded figure with frozen tears on his cheeks, crouched at the left, is certainly Urizen. The other seated figure would be Tharmas, while Los and Luvah are upside down, their heads almost—but not quite—submerged beneath the frozen waters of Udan-Adan.

The figures of the poets are much the same in both versions, as are the position and pose of Bocca degli Abati. However, the facial expression of the latter is more detailed and the resulting effect is a great improvement. The background is similar, except that the shaded area of the sky near the ice bridge extends much further across the page; also the horizon between the lake and the sky in the engraving meets the edge of the page on the left, and is no longer cut off by the rock, which is lower than in the drawing.

In spite of all these changes and of its much more developed character, the engraving is still not altogether finished. This is particularly noticeable in the lower left corner.

66. DANTE TUGGING AT BOCCA'S HAIR

Then seizing on his hinder scalp I cried:
"Name thee, or not a hair shall tarry here."
"Rend all away," he answer'd, "yet for that
I will not tell, nor show thee, who I am,
Though at my head thou pluck a thousand times."
Now I had grasp'd his tresses, and stript off
More than one tuft, he barking, with his eyes
Drawn in and downward, when another cried,
"What ails thee, Bocca? Sound not loud enough
Thy chattering teeth, but thou must bark outright?"

. . . .

We now had left him, passing on our way,
When I beheld two spirits by the ice
Pent in one hollow, that the head of one
Was cowl unto the other; and as bread
Is raven'd up through hunger, the uppermost

Did so apply his fangs to the other's brain,
Where the spine joins it.

Inferno XXXII, 97-106; 121-127

THIS DRAWING shows a continuation of the episode illustrated in the previous design. Dante stands in the center, crouching to get greater leverage as he pulls at Bocca's hair. The latter, as in the preceding illustration, is shown frozen in the ice as far as his chest. His mouth is open as he barks. Close to him and facing him another sinner is similarly buried in the ice. This is Buoso da Duero of Cremona, placed here for having accepted a bribe from the French not to molest with the troops under his command the army of Charles of Anjou as it advanced southward through Italy in 1265. He is shown in the act of revealing Bocca's name to Dante. To the left of Dante, Virgil stands watching. An unbroken expanse of icy lake and a dull sky with a few hints of cloud form the background.

Because of the description quoted from the very end of this canto, Blake has shown in the left background the figures of Count Ugolino and of Archbishop Ruggieri of Pisa, although Ugolino's story is not told until the following canto and the next two illustrations deal with it. In a small rocky or icy cavern behind Virgil and to his left, the two are seen, with Ugolino crouched over Ruggieri and gnawing his neck as described. The archbishop's crozier lies on the ice beside him.

Although Cary's translation here no doubt suggested the cavern in which the two are shown,[1] we must remember, as has been pointed out a number of times, that figures enclosed in caves or niches had a special significance for Blake. Both Ugolino and Ruggieri betrayed others for their own material ends, and their present relationship provides an excellent symbol of the cruelties of the Natural World in which all forms of life feed upon others.

[1] In the Italian the word used is *"buca,"* which can mean either "cave" or "hole." However, it is logical to assume that Dante intended to represent Ugolino and Ruggieri as frozen together in a hole similar to those which contain the other sinners of this region of Hell.

67. UGOLINO RELATING HIS DEATH

His jaws uplifting from their fell repast,
That sinner wiped them on the hairs o' the head,
Which he behind had mangled, then began:
"Thy will obeying, I call up afresh
Sorrow past cure; which, but to think of, wrings
My heart, or ere I tell on 't. But if words,
That I may utter, shall prove seed to bear
Fruit of eternal infamy to him,
The traitor whom I gnaw at, thou at once
Shalt see me speak and weep. Who thou mayst be
I know not, nor how here below art come:
But Florentine thou seemest of a truth,
When I do hear thee. Know, I was on earth
Count Ugolino, and the Archbishop he
Ruggieri. Why I neighbour him so close,

Now list. That through effect of his ill thoughts
In him my trust reposing, I was ta'en
And after murder'd, need is not I tell.
What therefore thou canst not have heard, that is,
How cruel was the murder, shalt thou hear,
And know if he have wrong'd me."

Inferno XXXIII, 1-21

COUNT UGOLINO DELLA GHERARDESCA was a leader of one of the Guelf factions of Pisa; the leader of the other was his nephew, Nino Visconti. In July 1288, Ugolino treacherously entered into an intrigue with the head of the Ghibellines, the Archbishop Ruggieri degli Ubaldini, with the object of driving out Nino and his followers. When this had been accomplished, Ruggieri turned on his confederate, Ugolino, and caused him to be imprisoned with his two sons and two grandsons. After many months of incarceration, food was withheld from them and they starved to death in March 1289. Dante places Ugolino in this circle for his treachery to his nephew and Ruggieri for his betrayal of his accomplice; Ugolino gnaws Ruggieri's head in vengeance for the manner of his death.

The setting of this drawing is similar to that of the previous one, except for the fact that Dante and Virgil have turned around and now look toward Ugolino and Ruggieri. These two are shown in much the same position as before, in a small cave within a low mound. Ruggieri, as previously, kneels bent over, blood dripping from his neck and an anguished expression on his face. Uglino has raised himself and kneels looking toward Dante and Virgil as he tells them his story. More of the mound to the left of the cave-mouth is visible than in the previous design, and on the bank near Ruggieri's head rests his episcopal hat.[1] His crozier still lies on the ice in the foreground. Both Ugolino and Ruggieri kneel on the ice instead of being frozen into it.

The poets stand in the center, Dante nearer Ugolino. Blake changed his mind concerning their position and alternative lightly sketched forms can be seen just to the right of where they are now standing, an early feature of the drawing not yet erased. Behind them, at the foot of the mound, a few very hasty pencil lines suggest that Blake probably intended to show some more of the sinners frozen into the surface. The icy lake stretches away into the distance in the right background, under a dull sky which is darkened just above the bank at the left.

The symbolism of the cavern has been mentioned in connection with the previous illustration. Blake has doubtless made the crozier and the episcopal hat so prominent because of his feelings concerning those who hold high clerical office. We have seen how frequently he associates ecclesiastics with kings and warriors, always with unfavorable connotations. Those in positions of authority in the church he regards invariably as cunning plotters who have no true love of God, but who use mankind's fear of punishment after death as a means of obtaining temporal power for themselves. The organized church is, in Blake's eyes, always linked to the support of worldly tyrannical

---

[1] An archbishop's hat is properly green with ten tassels on each side; this one is red with only one tassel. See *The Catholic Encyclopedia* under "Heraldry."

systems, which it accomplishes by means of a rigid code of man-made law which it claims is the law of God.[2] Thus, while profoundly religious in all his thought and art, Blake was uncompromisingly anti-clerical. He takes the opportunity offered by Dante's story of Ugolino to call attention to the wickedness and worldliness of which those in high ecclesiastical office are capable.

It will be noted that Ugolino in this illustration recalls the likeness of Job in that series, particularly in the eighth design, "Let the Day perish wherein I was Born."[3] Perhaps the similarity is intentional, both having suffered similar afflictions in the loss of their children. Job's error, according to Blake, was that he misunderstood the nature of God and worshipped the Angry God of This World. Certainly only a vindictive deity could have condemned sinners to eternal punishment and at the same time have granted to one the satisfaction of obtaining a cruel and painful retribution at the expense of another. Ugolino, the servant of the God of vengeance, may thus be likened to Job before his enlightenment: both also have to a certain extent the aspect of Urizen. The caption which Blake placed under his engraving of Ugolino in the Tower in *The Gates of Paradise*,[4] "Does thy God, O Priest, take such vengeance as this?" could equally well have served for the present illustration.

[2] For Blake's attitude toward the church, see J. G. Davies, *The Theology of William Blake*, Oxford, 1948, pp. 8-30. See also *Milton* 43, 37-39.

[3] W. M. Rossetti in his catalogue in Gilchrist's *Life*, II, p. 232, notes this resemblance.

[4] Reproduced in *Poetry and Prose*, p. 575.

68. UGOLINO IN PRISON

IN CANTO XXXIII, lines 29-91, is related Ugolino's tale of his imprisonment: his dream of evil portent, his hearing with his sons the nailing up of the door of their living tomb, their death one by one from hunger, and the death of Ugolino last of all on the eighth day. Having finished his account, Ugolino again sets his teeth to Ruggieri while Dante calls for vengeance against Pisa because of the cruel murder of the innocent sons.

Ugolino sits in the center of the design, staring straight ahead, with mouth tightly closed and knees drawn up to his chest; he has a long beard as in the previous drawing. On each side of him his two grandsons, Anselmuccio and Nino il Brigata, sit leaning against him and Ugolino places his arms about their shoulders. Behind and above them may be seen the barred window of the prison. Two angels hover gracefully over them. The two sons, Gaddo and Ugoccione, sit on the floor in the foreground to left and right. That on the left has his knees slightly bent and wears an agonized expression; the son on the right is very sketchily indicated with his legs stretched out straight before him. A few lines in the background suggest the walls and corners of the room.

This drawing is one of the least complete of the entire series, and is altogether in pencil. However, the composition of two triangles one within the other is effective, the mood is well conveyed, and the figure of Ugolino impressive, his intense gaze forming the focal point of the design. Solemnity, spaciousness, and a great deal of human feeling are all expressed in the simplest and most direct terms.

This subject no doubt appealed to Blake as an allegory of his concept of the Fallen

World as a prison of the soul. A political tyrant, and hence a follower of Urizen in the Fallen World, Ugolino now suffers from the terrors of that rule of law which, in his error, he was instrumental in supporting. However, while Natural Religion under the Law, as administered by Archbishop Ruggieri, may triumph momentarily, opposed to it is the loving forgiveness of God.[1] In the midst of what are to all appearances the most hopeless situations of his life, man can yet commune with God through his innate spiritual perceptions, personified in Blake's terms by the Emanations. They are here shown as hovering angels and serve to remind us that "Man's perceptions are not bounded by organs of perception; he percieves more than sense (tho' ever so acute) can discover."[2]

As was not the case with any of the other episodes of the *Divine Comedy*, Blake illustrated the subject of Ugolino's imprisonment on a number of different occasions apart from this particular series of drawings. The following is a list of other versions of the theme.

1. A very slight pencil sketch on page 59 of the notebook known as the "Rossetti Manuscript." A preparatory sketch for number 3 below, with which it is in the main identical. Very similar to the present version, except that the positions of the sons in the foreground have been reversed and there are no hovering angels.[3]

2. A pencil drawing now in the Victoria and Albert Museum, London. Inscribed in the hand of Frederick Tatham: "Original sketch for the Ugolino." This, like number 1, probably originated as a preparatory sketch for number 3, but numerous changes were later introduced. The sons in the foreground are similar, but the central group is not. Ugolino is shown cross-legged instead of with his knees straight up before him. The grandsons sit at a little distance apart and look at Ugolino who does not embrace them but has his hands straight down at his sides. The window behind is larger. The more compact grouping of number 1 and of the present design is much more successful.[4]

3. Plate 12 of *The Gates of Paradise*, line engraving published in 1793 and re-issued c. 1805. Very like number 1, except much more finished in detail.[5]

4. A version of this subject forms the background for the head of Dante in the series of heads of the poets done in tempera by Blake in 1800-1801 for William Hayley's library at Felpham (Fig. 103), and now, with the others of the group, in the Manchester City Art Gallery.[6] This is quite different from any of the other renditions of the theme. Ugolino sits in profile at the right-hand side of the painting, facing toward the center which is occupied by the portrait medallion. He holds one of his

---

[1] "Dost thou, O Priest, wish thy brother's death when God has preserved him?" (Annotation to Watson's *Apology for the Bible*, p. 752.)

[2] *There Is No Natural Religion, II*, p. 148. The angels in this drawing recall those of the fifteenth Job design and of the engraving to Blair's *Grave*, "The meeting of a Family in Heaven."

[3] See Keynes, *The Note-Book of William Blake called the Rossetti Manuscript*, London, 1935, pp. 83-84, 100, 156, and p. 59 of reproductions. The notebook is now in the possession of Mrs. F. W. Emerson of Cambridge, Massachusetts.

[4] Keynes, *Pencil Drawings*, plate 9.   [5] Reproduced in *Poetry and Prose*, p. 575.

[6] Thomas Wright, *Blake's Heads of the Poets*, Olney, Buckinghamshire, 1925; Gilchrist, *Life*, II, p. 211, no. 38 (d).

grandsons in his arms and the other kneels against him. The two sons are in the foreground, one seated and holding in his lap the head of the other who is already dead. An arch of heavy masonry is seen just above Ugolino's head, and his wrists and ankles are fettered. The half of the background to the left of the medallion shows only a masonry wall in which is set a ring to which a chain is fastened. Along each edge of the painting palm trunks reach upward and spread their branches across the top; they are, of course, emblematic of Christ's love, which alone offers man hope of salvation from the prison of the Moral Law.

5. A drawing given in W. M. Rossetti's list of Blake's work in Gilchrist's *Life*, II, p. 255, no. 3, and described as follows: "In outline; a preparation for the design in the 'Gates of Paradise.' " Dated by Rossetti, 1793.

6. A drawing of this subject, lent by A. A. Weston, Esq., is listed as number 8 in the catalogue of the Blake exhibition at the Burlington Fine Arts Club in 1876; it is not further described. Perhaps identical with number 5.

7. A. G. B. Russell, *Engravings of William Blake*, p. 63, in his account of number 3 above, speaks of having seen an india ink drawing of the subject; he gives no further description.

8. A fine tempera in brilliant colors has recently come into the possession of Geoffrey Keynes, Esq. It is identical in composition with the present drawing, of which it is clearly an elaboration, and includes the hovering angels which are not found in any of the other versions.[7] This is, in all probability, the work referred to by Blake in a letter to Linnell under the date of 25 April 1827: "As to Ugolino, &c., I never supposed that I should sell them; my Wife alone is answerable for their having Existed in any finish'd State."[8]

Among the number of renditions of the story of Ugolino in the Tower made by other artists during Blake's lifetime, the following should be mentioned as being by those with whose work he was certainly familiar.[9]

A. An oil by Sir Joshua Reynolds, exhibited at the Royal Academy in 1773. Very theatrical and stilted and quite different in composition from any of Blake's versions. The original painting is lost, but is known from engravings.[10]

B. An oil by Henry Fuseli, exhibited at the Royal Academy in 1806. The original

[7] A full discussion of this painting by Geoffrey Keynes and a reproduction of it will be found in *The Tempera Paintings of William Blake*, the catalogue of an exhibition organized in London by the Arts Council of Great Britain in the summer of 1951 (no. 10, pp. 18-19, and plate XI). It appears in W. M. Rossetti's catalogue of Blake's works in Gilchrist's *Life* (II, p. 251, no. 244), and in 1876 was lent to the Blake exhibition at the Burlington Fine Arts Club by J. W. White, Esq. (catalogue, no. 124); it was again exhibited in 1906 at the galleries of Messrs. Carfax & Co., Ltd., London (catalogue, no. 25). When in the possession of Mrs. Graham Smith, it was described by A. G. B. Russell (*Engravings of William Blake*, p. 63).

[8] *Poetry and Prose*, p. 928.

[9] Paget Toynbee, "Dante in English Art," *38th Annual Report of the Dante Society*, 1919, pp. 2-26.

[10] Toynbee, "The Earliest English Illustrators of Dante," *Quarterly Review*, CCXI, 1909, pp. 404-409; an engraving of the painting is reproduced.

is now lost; Ugolino was shown with the dead body of his younger grandchild on his knees.[11]

c. Two versions of the subject are included in Flaxman's series of illustrations to the *Divine Comedy*. Both are very different from any of Blake's renditions, other episodes of the story being shown. In the first, Ugolino and his sons are being led off to prison and, in the second, Ugolino gropes over the dead bodies. The original drawings are now in the Houghton Library of Harvard University; engraved by Piroli, they were published in Rome in 1793.

[11] *Ibid.*, pp. 410-412. For a letter written by Blake to defend this work against criticism, see *Poetry and Prose*, pp. 911-912.

69. LUCIFER

IN CANTO XXXIV, which is the last canto of the *Inferno*, Dante and Virgil reach the center of the world and there find Lucifer frozen from his waist up in the ice. The sinners in this region are wholly buried in ice and, looking down into it, Dante can see them frozen into various positions beneath the surface. Lucifer is described by Dante as having three faces, one mingled yellow and white in color, one black, and the central one red. Under each face he has two bat-like wings without feathers, the beating of which sets up three winds which serve to freeze the ice. In each mouth he has a sinner on whom he chews. Judas Iscariot is placed head first in the center mouth with only his legs sticking out; Lucifer bites him and also rends the flesh on his back with his claws. The two others, Brutus and Cassius, have their heads hanging down. After Virgil has pointed out these things to Dante, he makes him hold onto him while he grasps the hair on Lucifer's flanks. Carrying Dante thus, he climbs down between Lucifer's body and the ice. As they reach the thighs, they pass the center of the world and gravity changes, so that when they stand up they see Lucifer's legs held upward. They find themselves now in a narrow passage up which they climb on their journey to Purgatory.

This is obviously a complex canto to illustrate and Blake's drawing is confusing in certain respects, not only because of the involved nature of the symbolism, but because it is difficult to make out the details of the design itself. Most of the puzzling features will be found in the lower left portion of the page.

Lucifer fills the entire design and from the waist down is frozen in semi-transparent ice, through which his legs may be seen. They are not straight as though they bore his weight, but are bent to one side. He has bat-like wings, but only two are shown, instead of the six described in the text. He has three heads joined together into one at the back and each head is crowned. Of the three faces, only the center one is more than a slight sketch, and the legs of Judas may be seen protruding from the mouth; the other heads are so unfinished that the sinners in their mouths cannot be discerned.[1] As yet the differentiation in the color of the faces has not been made. Lucifer holds his hands raised on either side of him.

[1] Keynes has suggested (*Pencil Drawings*, note on plate 12) that some sketches in the Rossetti Manuscript of a flying figure with a body in its mouth might be a representation of Dante's Lucifer; however, as the figure is single-headed and is in all respects quite different from this version, the connection seems unlikely.

When we try to examine the details that are visible through the ice which covers the lower parts of Satan's body, there is much that is difficult to identify. The ice is not transparent at all points; rather, clear areas alternate with cloudy layers, reminding us of a figure frequently employed by Blake to symbolize the matter of the Fallen World. Completely buried in the ice are four giant forms, suggested by the sinners whom Dante sees frozen beneath the surface in the early lines of the canto. The heads of two of these appear to the right, one to the left and one—who wears a crown—is shown at the bottom of the page near Lucifer's right foot. In addition to these, close examination will reveal several much smaller figures at the left, the details of which are particularly difficult to distinguish.

Lucifer or Satan represents to Blake, of course, the limit of opacity. The triple head links him with the Threefold Accuser or Spectre of the Giant Albion and, as such, he is the counterpart of the Triple Hecate, the Fallen Goddess of Nature.[2] He stands at the nadir of error as the monstrous personification of the evil of the Fallen World, pure physical power and material bulk untouched by any of the essential human attributes of intelligence, feeling, or faith. God has created in him a state so monstrous that no man can fail eventually to recognize the nature of error, and thus be saved from the void.

At the lowest point of his fall, therefore, Albion is in the state Satan. Thus we see frozen beneath the ice of nonentity the forms of Albion's Fallen Zoas, their eyes closed in a death-like sleep which, like their frozen state, is the complete denial of the warmth and energy which is the essence of life. Urthona, Urizen, and Tharmas are shown as aged, bearded figures. Only Orc, the fallen aspect of Luvah, retains a youthful appearance; he too lies as if dead, and around his legs at the lower left may be seen coiled the serpent of materialism who always overcomes Orc when, having through misdirection spent his revolutionary force in vain, he falls victim to error.[3]

> No more remain'd of Orc but the Serpent round the tree of Mystery.
> The form of Orc was gone.
>
> Four Zoas viib, 211-212 (p. 328)

Near the serpent, and clinging to the legs of Orc, is the small figure of a man hanging upside down like a sloth. This creature of exceptionally dull senses and sluggish reactions, who lives upside down in the Tree of Mystery, is of course a perfect symbol of individual man at the nadir. This figure and the other small figures near it were no doubt suggested to Blake by the passage in which Dante and Virgil climb down close to the body of Lucifer until they reach the center of the world, when they have to turn themselves upside down in order to be again right side up. If we look closely, it will be observed that there are also four of these smaller figures. Near the sloth-man appears an indistinct head. Above this is a form in a crouched position and just above the beard of the recumbent giant on the left is another figure much like that of Dante

---

[2] Figgis, *Paintings of William Blake*, plate 76. This representation of Lucifer should be compared also to the three-headed demon found in the design of plate 50 of *Jerusalem*; see discussion of Drawing 12 above.

[3] Orc in this aspect is to be associated with Leviathan as he appears in the fifteenth Job design; note that there is a certain similarity with the serpent as shown here.

as he appears in many of the designs. As the giant forms are the Zoas of the Fallen Albion, so are these small figures the Fallen Zoas of the individual in error. That in the likeness of the poet, who is at the top, would be Los; below him are the caverned reason, the vague or "wat'ry" Tharmas, and the sloth-like form of human feeling at its lowest point bound upside down to the "stems of generation." All of this is probably an allegory of Dante in the pit of error and is a pictorial rendition of Blake's criticism of certain aspects of Dante's beliefs as discussed in the introduction.

2
PURGATORIO

There is from Great Eternity a mild & pleasant rest
Nam'd Beulah, a soft Moony Universe, feminine, lovely,
Pure, mild & Gentle, given in mercy to those who sleep,
Eternally Created by the Lamb of God around,
On all sides, within & without the Universal Man.
The daughters of Beulah follow sleepers in all their dreams,
Creating spaces, lest they fall into Eternal Death.

Four Zoas I, 90-96 (p. 254)

70. DANTE AND VIRGIL AGAIN BEHOLDING THE SUN AS THEY ISSUE FROM HELL

Then on the solitary shore arrived,
That never sailing on its waters saw
Man that could after measure back his course,
He girt me in such manner as had pleased
Him who instructed; and O strange to tell!
As he selected every humble plant,
Wherever one was pluck'd, another there
Resembling, straightway in its place arose.

Purgatorio I, 129-136

AFTER THEIR ascent from the infernal regions, Dante and Virgil reach the open air at the foot of the Mountain of Purgatory just as the dawn is approaching. Here they meet Cato, who asks them how they managed to reach Purgatory by this route. Satisfied by Virgil's reply, he commands Virgil to cleanse Dante's face of the grime acquired during the journey through Hell, and to gird him with one of the rushes which grow by the shore, and tells them that by that time the sun will have risen sufficiently to show them the route by which to climb the mountain. Accordingly, just as the sun rises Dante and Virgil go down to the shore, where Dante is washed and his head girded with a rush.

Blake shows the scene quite literally. The wall of the Mountain of Purgatory rises steeply at the extreme left of the page. Dante bends forward on hands and knees on the bank in the center foreground. Just to the right of him kneels Virgil who is in the act of binding a rush around Dante's head. Close behind them at the edge of the water grow the rushes which spring forth again miraculously when plucked. Beyond the expanse of sea and just behind the figure of Virgil, the rising sun appears upon the horizon. Above it is a clear sky and its rays seem to be pushing back banks of dark clouds toward the top of the page.

The sun has, of course, great significance for Blake as the symbol of the Poetic Imagination. Hence it is used here to frame the heads of the poets, particularly that of Virgil. The relationship of Virgil and Dante in this drawing is much the same as that of Milton and Blake in the fine design of plate 21 of *Milton*; the eternal poet places the wreath of inspiration upon the brow of the poet who still lives in the created world. However, this illustration is contemplative while that from *Milton* is dramatic. Art, in Blake's opinion, is the supreme link between man in the Fallen World and the eternal life of Eden, whose symbol is the sun. As man, by means of the power of spiritual perception which God has given him, rises from the pit of error and begins his ascent towards salvation, the sun of God's love, of the eternal warmth and energy of life, and of divine imagination, shines upon him.

> Awake, Awake, Jerusalem! O lovely Emanation of Albion,
> Awake and overspread all Nations as in Ancient Time;
> For lo! the Night of Death is past and the Eternal Day
> Appears upon our Hills.
>
> *Jerusalem* 97, 1-4

The sun then, as represented in this illustration, is the Spiritual Sun—the same Sun which is described in a famous passage at the end of *A Vision of the Last Judgment*: "I assert for My Self that I do not behold the outward Creation & that to me it is hindrance & not Action; . . . 'What,' it will be Question'd, 'When the Sun rises, do you not see a round disk of fire somewhat like a Guinea?' O no, no, I see an Innumerable company of the Heavenly host crying, 'Holy, Holy, Holy, is the Lord God Almighty!' "[1]

This drawing is very simple in its composition, yet in its sense of vastness, serenity, and quiet grandeur it is one of the finest designs of the series. The foreground is entirely in pencil; the horizon line has been inked, and washes are used in the sky and in the distance on the surface of the water. By means of them, a remarkable effect of light is obtained which emanates from the sun—itself uncolored—and pervades the entire composition with a radiance which well portrays the clear freshness of dawn.

[1] *Poetry and Prose*, pp. 651-652. "Holy, Holy, Holy" appears written in pencil upon the disk of the sun in the first of the Butts set of original watercolors to the Book of Job, now in the Pierpont Morgan Library, New York.

71. DANTE, VIRGIL, AND CATO

DANTE AND VIRGIL, having just issued from the infernal regions, are seen conversing with Cato whom they meet on the shore as day is dawning.[1] In the sky above them gleam four stars (I, 22-27), whose radiance as they shine upon Cato is suggested by the nimbus which surrounds his figure. His gestures indicate that he is questioning Dante and Virgil as to how they came to arrive by the narrow ascent from Hell instead of

[1] The subject of this drawing occurs earlier in the first canto of the *Purgatorio* than does that of the preceding one. It was misplaced by W. M. Rossetti in his list of the drawings in Gilchrist's *Life*, II, pp. 227-234, and consequently in the numbering of them in the National Art-Collections Fund portfolio; however, since it is convenient to accept that numbering as standard, it is followed here.

by the angelic boat. Virgil points toward the Mountain of Purgatory as he replies concerning the divine authority for his mission.[2]

Virgil is shown with his back turned. He gestures upward toward the mountain with his left hand and points down at the earth with his right. Dante stands in the middle, both hands raised in surprise. Cato is at the right, pointing down with his right hand and holding his left across his breast. It will be noted that Cato has much the appearance of the apparition of the ninth Job illustration, and is thus to be thought of as Urizenic in character. He points to the earth and is surrounded by a "cloudy vapour"[3] signifying perception which is purely of this world. Virgil, on the other hand, indicates by his gesture that his mission is to lead man from his present position to a realm above the stars.[4] The poet is thus shown standing between rationality which would bind him to the earth and imagination which seeks to lead him to spheres of infinite vision. This drawing perhaps symbolized for Blake his own position as a poet standing midway between the youthful spirit of dawning romanticism and the older classical tradition of the Age of Reason. Blake's own allegiance was, of course, clear; however, perhaps the fact that Dante here looks at Cato signifies once again Blake's feeling that Dante at times relied too strongly upon tradition and tended to support worldly systems at the expense of spiritual and intellectual freedom. To Blake it is the supreme task of the artist "To cast aside from Poetry all that is not Inspiration."[5]

With the exception of a few insignificant details in india ink, this is entirely a pencil drawing. A sense of spaciousness and calm is achieved by very simple means, but the effect is somewhat spoiled by conventional poses and gestures. The posture of Virgil will be found in more exaggerated form in a pencil drawing, "The Journey of Life,"[4] and in the design to plate 97 of *Jerusalem*. This pose and the facial types of both Dante and Virgil are similar to those of the fourth illustration of this series. Dante's gesture is an unfortunate variant of a type which appears frequently in these drawings and in the illustrations to the Book of Job.[6]

[2] This episode is described in *Purgatorio* I, lines 28-110, and the illustration suggests particularly lines 28-48.

[3] *A Descriptive Catalogue*, p. 607.

[4] Damon, *William Blake*, p. 474, interprets Virgil's gesture as that of "The Poet advancing inward towards Eternity." (See also Keynes, *Pencil Drawings*, commentary on the drawing, "The Journey of Life," plate 39.) Percival, *Blake's "Circle of Destiny,"* p. 57, sees in the constellation of four stars a symbol of the fourfold world of Eden.

[5] *Milton* 48, 7.

[6] E.g. the gesture of Job's wife in the seventh design and of Job himself in the eleventh of the series.

72. THE ANGELIC BOAT WAFTING OVER THE SOULS FOR PURGATION

THIS ILLUSTRATION combines a number of incidents, all of them described in the second canto of the *Purgatorio*. As Dante and Virgil linger by the shore, to which they have gone at Cato's command to wash Dante of the grime of his journey, Dante perceives a bright light advancing across the sea toward them. When it draws closer it proves to be a boat bearing more than a hundred souls and guided by an angel, who propels it by means of the beating of his wings. When they reach shore, the souls alight and the angel, having signed them with the cross, departs. The newly-arrived souls ask Dante and Virgil to indicate to them the path up the mountain; then, realizing from Dante's breathing that he is still alive, they turn pale and look at him curiously. One of them advances to embrace Dante and Dante recognizes him as his friend Casella. Casella tells him that those who after death are not sent down to Acheron assemble at the mouth of the Tiber, where they are met by the heavenly boat which brings them to Purgatory. Dante then asks Casella to sing for them as he used to when alive. All are absorbed in listening to the song when Cato again appears and chides them for tarrying by the shore instead of beginning at once their ascent of the mountain. The entire group at once hurries toward the hillside, Dante and Virgil among them.

A steep cliff rises to the left of the design. To the right of it the sea stretches off into the distance. Upon it may be seen the departing boat; it floats almost without displacement as described and in it stands the angel, propelling it by means of his wings which are held straight up. From him that brilliance radiates which makes it impossible for Dante to look directly at him. In the right foreground, on the shore with the sea behind them, stand the spirits who have just debarked; about ten are indicated, although the group is so sketchy that it is impossible to count them exactly. Virgil stands a little apart to the right and next to him Dante and Casella are seen embracing. Off to the left, with the cliff behind him, stands Cato.[1]

While much of the detail of this illustration is literal, there are two features which are quite different from anything described in the text, and for which an explanation must be sought in terms of Blake's own symbolism. First, it will be noted that the ship is shaped like a half-moon; also, behind Cato a cave-mouth is seen in the face of the cliff and within this upon a table stands a burning lamp before what appears to be a painted shrine in the form of a diptych.

It will be recalled that the in-between realm of Blake's mythology, which corresponds to Purgatory in Dante's *Divine Comedy*, is Beulah. Beulah is the abode of ideal love; its inhabitants are the Emanations, whom Blake depicts as hovering angels, and its symbol is the moon. The presence here of the moon-like boat, and of the angel, and the prominence given to the embrace of Casella and Dante all indicate that Blake associates this scene of the spirits arriving in Purgatory with Beulah, for Beulah too is a place where spirits come and go. Created to be a place of repose from the intensity of Eden, it serves also as the threshold of the Fall when it begins.[2]

However, instead of restoring his powers for return to Eden, man may become enamoured of the inaction of Beulah. With this acceptance of error, the Eternal Man sinks into slumber in the Caves of Sleep of Beulah and the Fall begins, for "if dwelt in too long, Beulah will soon turn into Ulro."[3] It is this cave which appears in the cliff behind Cato, who is to be associated with the rational Zoa who rules over the Fallen World. Suggested by the dark passage out of which Dante and Virgil have come

[1] Cato's name is written faintly in pencil just over his head.
[2] For Beulah see especially *Milton* 33, 1-34, 11.
[3] Frye, *Fearful Symmetry*, p. 234. For a discussion of Beulah see *ibid.*, pp. 227-235; and Percival, *Blake's "Circle of Destiny,"* pp. 52-59.

after their ascent from the infernal regions, Blake sees in the cavern the entrance to the vortex which leads from Eternity to Ulro . . . "the descent of the mind into abstraction and unbelief is the archetypal sleep which precedes the fall."[4] This is, of course, the realm of Natural Religion, and, as such, the lamp burns before the shrine of Mystery.

Man is thus shown in this design in the in-between realm of Beulah. As the spirits embrace on the shore, the angelic boat guided by the Divine Imagination waits to take them back to the eternal joy of Eden; however, the Caves of Sleep are also here with their Urizenic guardian as a reminder that Beulah can also become the gateway of the Fall.

The moon-boat as seen here is found again in the design at the top of plate 24 of *Jerusalem*, which depicts a boat shaped like a half-moon and containing a winged figure, riding serenely upon a stormy sea: the love of God as represented by the Emanation in Beulah is man's protection from annihilation beneath the waters of Ulro.[5]

Much of this drawing is in pencil, but washes appear upon the ground, on the surface of the sea, and in the sky. The effect of light which is produced by the washes radiates from the figure of the angel and suggests the misty brilliance of early dawn. The lack of detail in the figures themselves adds to the impression of immateriality which is appropriate to them as spirits and increases the sense that all are bathed in a shimmering radiance of light.

[4] Percival, *op. cit.*, p. 58.

[5] A similar boat-shaped crescent moon in which is cradled an Emanation who holds a lighted lamp is a prominent feature of the drawing which illustrates page 16 of "Night the Fifth" of Young's *Night Thoughts*.

73. THE MOUNTAIN LEADING TO PURGATORY

CANTO IV, lines 18-52, describes the beginning of the ascent of the Mountain of Purgatory. Dante and Virgil climb up a steep path within a narrow cleft, until at last they reach a ledge where they stop to rest.

This is one of the least detailed drawings of the series. Even its connection with the text is a very general one. To the right is the precipitous side of the mountain with the sea far below. The ledge takes up the center of the page, and in the upper left the cliff-like wall of the mountain again towers up out of the design. In the lower left near the margin may be seen the steep path up which Dante and Virgil have come. They appear as two tiny figures who have sat down to rest near a boulder by the rock wall in the upper left portion of the drawing. Behind them another cleft suggests the continuation of the path. The sun is not visible; heavy clouds tower up into the sky and some form a roll of mist which hangs down over the ledge.[1]

The symbolism here—if any is intended—is also very general in character. Perhaps

[1] Damon, *William Blake*, p. 219, assumes that this is the smoke from a fire and, comparing this design to the eighteenth of the Job series, comments that "the poets tend the same flame which Job tends." However, this is certainly a bank of mist. Damon's interpretation of it goes to show how difficult it is to make out the details of this particular drawing.

the long road to be travelled in the World of Generation from the sea of Materialism below to the celestial heights above is to be suggested by this illustration. The banks of cloud would then represent different stages of limited vision to be overcome along the way; in this sense they have a similar significance to the cloud layers of many of the Job engravings.

Although the washes in this design are more developed than those of the previous few drawings, this is one of the most incomplete in detail of any of the series. In spite of its sketchy character, however, the effects of immense space, loneliness, and of the atmospheric conditions peculiar to a mountain top are well conveyed and are the principal features of this illustration.

74. DANTE AND VIRGIL ASCENDING THE MOUNTAIN OF PURGATORY

> We through the broken rock ascended, close
> Pent on each side, while underneath the ground
> Ask'd help of hands and feet. .   .   .
>
> .   .   .   .
> I, wearied, thus began: "Parent beloved!
> Turn and behold how I remain alone,
> If thou stay not."   Purgatorio IV, 30-32; 42-44

THE ROCKY CLIFF and the path up it occupy the left half of the page. Dante is below;[1] he is seen from behind as he pulls himself up with his hands and also uses his left knee to help him climb. Above, Virgil has turned to look back at him, but is still in the position of climbing. Beyond Virgil, the path curves to the left out of sight. The right side of the design is taken up by a fine view over the sea, reaching from the bottom to well above the middle of the page. In the sky the sun is seen with part of its disk covered by a dark cloud in such a way as to leave only a half-moon shaped piece of the top of the sun visible. Light gleams across the water and the whole design achieves a fine effect of space.[2]

The only puzzling feature in this illustration is the veiling of the sun in this unusual way. This was no doubt done to remind us that we are still at the level of Beulah. In Blake's symbolism, the full disk of the sun would be revealed only in Eden,[3] while as we have seen the emblem of Beulah is the moon. Guided by his Poetic Genius, Dante toils upward,[4] pursuing a course away from the materialistic oblivion which the sea threatens and to which man may fall victim while in Beulah. In imagination, action,

---

[1] This drawing should properly have been numbered in the National Art-Collections Fund portfolio ahead of the previous one, for it shows a slightly earlier episode. Dante and Virgil are here seen climbing up the path before reaching the ledge upon which they were shown in the preceding design.

[2] Although much more finished, the general composition of this illustration is very similar to that of the forty-fifth of the series.

[3] The unveiled disk of the sun does not appear in any of the illustrations to the *Purgatorio*.

[4] Note that in this drawing Dante has his left foot advanced, while Virgil steps forward with his right foot. For Blake's right-and-left symbolism, of which this is clearly an intentional example, see the commentary on the first illustration to the *Inferno*.

and vision is to be found the pathway back to Eden and escape from the danger of falling again into error.

The wearisome journey of Dante upward toward grace and his appeal to Virgil to turn and aid him recall a passage in one of Blake's letters in which he describes to his patron, Thomas Butts, a similar experience of his own earthly journey which occurred during his Felpham years: "Temptations are on the right hand & left; behind, the sea of time & space roars & follows swiftly; he who keeps not right onward is lost, & if our footsteps slide in clay, how can we do otherwise than fear & tremble?"[5]

[5] January 10, 1802 (p. 855).

75. THE SOULS OF THOSE WHO ONLY REPENTED AT THE POINT OF DEATH

BEGINNING with line 22 of Canto V and continuing to line 26 of Canto VI, Dante describes his meeting in Antepurgatory with a group of those who had repented only at the point of death. Recognizing by his shadow that he is a living being, they cluster around him in great numbers, requesting that he bear news of them back to the world, so that their friends may pray for them and thus help them on their way toward salvation.

The Mountain of Purgatory appears at the right of the page, rising out of sight at the upper right and falling away toward the sea at the lower center. A view over the sea occupies the left side of the design. Dante and Virgil stand on a path which ascends the mountain at the right. Dante is looking at the spirits with a welcoming gesture, while Virgil looks back over his shoulder at him and seems to exhort him to continue the ascent (V, 43-45):

> "Many," exclaim'd the bard, "are these, who throng
> Around us: to petition thee, they come.
> Go therefore on, and listen as thou go'st."

The group of spirits are shown in an unusual manner, for while in the text there is no mention of their coming otherwise than by running, in the illustration they are portrayed in wingless flight, and float across the design with a counter-clockwise motion. The group begins with a column of vapor on the side of the mountain near the feet of the poets; it rises toward the top of the page and as it circles to the left indistinct forms begin to appear. The motion then turns downward toward the lower left, the forms becoming always more distinct. Two seem just about to plunge into the sea in the left corner, but at the last moment their direction of movement is changed and the remaining figures float lightly and gracefully toward Dante. Approximately sixteen forms can be discerned in the group of repentant spirits, although some at the top of the page are very indistinct. In all cases male and female figures are paired; this is Beulah and the Spectres and Emanations, while divided, are still closely linked.

This illustration is in many ways related to the thirteenth design of the Job series, "Then the Lord Answered Job out of the Whirlwind." In both, figures appear caught up in a rotating movement, a motion which in the Job engraving is carried out both in the design and in the surrounding marginal decoration. It will be observed, however, that the direction of the movement is different: it is clockwise in the Job engraving, counter-clockwise here. Of the Job design, Wicksteed says, as noted in the discussion of Drawing 19: "The margin carries on the motion of the whirlwind, the time current of creation, and shows Job's vision of his own spirit swept along in the endless round of Nature."[1] For the reverse movement we must recall the passage from page 77 of *Jerusalem* quoted in connection with the forty-fourth illustration above, in which Natural Religion is symbolized as a wheel turning "from west to east, against the current of Creation."

We have already pointed out that in Beulah the acceptance of error is possible. Here, then, we have a group of spirits who, because their vision had grown clouded in the "Caves of Sleep," became a prey to Natural Religion and were caught up in its reverse motion. Just before their fatal plunge into the waters of Ulro, however, they recognize their error through the power of spiritual perception which God has given to all men as a means of salvation—that is, they repent on the point of death. Their downward movement is arrested and they float upward toward Dante who, as the Divine Imagination, is now their guide and who receives them with his hands spread in the gesture of the cross, signifying God's forgiveness.[2] In a wider sense this design depicts the whole Circle of Destiny as Blake conceived it: man's fall into error, his escape through God's mercy from annihilation, and his redemption through God's love and forgiveness. It is again Blake's dominant theme of Fall, Regeneration, and Apocalypse. As so often in this series, Blake uses the poets as symbols of the truth of God revealed to men, since to him spiritual perception and imagination are one, and art is the closest link which binds Fallen Man to God.

"Truth has bounds, Error none."[3] Blake in this as in many passages insists that the test of the truth of perception rests in its distinctness. Thus in this drawing as long as error persists all is cloudy and indistinct, but with salvation, through the power of imagination, comes clarity of vision. "The clearer the organ the more distinct the object. A Spirit and a Vision are not, as the modern philosophy supposes, a cloudy vapour, or a nothing: they are organized and minutely articulated beyond all that the mortal and perishing nature can produce."[4]

This group of floating figures is, of course, somewhat akin to that of the illustration of the episode of Paolo and Francesca, except that the direction of movement is reversed. A number of Blake's other works have groups of forms which are similar. Plate 19 of *Jerusalem* is particularly close, in that the group which rises from the form of the sleeping Albion circles in the same direction as here: the symbolism of the two is evidently akin. The floating figures of the repentant souls in themselves recall vividly those of the rejected design for the title page of Blair's *Grave*, "The Ascension of the Dead."[5]

[1] *Blake's Vision of the Book of Job*, p. 99.
[2] Although nine of the spirits are named by Dante, it is impossible to identify any of those shown in the drawing specifically with those mentioned in the text.
[3] *Book of Los*, line 79 (p. 244).
[4] *A Descriptive Catalogue*, p. 607.
[5] Reproduced in Keynes, *Bibliography*, f.p. 219.

76. THE LAWN WITH THE KINGS AND ANGELS

AFTER THEIR MEETING with the spirits who repented only at the point of death, Dante and Virgil continue on their journey. Presently they meet a soul who is by himself and stop to ask him the way. He identifies himself as Sordello, the famous troubador of Mantua. After Virgil, also a Mantuan, has told him who he is, Sordello offers to guide him and Dante upward as far as he is permitted to go. However, darkness is coming on; Sordello tells them that at night it is impossible to ascend the mountain and suggests that he lead them to a pleasant resting place where they may remain until morning. He conducts them to a little valley recessed in the side of the mountain; here repose the spirits of those who delayed their repentance because of the pressure of worldly cares. The dell is filled with grass and many-colored flowers and in it the spirits, most of whom were kings on earth, are seated. Sordello proceeds to name many of them to Dante and Virgil. Presently, as night draws on, the spirits begin to sing a hymn, and two angels with fiery swords arrive to guard them during the hours of darkness. After a time, a large serpent appears among the grass and flowers and starts to glide into the vale, only to be driven off by the angels.[1]

In many respects Blake has followed the text closely. The hollow is shown with the side of the mountain behind it, above which is the sky. In the center foreground, with their backs turned, Dante, Virgil, and Sordello look at the spirits who sit under some trees in the middle distance. There are twenty spirits in all; several at the left of the group wear crowns and one a monk's cowl. It will be noted, however, that instead of flowers the dell contains many small trees and bushes. Above in the sky the two angels are flying and holding out their fiery swords so that they form a cross. Faint haloes around their heads suggest the radiance which Dante cannot look upon (VIII, 34-37). The serpent is gliding toward the vale from the right background, and turns to lick himself.[2]

We have already had several occasions to speak of the significance which Blake attaches to worldly power. It is to be inferred that the same connotation is intended here, and lest, because of a merely literal interpretation of the text, we should miss the significance of the crowned and cowled figures, Blake has placed them beneath a grove of trees—no such feature being mentioned in the poem. As brought out in the discussion of the first design of the series, Blake frequently symbolizes the error of the Fallen World by a dense growth of trees or other foliage.[3]

Here, then, is represented man in our present world. Wearing the attributes of that worldly power which the selfhood seeks so eagerly, and seated beneath the groves of

---

[1] The meeting with Sordello is described in *Purgatorio* VI, 59-75. Cantos VII and VIII tell of the vale and of the spirits within it, and of the events which the poets witness there.

[2] This detail follows very exactly lines 99-102 of Canto VIII.

[3] Note that the figures at the left are shown beneath oak trees with their characteristic leaves and acorns:

> Now Man was come . . . to the Oak of Weeping
> Which stands upon the Edge of Beulah.
> Four Zoas I, 456-457 (p. 264)

It will be observed that the crowned figure at the extreme left is shown as weeping. See also *Jerusalem* 16, 3-5.

deeply-rooted error, he is preyed upon by the serpent of materialism. God has not abandoned him in his Fall, however. Outside the grove stand the poets and artists, those men of imagination who retain a perception of their eternal life and who keep alive in man a knowledge of his spiritual heritage.[4] They can see in the open sky above them the angels of God's grace as they make, with the fiery swords of imagination,[5] the redeeming sign of the cross which wards off the evil of the Natural World.[6]

This drawing is largely in india ink and is tinted with light washes. A few uncompleted portions are still in pencil, notably some of the foliage in the lower right. There is, however, considerable highly finished detail.

[4] Note that Dante and Virgil each have their right, or spiritual, feet advanced and that Sordello's feet do not touch the ground, but that he seems to float just above it. While this latter feature is derived from the fact that Dante's text dwells upon the immaterial nature of the spirits in Purgatory, Blake probably also intends to indicate here the ability of the artist to transcend the created world.

[5] These are, of course, Spiritual as opposed to Natural Swords. See plate 52 of *Jerusalem* and the last stanza of the famous poem in the Preface to *Milton* (p. 376).

[6] As Dante compares the serpent to that which gave the fruit to Eve (VIII, 98), so Blake depicts him very much in the manner of the serpents in his own drawings of "The Temptation of Eve" and "Satan Exulting over Eve." (Figgis, *Paintings of William Blake*, plates 12 and 20.)

77. LUCIA CARRYING DANTE IN HIS SLEEP

> . . . "Ere the dawn
> Usher'd the day-light, when thy wearied soul
> Slept in thee, o'er the flowery vale beneath
> A lady came, and thus bespake me: 'I
> Am Lucia. Suffer me to take this man,
> Who slumbers. Easier so his way shall speed.'
> Sordello and the other gentle shapes
> Tarrying, she bare thee up: and, as day shone,
> This summit reach'd: and I pursued her steps.
> Here did she place thee. First, her lovely eyes
> That open entrance show'd me; then at once
> She vanish'd with thy sleep." Purgatorio IX, 47-58

THE MOUNTAIN rises by a series of steps from lower right to upper left. On the central step, Lucia is seen climbing upward with the sleeping Dante in her arms. She supports Dante's body with her left hand and her right hand holds his head against her bosom. Their heads are faintly shown against the dazzling disk of the full moon. Behind them, two steps lower, Virgil follows with his eyes intently fixed on Dante. The sky behind him is becoming bright with approaching dawn and the nearest of the group of stars which dot the sky are beginning to pale.

Here again we are in Beulah, ruled over by the moon. Tired out by the active life of Eden, the soul now reposes guarded by the Emanation, here represented by St. Lucy, Dante's patron saint. The left and right symbolism seems to be followed here, the Emanation going left foot first while the male spiritual guardian advances his right foot. Similarly, the Poetic Genius is placed before the rising sun of inspiration, while the Emanation has the moon for a halo. As the day of Eden dawns, the stars, which testify to God's love of man even through the darkness of night, begin to fade. This is the eternal aspect of Beulah as the place of repose in which the soul is ministered to by the Emanation and restored to new vigor for its return to Eden. The strange and rather sinister vegetation on the ground at the left, however, serves as a reminder that the sleep of Beulah, if too prolonged, can be as well the prelude to the Fall.

We have previously commented on Blake's theory that there are two avenues of communication by which man in the Fallen World can escape briefly from the limitations imposed upon him by his environment, and experience immediate perception of Eternity. These avenues are those of artistic creation and of an ideal sexual relationship. As the preceding illustration portrays vision expanded through art, so does this one show human love as a gateway to Eden. The poet falls into repose in Beulah and, as he does so, his Emanation separates from him and watches lovingly over the sleeping form. However, just as Beulah is a realm from which a fall is possible, so is physical love which originates here a source of great danger. In its unselfish ideal aspect it can make the soul one with God, but as a means of self-gratification and of obtaining control over others it is responsible for much of the misery of the Fallen World. Hence as Lucy mounts upward with Dante in her arms, the evil forms of earthly vegetation are ever near as a warning that the pathway of true joy is a narrow one, and as a reminder that Beulah is the realm where contraries exist side by side.[1]

This drawing recalls in a striking manner the following passages from Blake's prophetic poems:

> There is a place where Contrarieties are equally True:
> This place is called Beulah. It is a pleasant lovely Shadow
> Where no dispute can come, Because of those who Sleep.
>
> . . . .
>
> Beulah is evermore Created around Eternity, appearing
> To the Inhabitants of Eden around them on all sides.
> But Beulah to its Inhabitants appears within each district
> As the beloved infant in his mother's bosom round incircled
> With arms of love & pity & sweet compassion. But to
> The Sons of Eden the moony habitations of Beulah
> Are from Great Eternity a mild & pleasant Rest.
>
> Milton 33, 1-3; 8-14

> The Female searches sea & land for gratifications to the
> Male Genius, who in return clothes her in gems & gold
> And feeds her with the food of Eden; hence all her beauty beams.
> She Creates at her will a little moony night & silence
> With Spaces of sweet gardens & a tent of elegant beauty,

[1] As a portrayal of the ideal aspect of love, this illustration should be contrasted with the ninth of the series which deals with the perversion of love in the Fallen World.

Closed in by a sandy desart & a night of stars shining
And a little tender moon & hovering angels on the wing.

Jerusalem 69, 16-22

This episode in Dante's poem of the wearied soul falling asleep in the garden—under the stars and with the protection of the angels of God's love—and then being carried upward in its sleep by the power of feminine love, is so close to Blake's conception of Beulah that it must have served to confirm him in the truth of his belief in the oneness of inspired vision. Certainly, Blake was seldom able to combine literal illustration of a text and symbolical interpretation of the life of the soul with happier artistic effect than in this beautiful watercolor. Among all of Blake's work it is probably the finest from the standpoint of rich and harmonious color effects. Simple but perfectly balanced in composition, it suggests the imaginative beauty of the poem and creates convincingly a reality beyond the range of the physical senses. Although the drawing portrays a world which we can never enter in the body, it is humanly appealing in a spiritual and imaginative sense; hence it is simple and beautiful without being in the least unreal or fantastic.

78. DANTE AND VIRGIL APPROACHING THE ANGEL WHO GUARDS THE ENTRANCE OF PURGATORY

> . . . Nearer now we drew,
> Arrived whence, in that part, where first a breach
> As of a wall appear'd, I could descry
> A portal, and three steps beneath, that led
> For inlet there, of different color each;
> And one who watch'd, but spake not yet a word.
> As more and more mine eye did stretch its view,
> I mark'd him seated on the highest step,
> In visage such, as past my power to bear.
> Grasp'd in his hand, a naked sword glanced back
> The rays so towards me, that I oft in vain
> My sight directed.   .   .   .   .   .
>
> .   .   .   .
>
> The lowest stair was marble white, so smooth
> And polish'd, that therein my mirror'd form
> Distinct I saw. The next of hue more dark
> Than sablest grain, a rough and singed block,
> Crack'd lengthwise and across. The third, that lay
> Massy above, seem'd porphyry, that flamed
> Red as the life-blood spouting from a vein.
> On this God's Angel either foot sustain'd,
> Upon the threshold seated, which appear'd
> A rock of diamond.   Purgatorio IX, 66-77; 86-95

IN THE FOREGROUND of the illustration appears the top of the cliff and along its edge curves the pathway up which Dante and Virgil have come. To the left and far below, the sea stretches to the horizon, with a fine effect of reflected light upon its surface. In accordance with the text, the sun has not yet risen very high into the sky, it being still early morning; its face, however, is veiled with heavy rolls of blood-red clouds which completely cover it. Light gleams from between the clouds and three great rays reach down to the sea.

To the right rises the wall and in it is the gateway, its top a pointed arch. The three steps are shown of varying colors and textures as described. The angel sits upon the threshold with his feet upon the top step. He is a venerable, bearded figure; his wings are seen behind him, light radiates from his head, and a scroll lies across his knees. Just to the left of the portal, and with the sun behind them, stand Dante and Virgil, their heads bent and their hands raised as though in prayer. Both face the angel and Virgil is shown a step ahead of Dante.

The text is followed quite exactly, but several features have evidently been introduced by Blake to accord with his own beliefs. It is clear, for instance, that Blake wishes us to associate the angel with Urizen. He is bearded and blind and has a long scroll across his knees: all these details are common attributes of Urizen.[1]

In Drawing 72, "The Angelic Boat Wafting over the Souls for Purgation," we saw the bearded figure of Urizen standing outside a cave—the mouth of which was the same shape as the portal here—while the moon-boat was shown upon the sea. In discussing that design, we concluded that it portrayed the two aspects of Beulah as midway between Eden and the Fall. Here we have the same symbolism, only now the face of the sun—which has the same significance as the radiance emanating from the angel in the other illustration—is veiled; also Dante and Virgil bow before the Urizenic figure who sits within the Caves of Sleep, while their backs are turned to the source of light. Obviously then, this drawing depicts the moment in Beulah when man accepts error and the Fall begins.

We find in the present illustration a statement by Blake of a point of view which will recur numerous times in the succeeding designs as Dante and Virgil proceed on their journey through Purgatory and Paradise. The pathway which they follow, as described by Dante, is that of orthodoxy or, in Blake's terminology, of Natural Religion and the Wastes of Moral Law. Blake expressed his own conception concerning the road which leads to salvation very succinctly: "Mutual Forgiveness of each Vice, Such are the Gates of Paradise."[2] Dante and Virgil, however, turn their backs on the sun of divine love and choose the path which leads through the narrow gate of the Moral Law, guarded by the "angel" of unforgiving rationalism. As the poets bow before the God of This World in his cavern, the blood-red clouds of war—the in-

---

[1] See *Ahania*, 103-106 (pp. 237-238), and *Urizen*, 82-91 (p. 222); the latter is quoted in the introduction. The figure of the angel in the present drawing is much like that of plate 22 of *Urizen*, in which Urizen appears in fetters. In pose it recalls the form which sits in the shattered gateway in the frontispiece of *America*. In the color-printed drawing, "The Lazar House" (Figgis, *Paintings of William Blake*, plate 73), Urizen is shown as a blind, bearded figure with a scroll; the scroll appears likewise in the design to plate 41 of *Jerusalem*. It is doubtless to emphasize this identification with Urizen that Blake substitutes a scroll in this illustration for the sword which is described in the text but which does not appear in the drawing.

[2] Prologue to *The Gates of Paradise*, p. 569.

evitable outgrowth of worldly systems—blot out the face of the sun. This illustration, then, presents Blake's conviction that Dante's vision is partial and that he tends at crucial times to be guided by traditionalism and to be blind to divine revelation.

79. THE ANGEL MARKING DANTE WITH THE SEVENFOLD "P"

> . . . Up the trinal steps
> My leader cheerly drew me. "Ask," said he,
> "With humble heart, that he unbar the bolt."
> Piously at his holy feet devolved
> I cast me, praying him for pity's sake
> That he would open to me; but first fell
> Thrice on my bosom prostrate. Seven times
> The letter, that denotes the inward stain,
> He, on my forehead, with the blunted point
> Of his drawn sword, inscribed. And "Look," he cried,
> "When enter'd, that thou wash these scars away."
>
> Purgatorio IX, 95-105

THE SETTING is much the same as the upper right portion of the preceding drawing. The gate is closer now, and but little of the foreground terrace is visible; however, the sea still appears to the left with sunlight filtering through the clouds above and reflecting from the surface of the water.

The three varicolored steps are in the foreground. Dante has climbed them and now kneels on the top step; he faces the angel and his hands are joined in supplication. The angel stands under the arch of the doorway and with the point of his sword traces the letters on Dante's brow. Both his hands hold the blade of the sword and the hilt may be seen above his head. Virgil stands just behind him to the right, his hands folded on his breast as he watches. The angel has partly spread his wings so that they frame his head and Virgil's as well.

The text is followed closely and the symbolism is merely an extension of that of the previous illustration. Dante now kneels in subjection to Urizen before entering the Cave of Sleep which will lead to the Fall. As a result, the sun has now completely disappeared and only the light which gleams from behind the rocky wall and reflects on the surface of the water testifies to its presence. The sword is, of course, the Natural Sword, emblematic of warfare, the characteristic evil of the Fallen World.[1]

[1] The angel here is to be identified with the "Covering Cherub" who guards the Tree of Life with a sword and whom Frye (*Fearful Symmetry*, pp. 137-141) describes as "man's Selfhood or desire to assert rather than create."

80. THE ROCK SCULPTURED WITH THE RECOVERY OF THE ARK AND THE ANNUNCIATION

AFTER HAVING been admitted into Purgatory by the angel who unlocks the gate for them, Dante and Virgil climb upward for a long time through a narrow passage and finally come out upon a ledge which runs entirely around the mountain, but which is only five or six yards wide. One side of the ledge borders upon the void and the other is formed by a perpendicular cliff of white marble. Upon this are sculptured three scenes: the Annunciation, the Recovery of the Ark, and the story of Trajan and the Widow. All are examples of humility, set up as an object lesson for the Proud who expiate their sin at this level of Purgatory. The description of the ledge and of the sculpture will be found in *Purgatorio* x, lines 13-89.

Dante and Virgil stand upon the narrow ledge conversing and pointing to the sculptured scenes before them. To their left is seen the precipice with the sea far below; the cliff with its carved reliefs is at the right, and above it the mountain side recedes. Only two of the sculptured scenes are shown, these being the Recovery of the Ark at the left and the Annunciation at the right. It should be noted that Blake has reversed the scenes, for in the text the Annunciation is described as being to the left.

The description of the Annunciation in the poem is very general. Blake has shown it much in the manner in which it frequently appears in the late Gothic art of northern Europe. The Virgin sits at a desk with a book before her, and turns to look over her shoulder at the angel who approaches from behind. The hovering angel recalls many similar figures in Blake's work; tongues of flame form an aura behind his head.

On the other hand, Dante describes the scene of the Recovery of the Ark in considerable detail. The passage is quoted here for comparison with the illustration.

> There, in the self-same marble, were engraved
> The cart and kine, drawing the sacred ark,
> That from unbidden office awes mankind.
> Before it came much people; and the whole
> Parted in seven quires. One sense cried "Nay,"
> Another, "Yes, they sing." Like doubt arose
> Betwixt the eye and smell, from the curl'd fume
> Of incense breathing up the well-wrought toil.
> Preceding the blest vessel, onward came
> With light dance leaping, girt in humble guise,
> Israel's sweet harper: in that hap he seem'd
> Less, and yet more, than kingly. Opposite,
> At a great palace, from the lattice forth
> Look'd Michol, like a lady full of scorn
> And sorrow.
>
> Purgatorio x, 50-64

Dante's account, which Blake has followed closely, is not strictly in accord with that of the Bible, in that two separate episodes are combined. While Dante does not mention Uzzah by name, he certainly alludes to him in line 52, and Blake has shown him behind the cart at the moment when he is smitten by lightning which issues from the ark.[1] In the Biblical account, at the time of the smiting of Uzzah the ark was mounted upon an ox-cart; however, because of his fear engendered by Uzzah's fate,

---

[1] Damon, *William Blake*, p. 219: "We also see the Ark guarded by the Cherubim, from between whose wings darts an electric flame smiting a follower, so that he falls backward in the same ecstasy as William and Robert in *Milton*." [The reference here is to the designs of plates 29 and 33 of *Milton*.]

David then ordered the ark to be carried to the house of one of his followers, where it remained for a period of three months. At the end of this time, the signs being propitious, David caused it to be borne into the city by the Levites. It was on this occasion that, as David danced before the ark, Michal, the daughter of Saul, observed him from the palace window and despised him in her heart.[2] She and the dancing David both appear at the left of the relief.

Of particular interest here are the two angels which float facing each other above the ark, their hands folded in prayer and their wings meeting above their heads. While they follow very closely the description given in the Bible of the golden cherubim placed above the mercy seat,[3] they have a further significance for Blake who frequently portrays in this manner the Daughters of Beulah as they watch over the Fallen Humanity.[4] Their identification is clearly established by the following passage:

> The Fallen Man stretch'd like a corse upon the oozy Rock,
> Wash'd with the tides, pale, overgrown with weeds
> That mov'd with horrible dreams; hovering high over his head
> Two winged immortal shapes, one standing at his feet
> Towards the East, one standing at his head toward the west,
> Their wings join'd in the Zenith over head;   .   .   .
>
> .   .   .   .
>
> Their wings touch'd the heavens; their fair feet hover'd above
> The swelling tides; they bent over the dead corse like an arch,
> Pointed at top in highest heavens, of precious stones & pearl.
> Such is a Vision of All Beulah hov'ring over the Sleeper.
>
> Four Zoas VIII, 4-9; 12-15 (p. 331)

We have seen in our discussion of the previous designs that Blake equates Purgatory with Beulah. On the basis of the above quotation, it is reasonably certain that here he intends the ark to represent the sleeping form of the Fallen Albion, guarded over by the Emanations. As early as 1788, in one of his annotations to Lavater's *Aphorisms on Man*, Blake had made this connection: "Man is the ark of God; the mercy seat is above, upon the ark; cherubims guard it on either side, & in the midst is the holy law; man is either the ark of God or a phantom of the earth & of the water; if thou seekest by human policy to guide this ark, remember Uzzah."[5]

Thus we have here another representation of the soul in Beulah. At the head of the ark dances the psalmist who reminds us that through art and imagination man can regain Eden; Uzzah, however, who reaches out to the law for his support, is smitten, for it is in Beulah also that the Fall begins. Michal, the daughter of Saul, who looks upon her warrior husband with contempt at the time of his prophetic ecstasy is, of

[2] II Samuel vi, 2-16. A very similar but somewhat more extended account will be found in I Chronicles, chapters xiii and xv; the latter version makes more explicit the fact that, when David brought the ark to the city, it was borne by the Levites and not mounted on an ox-cart.

[3] Exodus xxv, 18-20.

[4] See, for example, the drawing "Angels Hovering over the Body of Jesus" (Figgis, *Paintings of William Blake*, plate 48) and the illustration to Blair's *Grave*, "The meeting of a Family in Heaven."

[5] *Poetry and Prose*, p. 727. For the ark, see also *ibid.*, p. 569 (Prologue to *The Gates of Paradise*) and *Jerusalem* 75, 15.

course, a perfect example of the Female Will. "I have mock'd those who refused cruelty, & I have admired the cruel Warrior." So Michal, who loved David when he won her to wife by presenting to Saul two hundred foreskins of the Philistines, now scorns him as a visionary.[6]

It seems clear, therefore, that Blake intends in this design to represent the Divine and Fallen aspects of Female Love. Opposed to the Female Will of Michal is the true love of the Madonna, to whom the angel of imagination pays tribute.[7] Michal and the Virgin become, in terms of Blake's mythology, representations of Vala and Jerusalem respectively. Thus the position of the reliefs has been changed from that described by Dante, the spiritual aspect of love now appearing properly on the right.

In closing, it should be recalled that Blake regarded sculpture, the most permanent physically of the creative arts, as a supreme symbol of eternal truth made manifest through imagination to man in the Fallen World. Thus Dante's description of the sculptured reliefs seen by him and Virgil upon the mountain had undoubtedly in itself a special significance in Blake's mind.

> All things acted on Earth are seen in the bright Sculptures of
> Los's Halls, & every Age renews its powers from these Works
> With every pathetic story possible to happen from Hate or
> Wayward Love; & every sorrow & distress is carved here,
> Every Affinity of Parents, Marriages & Friendships are here
> In all their various combinations wrought with wondrous Art,
> All that can happen to Man in his pilgrimage of seventy years.[8]
>
> Jerusalem 16, 61-67

[6] *Jerusalem* 81, 1-2. I Samuel xviii, 20-27.

[7] In *A Vision of the Last Judgment*, p. 643, Blake describes Mary as "ignorant of crime in the midst of a corrupted Age."

[8] The well-known story, told by Blake at a dinner party, concerning sculptured sheep (Gilchrist, *Life*, I, pp. 362-363) is another example of his identification of sculpture with the representation in artistic form of eternal truth.

81. THE PROUD UNDER THEIR ENORMOUS LOADS

CANTOS X, XI, and XII are all concerned with the ledge of Purgatory which is devoted to the punishment of the Proud. After having admired the rock sculptures, Dante and Virgil observe a group of people coming toward them who are moving in a doubled-up position. When they draw closer, they are seen to have heavy stones upon their backs which force them to walk bowed down and to look at the ground. In reply to Virgil's request for directions to the next stairs up which they can continue their ascent of the mountain, one of the burdened indicates the route and identifies himself as Omberto Aldobrandesco, Count of Santafiora, who has been placed here to expiate the sin of family pride. Another spirit then speaks to Dante, who recognizes him as Oderisi d'Agobbio, a noted miniature painter who had been inordinately proud of his skill. Dante walks along beside him for a time; they converse further and Oderisi points out another of the Proud whom he identifies as Provenzan Salvani, a Sienese leader at the time of the Battle of Montaperti. Dante and Virgil then leave the Proud, whose pace is slow owing to their loads, and go on ahead in search of the upward path.

Although the poem indicates that all of this scene takes place on a flat, narrow ledge as shown in the previous illustration, Blake shows the Proud climbing with the occasional aid of their hands up a steep path with steps like a flight of stairs. The sheer side of the mountain ascends to the left and at the right of the path a high rocky bank rises like a wall between the pathway and the edge of the cliff. Dante and Virgil stand near the bank at the foot of the path, looking at the figures who are climbing. Virgil gestures upward with his right hand and Dante stoops slightly in order better to see one of the Proud who, holding a huge rock on his back and walking almost on all fours, twists his head around in order to look at the poets.[1] Just behind this figure and close to the cliff is another burdened form and further up the path two more may be seen. The steps curve out of sight near the upper left of the page. The portion of the design on the right is taken up by a view over the sea. In the dark sky above, the moon is just about to set and streaks of moonlight are reflected from the surface of the water. The moon is in a crescent phase, but the full disk can be faintly discerned between its horns.

If we go back to the beginning of the tenth canto we shall find that the description of the narrow path up which Dante and Virgil climb from the gate of Purgatory to the Circle of the Proud fits well with that shown here. By depicting the Proud in this defile, Blake seems to link pride with the choice by Dante of the narrow path of the law. Regeneration in all of Blake's prophecies comes only after the annihilation of the selfhood; and pride is, of course, the particular sin of Fallen Man. In our discussions of drawings 78 and 79, we saw how Dante turned his back upon the sun of imagination to pass through the gate of rationalism. Now that he has entered upon the path of the Moral Law, he at once encounters the spirits of pride. Similarly, ever since Dante made his choice the sky has been darkened and now the moon of Beulah is about to set.[2] This indicates that we are approaching the limit of Beulah which heralds the Fall, as opposed to that shown in Drawing 77 when the return to Eden seemed to be at hand.

> In one night the Atlantic Continent was caught up with the Moon
> And became an Opake Globe far distant, clad with moony beams.
> The Visions of Eternity, by reason of narrowed perceptions,
> Are become weak Visions of Time & Space, fix'd into furrows of death.
>
> .   .   .   .
>
> Ah! weak & wide astray! Ah! shut in narrow doleful form!
> Creeping in reptile flesh upon the bosom of the ground!
> The Eye of Man, a little narrow orb, clos'd up & dark,
> Scarcely beholding the Great Light, conversing with the ground.
>
> Jerusalem 49, 19-22; 32-35

[1] This figure so closely resembles Oderisi d'Agobbio as he is described in the poem (xi, 73-81) that Blake doubtless had him in mind.

[2] Wicksteed (*Blake's Vision of the Book of Job*, p. 49n.) points out that Blake's representations of heavenly bodies are always ideal, being based upon symbolic rather than astronomical considerations. Thus the moon has waned considerably here, although only the night before in Drawing 77 it was shown as full. Conversely, Dante takes great pains to be astronomically consistent in his poem.

Numerous details of this drawing are still in pencil. In spite of the unfinished character of the washes, a fine effect is obtained of moonlight upon the surface of the dark sea.

82. THE ANGEL DESCENDING AT THE CLOSE OF THE CIRCLE OF THE PROUD

After Dante and Virgil leave the group of the Proud burdened by their heavy loads and pass on in search of the ascent to the next ledge, Virgil calls Dante's attention to the surface of the path on which they are walking. The entire roadway from the cliff to the edge is carved in low relief with scenes depicting those who fell through pride; they are so placed in order to be visible to the Proud as they walk with faces bowed down under their burdens. Examining the reliefs, Dante observes Lucifer, Briareus, Nimrod, Saul, Sennacherib, Holofernes, and numerous others. Presently Virgil calls Dante's attention to an angel who appears hurrying toward them; when he comes close, he reveals to the poets the steps which lead upward. The incidents illustrated here will be found in *Purgatorio* XII, lines 9-86.

Dante and Virgil are to be seen at the lower left, their backs turned as they advance along the path. Virgil raises his left arm above his head and rests his right hand solicitously on Dante's shoulder; Dante gestures toward the sculpture. The wall of the mountain rises steeply at the left and to the right the cliff falls away precipitously to the sea far below. The path curves around in the center background and beyond it more of the sea can be seen, stretching across the page. In the top center the angel appears running swiftly along the ledge toward the poets, with arms and wings outspread. His body hides the sun from view; rays of light pierce through the clouds behind and shine upon the surface of the water.

The most interesting feature of this illustration is the sculpture upon the path. Only a few of those listed in the text as being represented here can be recognized and all of them are deeply involved with Blake's personal symbolism. At the bottom of the page, in an upside down position and entwined in the coils of a serpent, lies Lucifer; he is shown crowned and with three faces as in the last of the designs to the *Inferno*. To his right and at the very edge of the cliff a figure lies upon a brick or masonry tower to which it is tightly bound by the coils of another serpent: this must be Nimrod.[1] The other forms cannot be identified, unless the group of many wild-looking heads from which rise arms bearing swords is intended to represent the giant Briareus, to whom legend ascribes fifty heads and a hundred arms. It is more likely, however, that this group symbolizes the violence and cruelty of the Fallen World in which men who have lost the gift of vision war against each other. Above the swords squats the crowned and bearded form of Urizen; next to him is Vala, the Goddess of Nature.[2] Surrounding the entire group, and most noticeable at the base of the cliff and above the seated figure of Urizen, is a large rope. This is doubtless intended to represent the edge of the Net of Natural Religion in which those in the Fallen World are en-

[1] See discussion of Drawing 61 above.

[2] Save for being reversed, this figure is much like that of a representation of Vala in the manuscript of *The Four Zoas* (reproduced in Keynes, *Bibliography*, f.p. 36).

meshed; the webbing of the net is lightly indicated in pencil at the upper right of the path.[3]

These forms carved upon the pathway are, of course, to be identified in symbolism with those previously shown as petrified in rock bridges or frozen beneath the ice.[4] Blake has included in the group kings, warriors, the all-devouring reason, the Female Will, and Satan—in short, those who in his mythology set material things above spiritual, and whose blind avarice leads to the death of the soul, to the Fall, and to war. Only the love of God as revealed to man through vision can save those in the Fallen World, and thus the angel appears outlined against the sun of Eden.

[3] The Net of Natural Religion is shown much as here—only more clearly—in the design on the last page of *The Book of Urizen*, in which Urizen appears tangled up in it. Folio 8r of the manuscript of *The Four Zoas* also shows an aged man in a similar situation. For a description of the Web of Religion, see *Urizen*, 459-476 (p. 232).

[4] This illustration, in which Virgil shows the sculptured reliefs to Dante, should also be compared with the twentieth design of the Job series in which Job points out to his daughters pictures representing the terrors of the Fallen World.

83. THE SOULS OF THE ENVIOUS

THIS ILLUSTRATION is based upon Canto XIII. Having arrived upon the ledge of the Mountain of Purgatory where the Envious expiate their sin, Dante and Virgil set out in search of the path upward to the next terrace. As they go along they hear voices whose source they cannot discover citing texts associated with generous love. These, being intended as an example for the Envious, fulfill the same function as did the sculptures of the previous ledge. After a time they come upon a group of the Envious Souls seated upon the ground and leaning upon each other and against the face of the cliff. Their punishment is to have their eyelids sewn shut with wire so that they cannot see the Divine Light; from beneath their closed lids tears well out. Dante speaks to them and asks if any are Italian. One of them identifies herself as Sapia of Siena and tells Dante how she sinned by rejoicing more in the misfortunes of others than in her own good fortune. She asks Dante to bid her relatives pray for her when he returns to earth.

This drawing is entirely in pencil and is one of the most sketchy of the entire series; its symbolical significance for Blake is apparent: the tragic lot of those who permit material cares and interests to blind them to spiritual light. The setting is much like that of Drawing 80: the cliff rises to the right, the ledge is in the center, and to the left is the sea. Light clouds fill the sky and rays of sunlight filter through them; the sun is so high in the sky as to be out of sight. Dante and Virgil stand at the edge of the path near the cliff. Leaning against the cliff at the right and against each other are the blinded spirits; most of them stand, although in the text they are described as seated. Above them is what appears to be a cleft in the face of the rock in which more forms can be seen. Everything in this passage is so indistinct that it is impossible to be sure what Blake wished to represent. Either these are souls climbing to the next ledge up one of the narrow stairs or they are intended to indicate the invisible spirits from whom the mysterious voices proceed. From the group of those below who lean against the cliff, one form has detached itself and floats gracefully and lightly toward Dante. This represents the spirit of Sapia of Siena; the figure recalls the hovering cherubim above the ark in the eightieth illustration.

84. THE ANGEL INVITING DANTE TO ENTER THE FIRE

THIS DRAWING illustrates lines 5-42 of Canto XXVII of the *Purgatorio*. A considerable number of cantos have passed since the last design and Dante and Virgil have now reached the seventh and topmost ledge. Here the Lustful undergo purgation in flames which shoot out from the base of the rock wall. In order to proceed, Dante and Virgil must keep very close to the precipice, as there the wind blowing up the mountain side beats the flames back. They are now accompanied by the shade of Statius, a Roman poet of the first century after Christ, who has just been released from Purgatory and is on his way upward to Paradise. As they reach the end of the ledge, an angel appears and informs them that they can go no farther without passing through the fire. Dante hangs back in terror and, to reassure him, Virgil tells him that while the fire may give pain, if he should remain in it for a thousand years not a hair would be singed. Dante still hesitates, but finally enters the fire when Virgil informs him that he will find Beatrice on the other side.

A vast expanse of sea appears at the right. On the horizon the sun is just setting (XXVII, 6); only a small portion of its disk remains above the water and five rays from it light up the sky.[1] To the left is the narrow path which is shown as a flight of stairs, although in the text Dante passes through the fire before reaching them. Flames clothe the side of the mountain as described, forcing the poets to walk near the edge. At the top of the steps the fire reaches right across the path, and just in front of it the angel is seen as though hovering slightly above the steps. His left arm is raised and with his right he indicates the way through the flames which the poets are to take. In the center of the group of three at the bottom of the steps is Dante, his face raised to look at the fire and his hands clasped in dismay above his head. Statius follows behind him and Virgil, who is a step ahead, looks back. Both exhort Dante with gestures to do the angel's bidding.

Having now reached the upper limit of Beulah, Dante is brought face to face with the fact that salvation can be achieved only by passing through the purging fire of imagination. Still beset by rational doubts, he hangs back, but is urged on by his spiritual guides. As this is still Beulah, the sun of Eden is as yet only partially visible. In some such terms as these, no doubt, Blake equated Dante's vision with his own.

It is significant that both *The Four Zoas* and *Jerusalem* end with scenes in which the soul is purged with fire just before its reunion with God.[2] The similarity of this episode of the *Divine Comedy* must have impressed Blake and he no doubt regarded the passage through the fire as a significant climax of Dante's journey. The soul, won over by love, summons the boldness to throw itself into the flames, only to find that its fears were but an illusion. At the close of *Jerusalem*, the regeneration of Albion

[1] Wicksteed (*Blake's Vision of the Book of Job*, p. 121) has suggested that in the eighteenth Job design the presence of a greater number of rays on the sun's right side than on its left is an indication that the spiritual sun of Eden is represented. It will be noted that the same is true here.

[2] See the design to plate 99 of *Jerusalem* in which the soul is reunited with God amid flames.

is accomplished in precisely this manner, following upon his recognition of error through the example of Jesus' denial of the selfhood.

> So Albion spoke & threw himself into the Furnaces of affliction.
> All was a Vision, all a Dream: the Furnaces became
> Fountains of Living Waters flowing from the Humanity Divine.
> And all the Cities of Albion rose from their Slumbers, and All
> The Sons & Daughters of Albion on soft clouds, waking from Sleep.
> Soon all around remote the Heavens burnt with flaming fires,
> And Urizen & Luvah & Tharmas & Urthona arose into
> Albion's Bosom. Then Albion stood before Jesus in the Clouds
> Of Heaven, Fourfold among the Visions of God in Eternity.
>
> *Jerusalem* 96, 35-43

85. DANTE AT THE MOMENT OF ENTERING THE FIRE

THIS ILLUSTRATION shows the same episode as the preceding one, only Dante has now approached much closer to the fire. Virgil has already stepped into the flames and he and the angel both urge Dante to follow, but Dante still hesitates.

The face of the cliff, with vine-like vegetation on its surface, occupies most of the bottom of the page; to the left is a small glimpse of the sea, with a cloudless but dark sky above. To the right the face of the mountain rises steeply.[1] At the foot of it, upon the narrow path, stand Dante and Statius; above them against the mountainside is a tree. Dante stands to the left of Statius, his hands clasped above his head, as he looks apprehensively at the fire. Just to his left the flames begin, covering the entire width of the ledge and licking upward across the face of the mountain. Virgil already stands within the first flame; he looks back over his shoulder at Dante and extends his right hand to him to encourage him to follow. Above Virgil's head, the angel hovers in the flame, with hands spread in a graceful solicitous gesture and with an expression of watchful and tender sympathy; the angel's wings are raised behind and blend into the shape of the flame. Within the flames to the left of Virgil and the angel, four female figures float in varied poses as though engaged in a dance.[2]

Virgil is here to be regarded as the eternal poet, walking amidst the flames of intellect and encouraging his earthly counterpart, Dante, to accompany him.[3] Virgil bears the same relationship to Dante in this drawing as does Los to Blake in the design

[1] It will be noted that the positions of the mountain and of the sea have been reversed from those shown in the previous illustration, although consistency would require them to be the same; also, the steps are not shown. As the two drawings illustrate the same passage of text, it is perhaps unlikely that Blake originally planned two illustrations of this episode. Rather, as in the case with the two versions of Cerberus, it seems probable that he was not altogether pleased with his first effort, and so repeated the subject. This explanation would account for the very incomplete character of the preceding drawing as compared to the highly finished state of the present one.

[2] These forms recall the principal figure in the engraving for Milton's *L'Allegro*, "Mirth and her Companions" (reproduced in L. Binyon, *The Engraved Designs of William Blake*, London and New York, 1926, plate 14; Keynes, *Engravings*, plate 41).

[3] "I was walking among the fires of hell, delighted with the enjoyments of Genius, which to Angels look like torment and insanity." (*Marriage of Heaven and Hell*, p. 183) Compare also *Four Zoas* IX, 842 (p. 371): "How is it that we have walk'd thro' fires & yet are not consum'd?"

of page 21 of *Milton*.[4] It will be noted that the angel who hovers over Virgil within the same flame is now distinctly feminine in appearance and is to be identified as his Emanation, Enitharmon. She and Los urge Dante to take the bold step into the flames of inspiration but, in the created world beneath the Tree of Mystery, the earthly poet hesitates. Statius is shown as a small figure with back turned and was probably intended by Blake to be thought of as feminine—the Emanation of the poet of this world as the angel is that of the eternal poet.

The four female figures clad in almost transparent garments are the Daughters of Beulah or Inspiration; they symbolize the complete joyous liberty of that active intellectual and spiritual life which opens the gateway of Eden,[5] and whom the poet will find when he leaves the temporal and vegetative world to enter the fires of imagination. It should be noted that there is no mention of them in the *Divine Comedy* and that Blake has thus clearly introduced them for purposes of his own. Just as in the Bible the three figures who are cast into the burning fiery furnace become four, so do they here; in Blake's terms, this represents the transformation of the threefold realm of Beulah into the fourfold world of Eden.[6]

The light upward movement of the flames and of the figures within them is beautifully portrayed. The graceful motion within the flames, contrasted with the static areas outside and with the angular pose of Dante, serves to emphasize the conflict between imaginative confidence and rational doubt which is the symbolical significance of the illustration. Save for a few minor details, this is a finished watercolor.[7]

[4] This comparison has also been made in connection with Drawing 70.

[5] "Imagination is surrounded by the daughters of Inspiration, who in the aggregate are call'd Jerusalem." (*Vision of the Last Judgment*, p. 638.)

[6] Daniel iii, 24-25; see also Frye, *Fearful Symmetry*, p. 300. The four women also appear accompanying Los in the design of plate 15 of *Milton*, in which both they and the poet carry musical instruments.

[7] The British Museum has a pencil sketch (9¾ x 11¾ in.) of this design, much as it appears in its final form. Although listed in the catalogue, its connection with this illustration is not noted, nor even that the subject is derived from the *Divine Comedy*. See L. Binyon, *Catalogue of Drawings by British Artists . . . preserved in the Department of Prints and Drawings in the British Museum*, London, 1900, I, p. 126, no. 17.

86. DANTE AND STATIUS SLEEPING, VIRGIL WATCHING

> Nor many stairs were overpast, when now
> By fading of the shadow we perceived
> The sun behind us couch'd; and ere one face
> Of darkness o'er its measureless expanse
> Involved the horizon, and the night her lot
> Held individual, each of us had made
> A stair his pallet; not that will, but power,
> Had fail'd us, by the nature of that mount
> Forbidden further travel.　　.　　.　　.　　.
>
> 　　.　　.　　.　　.　　.　　.　　.　　.
>
> A little glimpse of sky was seen above;

Yet by that little I beheld the stars,
In magnitude and lustre shining forth
With more than wonted glory. As I lay,
Gazing on them, and in that fit of musing,
Sleep overcame me, sleep, that bringeth oft
Tidings of future hap. About the hour,
As I believe, when Venus from the east
First lighten'd on the mountain, she whose orb
Seems always glowing with the fire of love,
A lady young and beautiful, I dream'd,
Was passing o'er a lea; and, as she came,
Methought I saw her ever and anon
Bending to cull the flowers; and thus she sang:
"Know ye, whoever of my name would ask,
That I am Leah: for my brow to weave
A garland, these fair hands unwearied ply,
To please me at the crystal mirror, here
I deck me. But my sister Rachel, she
Before her glass abides the livelong day,
Her radiant eyes beholding, charm'd no less,
Than I with this delightful task. Her joy
In contemplation, as in labour mine."

Purgatorio xxvii, 68-76; 88-110

THE STAIRS rise in the center of the design, curving to the left slightly so that they disappear just above the middle of the page. The side of the mountain is at the left. Between it and the stairs is a low bank covered with foliage; the right edge of the flight of steps also terminates in a low bank upon which a leafy vine is growing.[1] Beyond this bank, the cliff falls away precipitously to the sea, a narrow strip of which is to be seen at the right. On the steps the three poets recline. Statius is at the bottom, Dante in the middle, and at the top Virgil leans on his left arm and gazes upward in contemplation.

The most interesting feature of the illustration is the enormous full moon. Bright rays shine out from it and its light gleams on the water. Four large stars appear below it. Lightly sketched within the disk of the moon is Dante's vision of Rachel and Leah. At the left Rachel sits looking at herself in the mirror, while at the right Leah is seated beneath a tree.[2]

Night has fallen and the moon and stars of Beulah now shine upon the scene.[3] After

[1] The text (xxvii, 87) implies, however, that the banks were high on both sides.

[2] There are two inscriptions in pencil within the disk of the moon, but the writing is so faint as to be difficult to decipher. That to the right of the mirror among the leaves is probably "Leah and Rachel," while that in the lower center close to the figure of Leah appears to be "Dante's Dream."

[3] There is no mention in the poem of the moon being visible at this time; it now being Tuesday night or early Wednesday morning after Easter (Rev. H. F. Tozer, *An English Commentary on Dante's Divina Commedia*, Oxford, 1901, p. 358), the moon would be well past the full. This is another example of Blake's disregard of all but symbolic considerations in his portrayal of heavenly bodies.

160

passing through the intense fires of Eden, the poets rest. As they do so, the dangers inherent in the Caves of Sleep are shown to them in a vision of feminine passivity. The creeping vegetation also serves as a reminder that when rest leads to inaction instead of to the restoration of energy, the Fall begins.

Rachel and Leah, as the text quoted makes plain, symbolize the active and the passive life. The tasks in which they are engaged would, however, be interpreted by Blake as selfish: one gathers flowers for the purpose of adorning herself and the other admires her beauty in the mirror. Inaction and satisfaction with one's own perfection are prime evils of the selfhood and as such herald the Fall, which comes in terms of Blake's mythology with the dominance of that passive attitude of mind which he identifies with the feminine aspect of the human personality.[4] To emphasize the dangers of this state, Blake has taken a characteristic liberty with the text. Rachel appears much as described—"a self-contemplating shadow"[5] seated before her mirror, in which her reflection may be seen; Leah, however, is not shown walking as she gathers flowers, but is seated upon the ground beneath the Tree of Error and Mystery.[6]

This drawing is approaching completion; however, details of the foliage and of the vision in the moon are unfinished. In spite of this, the design is decoratively one of the most beautiful in the series. The pale brilliance of the moonlight and the weirdly graceful foliage give the entire composition a mysterious unearthly quality as of the dream itself.[7]

[4] "Active Evil is better than Passive Good." (Annotation to Lavater's *Aphorisms*, p. 721.)
[5] *Urizen*, line 28 (p. 220).   [6] See also note 15 to Drawing 88 below.
[7] For a comment upon this design by W. B. Yeats, see *Ideas of Good and Evil*, p. 195.

87. BEATRICE ON THE CAR, DANTE AND MATILDA

THIS ILLUSTRATION, although inscribed "P-g- Canto 29," is actually based upon Cantos XXVIII, XXIX, and XXX. Having reached the Terrestrial Paradise, Dante finds himself at the edge of a beautiful forest, the floor of which is covered with flowers. Virgil and Statius follow him as he enters. After going only a short distance, they come to a clear stream which winds through the wood. Pausing by its bank, Dante looks across and sees on the opposite shore a beautiful young woman who is gathering flowers and singing as she does so. She is later identified as Matilda, countess of Tuscany and supporter of Pope Gregory VII in his contentions with the Holy Roman Empire.[1] In reply to Dante's inquiries, she tells him whence comes the wind which blows through the trees and the water which forms the stream which she identifies as Lethe. She then starts to walk upstream, Dante keeping pace with her upon the other bank. After they have gone a short distance, she calls Dante's attention to a light in the forest, which grows in brightness. As they draw nearer, Dante believes that he sees seven trees of gold, but these turn out to be candlesticks which, as they move, leave behind

[1] *Purgatorio* XXXIII, 119. There has been considerable controversy concerning which Matilda Dante had in mind. Here, as in other questions of identification throughout the series, I follow Paget Toynbee, *A Dictionary of Proper Names and Notable Matters in the Works of Dante*, Oxford, 1898.

them in the air bands of color like banners. Behind the torches march twenty-four elders two by two and after them comes a chariot drawn by a gryphon and surrounded by the four beasts of Ezekiel's vision, having wings filled with eyes. The gryphon's wings rise up out of sight, passing between the streams of light left behind by the torches. Alongside the right wheel of the chariot three women dance in a ring, one of them being red, one green, and one white; by the other wheel are four women clad in purple, of whom the leader has three eyes. Behind the chariot, seven more male figures bring up the rear. When the car is abreast of Dante, the procession stops and bursts into song. A hundred angelic ministers rise from the car, strewing flowers, and in the cloud of petals Dante first sees Beatrice standing upon the chariot.[2]

As may be gathered from the above brief synopsis, this is a tremendously complex scene to illustrate, and yet Blake manages both to show it quite literally and also to create a composition which gives harmony to the many figures and which, with its sweeping curves and rich yet extremely delicate coloring, suggests much of the splendor and visionary character of the poet's description.

The stream winds across the design in an s-curve; by its edge in the foreground stands Dante. Two trees rise gracefully in the right foreground, their branches arching across the top of the page to meet those of another tree which stands at the extreme left upon the farther bank. Behind Dante and between the two trees stand Virgil and Statius. Grass and flowering plants cover the ground.

Directly opposite Dante on the other bank of the stream, Matilda stands looking toward him. Behind her is the procession. The candelabrum is seen at the left next to the tree. Its stem is like the trunk of a palm tree, from which branches spring, each supporting an angel who tends one of the seven flames. From the torches bands of colored light stream entirely across the page, and reflections of the flames can be seen in the water. The candelabrum rests upon a bank of cloud which trails backward, supporting the entire procession; another bank of cloud appears above the chariot.

Two angels carrying books stand beside the candelabrum and behind them is the procession of elders, an indistinct group whose number cannot be counted. Seen in profile in the center of the design is the chariot. The gryphon draws it, his wings rising up until lost from sight in the clouds above. The wings with eyes flank the car, upon which Beatrice stands. The forms of the beasts can be faintly seen surrounding her; the eyes of their wings are reflected in the stream between Matilda and Dante. The left wheel of the car is shown in the form of a fiery vortex.[3] Beside it the four women described in the text dance in a ring. The hundred angelic ministers are not shown, but the shower of petals is indicated just to the left of the wings of the gryphon. The group which follows the chariot is very accurately portrayed. First come two aged men, one bearing a sword; then a group of four; and finally, well separated from the rest, the single figure who is seen in the distance between the two trees.

[2] For the symbolism of this scene as probably intended by Dante, see John D. Sinclair (ed.), *The Divine Comedy of Dante Aligheri*, London, 1948, II, pp. 373-375, 387-390; Rev. J. S. Carroll, *Prisoners of Hope*, London, 1906, pp. 376-432; Tozer, *Commentary*, pp. 367-377. As we shall see in our discussion of this and of the following design, Blake interprets much of this vision in terms of his own mythology.

[3] See discussion of the following design.

In spite of the closeness with which Blake follows the poem, there are a number of features which indicate the presence of his own symbolism. We shall first consider the candelabrum, with its trunk like a palm tree and angels in its branches. Just as the oak represents error and the Fall,[4] so the palm tree, whose branches were strewn before Christ as He rode into Jerusalem to die, is a symbol of forgiveness and salvation. Thus in the fine design on page 37 of *Jerusalem* the trunk of a palm tree is seen beside the kneeling figure of Christ, who is supporting the body of Albion as he faints beneath an oak. The Fall both begins and ends in Beulah, and hence both these trees grow there:

> He stood between the Palm tree & the Oak of Weeping
> Which stand upon the edge of Beulah.
>
> Jerusalem 23, 24-25

At the Fall, the Eternals ordained the Seven Eyes of God to watch over Man in his journey of sorrow, and to be messengers of God's love in order to save him from annihilation.[5] These eyes, or lights, representative of God's forgiveness, are borne by the Daughters of Beulah, the loving Emanations who guard the eternal but sleeping Humanity of the Fallen Man.

> . . . Then they Elected Seven, called the Seven
> Eyes of God & the Seven Lamps of the Almighty.
> The Seven are one within the other; the Seventh is named Jesus,
> The Lamb of God, blessed for ever, & he follow'd the Man
> Who wander'd in mount Ephraim seeking a Sepulcher,
> His inward eyes closing from the Divine vision, & all
> His children wandering outside, from his bosom fleeing away.
>
> Four Zoas I, 545-551 (pp. 266-267)

The candelabrum with the palm trunk and angels tending the lights is, therefore, symbolic of the divine love and compassion which watches over Man in the Fallen World.[6] On the other hand, as will be seen in the discussion of the next design, Beatrice on the car is clearly intended to represent the Female Will. Thus this illustration presents, somewhat in the same manner as Drawing 80, the contrast between the eternal and fallen aspects of feminine love. Matilda here symbolizes Dante's earthly Emanation and behind her appear visions of spiritual and selfish love.[7] The next design shows Dante paying homage to the Female Will. Thus again Blake presents his view, as so often in these illustrations, that when confronted with a choice between the pathway of conventional error or of imaginative truth, Dante is likely to choose

[4] As, for instance, in Drawing 76 of this series.

[5] For the Seven Eyes of God, see Frye, *Fearful Symmetry*, p. 128.

[6] . . . Seven . . . loves attend each night
Around my couch with torches bright.
MS poem, p. 105

[7] In Beulah, the sexes have divided; it will be noted that only men are on the nearer bank and that the most important figures on the farther shore are women. The fact that, in the procession, "states" are represented is indicated by the clouds which separate the space of the vision from that of the rest of the design.

the former.[8] In this lies Dante's fundamental lack of vision which, in spite of his greatness as a poet, made him in Blake's eyes "an 'Atheist,' a mere politician busied about this world."[9]

[8] As in Drawings 78 and 79. It will be noted also that in Drawings 84 and 85 Blake does not show Dante actually entering the fire of imagination; in both cases he draws back.

[9] A remark, as already noted in the introduction, made by Blake to Henry Crabb Robinson; quoted from Symons, *William Blake*, p. 262. In this respect Blake would consider Dante the direct antithesis of Jesus, who "was all virtue, and acted from impulse, not from rules." (*Marriage of Heaven and Hell*, p. 191.)

88. BEATRICE ADDRESSING DANTE FROM THE CAR

> . . . After that the flowers,
> And the fresh herblets, on the opposite brink,
> Were free from that elected race; as light
> In heaven doth second light, came after them
> Four animals, each crown'd with verdurous leaf.
> With six wings each was plumed; the plumage full
> Of eyes. . . . .
>
> . . . .
> The space, surrounded by the four, enclosed
> A car triumphal: on two wheels it came,
> Drawn at a Gryphon's neck; and he above
> Stretch'd either wing uplifted, 'tween the midst
> And the three listed hues, on each side, three;
> So that the wings did cleave or injure none;
> And out of sight they rose. The members, far
> As he was bird, were golden; white the rest,
> With vermeil intervein'd. . . . . .
>
> . . . .
> . . . . . Three nymphs,
> At the right wheel, came circling in smooth dance:
> The one so ruddy, that her form had scarce
> Been known within a furnace of clear flame;
> The next did look, as if the flesh and bones
> Were emerald; snow new-fallen seem'd the third.
> >> Purgatorio XXIX, 85-91; 102-110; 116-121
>
> . . . in white veil with olive wreathed,
> A virgin in my view appear'd, beneath
> Green mantle, robed in hue of living flame.
>
> . . . .
> Towards me, across the stream, she bent her eyes;
> Though from her brow the veil descending, bound
> With foliage of Minerva, suffer'd not
> That I beheld her clearly: then with act
> Full royal, still insulting o'er her thrall,

Added, as one who, speaking, keepeth back
The bitterest saying, to conclude the speech:
"Observe me well. I am, in sooth, I am
Beatrice. What! and hast thou deign'd at last
Approach the mountain? Knewest not, O man!
Thy happiness is here?" Down fell mine eyes
On the clear fount; but there, myself espying,
Recoil'd, and sought the greenswerd; such a weight
Of shame was on my forehead. With a mien
Of that stern majesty, which doth surround
A mother's presence to her awe-struck child,
She look'd; a flavour of such bitterness
Was mingled in her pity.

Purgatorio xxx, 31-33; 64-81

THE CHARIOT appears in profile in such a manner that the right wheel is seen and the gryphon who draws it faces toward the right. Strips of cloud suggest the streaming banners of light; they are parted by the gryphon's wings, which rise up so high that the tips of them are cut off by the top of the page.[1]

At the four corners of the chariot are the four beasts with wings full of eyes. Except for the wings, only their heads are visible; these are surrounded with haloes of light. At the rear of the car is the eagle with the lion behind him; in the front we see the bull behind the angel. Between the beasts and over the wheel is a platform, all but a portion of the front edge of which is hidden behind the wheel; this edge bears a design of lotus blossoms.[2] On the platform stands Beatrice in a mandorla of light. She is crowned, and dressed in a transparent garment of mingled red and yellow, over which she wears a blue-green cloak. The wheel of the car is formed of circling flames of many hues; in form it recalls a vortex or whirlpool and, in the manner of the wheels of Ezekiel's vision, it also is full of eyes.[3] Three indistinct forms appear caught up in the whirlpool, two at the edge and one in the center.

In the foreground near the wheel are the three women whom Dante describes as dancing by the right side of the car. Two of them are near the left margin of the page. The one at the extreme left raises her hands above her head and walks on her toes; she is dressed in dark green. Next to her another stands by the wheel; she is crowned with jewels, robed in red, and is shown in much the same pose as Beatrice. Close beside her legs float five infants, shaped like roots. The third woman stands to the right of the wheel. Dressed in white, she steps toward Dante, but turns her body sharply and looks over her left shoulder at Beatrice on the car. With her right hand she

---

[1] The layer of cloud formed over the figure in the chariot serves to remind us that here, with the Female Will dominant, eternity is closed from view.

[2] Piloo Nanavutty, "A Title-Page in Blake's Illustrated Genesis Manuscript," *Journal of the Warburg and Courtauld Institutes*, x, 1947, pp. 114-122, points out that lotus blossoms are an emblem of fertility. As will be seen later in the discussion of this design, Beatrice is here to be associated with Vala, the Goddess of Nature; this symbol thus serves to support the identification.

[3] Ezekiel i, 15-18. The beasts, of course, derive from the same vision of Ezekiel; they appear again in Revelation iv, 6-9, and are the traditional symbols of the evangelists.

gestures toward Dante while, with her left, she points to a text in a book which seems to float on a cloud of bluish smoke which emanates from the vortex.

Dante is shown at the extreme right of the picture. He bows his head as he glances toward Beatrice with a guilty and pleading expression and raises his hands in a gesture of supplication. Between him and the chariot the gryphon stands impassively. Around the beast's head is a halo edged with a roll of cloud. Beneath his body some flowers appear on the ground. The sky in the upper corner is brilliantly colored in many hues.

In the *Divine Comedy*, the gryphon and Beatrice on the car symbolize Christ and the Church respectively.[4] Blake has in the main followed the highly descriptive text. However, if this drawing is compared closely with the poem, it is evident that there are a number of significant variations. On the basis of these, it eventually becomes apparent that, while the scene at first glance appears much as Dante describes it, the symbolism is entirely Blake's own and very different from that of the poem. Detailed study will show that, of all the illustrations, this is perhaps the one in which Blake's personally-contrived mythological system figures to the greatest extent.

In order to demonstrate clearly that Blake does intend to suggest his own interpretation of the subject, and that difficulties are not deliberately being sought where none exist, it will be well first to list the features of the design which cannot be accounted for in the text, or which differ in important respects from the descriptions given there. These variations must then be examined in an attempt to show why Blake introduced them.

The important differences between the illustration and the poem are five in number, as follows:

A. The stream is no longer shown as flowing between Dante and the heavenly procession as it did in the previous drawing. In the poem, Dante does not cross to the same side of the stream as Beatrice until the latter part of Canto xxxi; however, as Blake has inscribed "P - g Canto 29 & 30" on the ground in the lower right of this illustration, he evidently intended it to be associated with the first appearance of Beatrice.[5]

B. Beatrice wears a golden crown, not an olive wreath as described by Dante.

C. The poem does not describe the wheels of the car as being anything unusual. The vortex has evidently been deliberately introduced by Blake for some purpose of his own.

D. The infants which float beside the female figure just to the left of the wheel are not mentioned in the text.

E. There is no explanation in the poem for the book to which the female figure by the right side of the wheel is pointing.

The vortex is the most unusual feature of this drawing and is at once recognizable as an important symbol in Blake's mythology. The best account of it will be found

---

[4] See footnote 2 to the preceding illustration.

[5] Except for the inscription, this drawing might very well illustrate the passage in Canto xxxi, lines 128-146, in which, after Dante has crossed the stream, the three women beg Beatrice to gaze upon him and to unveil her mouth.

in *Milton*. The Eternal Form of the poet has determined to forsake Eden and to go down into the Fallen World in order to free his Spectre from error. His downward passage is thus described:[6]

> The nature of infinity is this: That every thing has its
> Own Vortex, and when once a traveller thro' Eternity
> Has pass'd that Vortex, he perceives it roll backward behind
> His path, into a globe itself infolding like a sun,
> Or like a moon, or like a universe of starry majesty,
> While he keeps onwards in his wondrous journey on the earth,
> Or like a human form, a friend with whom he liv'd benevolent.
> As the eye of man views both the east & west encompassing
> Its vortex, and the north & south with all their starry host,
> Also the rising sun & setting moon he views surrounding
> His corn-fields and his valleys of five hundred acres square,
> Thus is the earth one infinite plane, and not as apparent
> To the weak traveller confin'd beneath the moony shade.
> Thus is the heaven a vortex pass'd already, and the earth
> A vortex not yet pass'd by the traveller thro' Eternity.
>
> Milton 17, 21-35

From this passage it is apparent that the vortex represents the gate of entry from Eternity into materialized existence. Here the Fall begins; forms lose their identity and we see figures in the vortex becoming indistinct as they are sucked downward. The forms in the whirlpool are all female, indicating that it is feminine passivity which precipitates the Fall, and there are three of them for, as we have seen on a number of occasions, three is a number which Blake associates with the Fallen World.[7] The eyes in the vortex probably represent the Seven Eyes of God and the shadowy Eighth Eye which is mentioned in *Milton* and *Jerusalem* and which seems to be a symbol of God's promise of Albion's eventual awakening. They attest to God's presence with Man even after the Fall, and remind us that "God is within & without: he is even in the depths of Hell!"[8]

As Blake continually associates Purgatory with Beulah, it is now clear that the vortex indicates that we have here a vision of the limit of Beulah at which the Fall begins. As we have seen, this comes about when the masculine imagination loses its energy and submits to the feminine aspect of the soul, which is materialistic rather than spiritual. In the poet who stands submissively while Beatrice chides him, we have clearly an instance of the Poetic Genius humbling itself to the Female Will. We now have an explanation of why the river has been eliminated, for the poet must

[6] The vortex will again be found portrayed in the drawing to *Paradise Lost*, "The Expulsion from Eden." (Figgis, *Paintings of William Blake*, plate 22.)

[7] Percival, *Blake's "Circle of Destiny,"* p. 70. Frye, *Fearful Symmetry*, p. 300, shows that the number three is associated with cyclic recurrence; it thus fits in appropriately with the symbolism of the vortex.

[8] *Jerusalem* 12, 15. See footnote 5 to the preceding design; in the same passage, Frye also identifies the Eighth Eye.

already have been submerged beneath the waters of materialism and forgetfulness, or he would not thus pay homage to the Female Will.

Further, in Blake's mythology the Female Will is associated with Vala, the Goddess of Nature in her fallen form of Rahab. Lest we miss this significance, Blake has given Beatrice, with her clinging transparent garment, the sensual appearance of Vala, and has placed a crown of gold upon her head instead of an olive wreath.[9]

> They took their Mother Vala and they crown'd her with gold;
> They nam'd her Rahab & gave her power over the Earth,
>
> . . . .
>
> . . to destroy the Lamb & usurp the Throne of God,
> Drawing their Ulro Voidness round the Four-fold Humanity.
>
> *Jerusalem* 78, 15-16; 19-20

We now see that Blake has represented in this illustration Vala-Rahab, crowned with gold, presiding over "Ulro Voidness," which is, of course, the vortex. The passage also indicates clearly that we are to regard the four beasts as the Zoas, who are the various aspects of the "Four-fold Humanity."

> Four Mighty Ones are in every Man; a Perfect Unity
> Cannot Exist but from the Universal Brotherhood of Eden,
> The Universal Man, To Whom be Glory Evermore. Amen.
> What are the Natures of those Living Creatures the Heav'nly Father only
> Knoweth. No Individual knoweth, nor can know in all Eternity.
>
> *Four Zoas* I, 6-10 (p. 252)

This, therefore, completes the picture of the Female Will usurping the Throne of God and presiding over the Fall.

> There is a Throne in every Man, it is the Throne of God;
> This, Woman has claim'd as her own, & Man is no more!
> Albion is the Tabernacle of Vala & her Temple,
> And not the Tabernacle & Temple of the Most High.
> O Albion, why wilt thou Create a Female Will?
>
> *Jerusalem* 34, 27-31

We must now pause to examine the beasts and to show, by means of quotations from Blake's prophecies, which Zoa is to be identified with each.[10]

First we have the eagle. He is to be identified with Tharmas, the physical body and instincts of man. As the Female Will is now dominant, all the Zoas are shown in their Fallen aspects, and all except Los appear brutalized, with fierce expressions. The bird of prey thus stands for the Natural Violence of the Fallen World and for

[9] Although Beatrice's garments, save for their transparency, are much as described by Dante, Blake doubtless associated the veil with "Vala's Veil," to which there are numerous references in the prophecies (e.g. *Jerusalem* 20, 22-41).

[10] Piloo Nanavutty, *op. cit.*, pp. 120-122, assigns the beasts to the Zoas in a different order, identifying the man with Urthona, the eagle with Urizen, the lion with Luvah, and the bull with Tharmas. On the basis of the quotations given in this discussion, I cannot agree with her identifications, and follow instead those given by Northrop Frye in the table on p. 277 of his *Fearful Symmetry*.

Warfare, the form in which Fallen Man expresses that violence. Thus the eagle is given the countenance of Caesar and wears the imperial laurel of military triumph.[11] He looks down into the vortex where worldly power and ambition originate.

> Tharmas beheld them . . . .
> And he said: . . . .
>   . . .   "All my hope is gone! for ever fled!
> Like a famish'd Eagle, Eyeless, raging in the vast expanse."
> Four Zoas IV, 6-7; 9-10 (pp. 285-286)

The lion represents Urizen, pure intellectual rationalism as dominant in this world, unsubservient to either imagination or feeling and thus calculatingly cruel as is the great beast which symbolizes it. Together with Tharmas, Urizen is dominant after the Fall; thus these two are placed behind the car, while the Zoas who rule in the eternal realms go before.

> Then seiz'd the Lions of Urizen their work . . .
> Four Zoas II, 135 (p. 271)

Luvah, the Zoa of emotion and feeling, is here symbolized by the bull, representative of passion on a brutal and physical level—another indication that the Zoas are shown in their Fallen aspects.

> The bulls of Luvah, breathing fire, bellow on burning pastures.
> Four Zoas VIIa, 16 (p. 309)

Finally there is Los, the Fallen form of Urthona:

> . . . the Sons of Eden praise Urthona's Spectre in songs,
> Because he kept the Divine Vision in time of trouble.
> Jerusalem 95, 19-20

> The Divine Appearance was the likeness & similitude of Los.
> Jerusalem 96, 7

As emblematic of God's love of Fallen Man, Los has the countenance of Jesus and looks down in deep thought and with infinite compassion upon the Fallen Void. As Christ died—that is, assumed the life of this world—to save man, so does Los labor endlessly in every human being to open his eyes to his oneness with God and to lead him back to the pathway of Regeneration.

> God becomes as we are, that we may be as he is.
> There Is No Natural Religion, II, p. 148

> Thou wast the Image of God surrounded by the Four Zoas.
> Three thou hast slain. I am the Fourth; thou canst not destroy me.
> Jerusalem 42, 23-24

This vision of Beatrice on the car may be summed up in the following passage:

> I see a Feminine Form arise from the Four terrible Zoas,

---

[11] Note that while Dante, in the passage quoted, speaks of each of the beasts as being crowned with foliage, Blake places wreaths only upon the eagle and the lion, who represent the Zoas who are dominant in the Fallen "vegetated" World.

Beautiful but terrible, struggling to take a form of beauty.

Jerusalem 74, 52-53

As to the gryphon who draws the car, he—like Leviathan and Behemoth of the fifteenth Job design—is representative of "the monstrous forms of the sea- and earth-powers, . . . terrible in their magnitude and their might, but unillumined by intelligence, or the knowledge of 'brotherhood.'"[12] The heavy belt of cloud which surrounds the head of the gryphon symbolizes its "single vision" and corresponds to the Mundane Shell which encloses Leviathan and Behemoth.

We must now turn to the three women who accompany the car, and whose number undoubtedly confirmed Blake in their Fallen identity. These are the Daughters of Albion who stand beside the vortex to assist in "weaving the 'natural' world of spiritual depravity."[13] The poet, having accepted the dominance of the Female Will, is now ruled by the Daughters of Memory rather than by the Daughters of Inspiration.[14]

It is possible, however, to go further, and to identify these women with the Fallen aspects of the Emanations of the Zoas, who have become dominant over their masculine counterparts following upon the triumph of error. We have already seen that Beatrice is to be recognized as Vala, the Emanation of Luvah. The figure at the extreme left seems to be Ahania, the Emanation of Urizen; she dances as befits her general character of purely worldly and corporeal pleasure. Next to Ahania stands Enion, the Emanation of Tharmas. As the Earth Mother, she brings forth the forms of life, shown as the infants floating beside her. She wears a crown of jewels, which suggest material but soul-less splendor. Her fair form and handsome attire recall the following words addressed to her by Tharmas:

> "O Enion, thou art thyself a root growing in hell,
> Tho' thus heavenly beautiful to draw me to destruction."
>
> *Four Zoas* I, 53-54 (p. 253)

As to the infants, there are five of them in order to symbolize the senses of the Fallen Man. Their root-like form is explained by the first plate of *The Gates of Paradise*, in which a female figure draws forth a child enrooted in the ground, who thus begins his "vegetative" existence. The explanatory lines written later to accompany this plate are as follows:

> . . . she found me beneath a Tree,
> A Mandrake, & in her Veil hid me.

"The appropriateness of the mandrake, the human-shaped vegetable which shrieks when uprooted, as a symbol for the natural man, needs no elaboration."[15]

Finally by elimination, the figure to the right of the wheel, who points to the book,

[12] Wicksteed, *Blake's Vision of the Book of Job*, p. 105.

[13] Percival, *op. cit.*, p. 45.

[14] See *A Vision of the Last Judgment*, pp. 637-638; also the Preface to *Milton* and *Milton* 15, 28-29.

[15] Frye, *op. cit.*, p. 369. The plate from *The Gates of Paradise* is reproduced in *Poetry and Prose*, p. 569; the quotation is from p. 577. It will be recalled that mandrakes are mentioned in the Bible in an episode of the story of Rachel and Leah (Genesis xxx, 14-16); Blake refers to this in *Jerusalem* 93, 8.

must be Enitharmon, the Fallen Emanation of the poet, Los. Properly his inspiration, whose function it is to restore his imagination for the creative life of Eden, she turns instead for guidance to the Female Will and points to the Book of the Law which is about to be swept up into the vortex. Art in a fallen world is all too often based upon sterile rules instead of upon inspiration. Blake, who lived in the heydey of the Royal Academy, knew this only too well. Hence he continually insists that the artist must "act from impulse, not from rules" and must "cast aside from Poetry all that is not Inspiration."[16] Here he presents the same theme in pictorial form. In summing up the significance of the three Daughters of Albion, we can do no better than to quote from Blake's most important prophecy:[17]

> .   .   .   . Three Women around
> The Cross! O Albion, why didst thou a Female Will Create?
>   Jerusalem 56, 42-43

Thus, without departing very far from Dante's poem in detail, and while creating a perfectly recognizable illustration of the triumphal car as it is described in the *Purgatorio*, Blake fuses with it a wealth of meaning all his own. Surely there is no finer example of the extraordinary and subtle fabric of symbolism which Blake can weave around another poet's images, nor of the remarkable counterpoint of theme and suggestion which he can contrive![18]

[16] *Marriage of Heaven and Hell*, p. 191; *Milton* 48, 7. The significance of the book in this drawing is explained by the inscription from II Corinthians iii, 6, which appears on the altar in the marginal design at the bottom of the first Job engraving: "The Letter Killeth, The Spirit giveth Life."

[17] The Daughters of Albion are, of course, the three women who dismember the body of the Fallen Albion in the design to page 25 of *Jerusalem*. While in the early prophetic book named after them (*Poetry and Prose*, pp. 194-200) they represent women in general in the Fallen World, in the later poems their significance is almost always sinister.

[18] A full-size color facsimile of this drawing has recently been published by the Ganymed Press, London.

89. THE HARLOT AND THE GIANT

AFTER BEATRICE appears, as illustrated in the two preceding designs, she chides Dante for his unfaithfulness to her since her death and for his wayward life, which finally made it necessary for her to send Virgil to his rescue. Dante confesses his sin and is so overcome with remorse that he swoons. While he is unconscious, Matilda bears him across the river Lethe and, as he recovers, plunges him beneath it to wash away the remembrance of his sin. He is then conducted to the car and the procession moves off through the wood with Dante walking beside the chariot. After a short interval, they come to a tall tree in the forest to which the gryphon attaches the pole of the car. Dante then falls asleep. When he awakens, Beatrice has descended from the car and sits on the ground under the tree, surrounded by the seven women who had accompanied the car and who now bear torches in their hands. The rest of the procession has departed, leaving the car still attached to the tree. Beatrice commands Dante to watch the car closely; it then undergoes a series of miraculous transformations in which the history of the church is told in allegorical form. It is the last of these which is illustrated here.

> The holy structure, through its several parts,
> Did put forth heads; three on the beam, and one
> On every side: the first like oxen horn'd;
> But with a single horn upon their front,
> The four. Like monster, sight hath never seen.
> O'er it methought there sat, secure as rock
> On mountain's lofty top, a shameless whore,
> Whose ken roved loosely round her. At her side,
> As't were that none might bear her off, I saw
> A giant stand; and ever and anon
> They mingled kisses.   Purgatorio XXXII, 141-151

The beast takes up much of the left part of the drawing. His body is serpent-like, with the tail coiled several times upon itself and then reaching upward along the left margin of the page to the top.[1] From the coiled body rise the seven heads, each of them crowned.[2] The four rear heads have but one horn each; of the other three, two have twin horns as described, but the most prominent head has no horns at all, being surmounted by the triple crown of the papacy with tassels hanging down from it as from ecclesiastical hats. Five of the heads have bestialized human faces, but the two which are most conspicuous—including the one with the triple crown—have monstrous animal heads.

Upon the beast sits the whore who is, of course, the Whore of Babylon of St. John's vision.[3] In her right hand she bears the cup of abominations, which is running over; a crown, earrings, and rings on her left hand suggest the rich raiment of the Biblical account. She bends forward to kiss the giant who stands at her left. He is a bestial, bearded figure; in his left hand he holds a rope with which he leads the seven-headed monster. Brambles grow on the ground near his feet.

Just to the right of the giant and in the background rises the trunk of a big tree. Its branches spread out to right and left and from them hang large fruits; some of these can be seen near the right margin of the page and others hang down from above into the upper left corner near the dragon's tail. At the foot of the tree, Beatrice kneels on the ground, looking at the harlot and the giant. Beside her and to the right of the tree stand the three women of the previous illustration; the one in white still holds a book, but it is now closed.

It is perhaps at first surprising to find Blake choosing to illustrate this incident from the wide range of subjects which offer themselves in the closing cantos of the *Purgatorio*. The reason he does so is that the Whore of Babylon has special significance for him; this demonstrates once again that Blake looks for parallels between Dante's ideas and symbolism and his own, rather than approaching his text with the purely pictorial interest of the average illustrator. Previous to this time, Blake had made

[1] The coils of the serpent's body recall the vortex of the preceding design. For the symbolism of serpents in Blake's work, see the discussion of Drawing 47 above.
[2] For the crowns, see Revelation xii, 3.   [3] Revelation xvii, 1-6.

several designs showing the Biblical whore,[4] and "Mystery, Babylon the Great" is also an important figure in his prophetic books. She serves, in fact, as the antithesis of Jerusalem, and represents the fallen form of Vala in much the same manner as her counterpart Rahab, with whom she is often identified. She may be thought of as the summation of the blind materialism of human ambition. As the woman with whom the kings of the earth commit fornication, she represents the cravings for worldly power, fame, and riches which obsess those at the nadir of the Fall, when all spiritual illumination has been lost and the selfhood has supreme control. As such she properly sits upon the serpent of the Fallen World. Her lover is, of course, the God of that world, Satan. Her cup represents Natural Religion, the stupefying draught with which she reduces man to servitude.[5] As Mystery, she is symbolic of the paralyzing hold which ingrown ideas and tradition have upon men's minds, making them the easy prey of those who would destroy their liberty. In order to keep her position secure, she must uphold all systems of oppression; she is thus the instigator of warfare, upon which all tyrannies thrive.[6]

> No sooner had she spoke but Rahab Babylon appear'd
> Eastward upon the Paved work across Europe & Asia,
> Glorious as the midday Sun in Satan's bosom glowing,
> A Female hidden in a Male, Religion hidden in War,
> Nam'd Moral Virtue, cruel two-fold Monster shining bright,
> A Dragon red & hidden Harlot which John in Patmos saw.
>
> Milton 46, 17-22

Associated with Mystery is the Tree of Mystery—deeply enrooted error displaying its enticing fruits to make man forget his eternal role in the desire of the moment. The fruit of this tree was the bait by means of which the serpent of this world and the Female Will, conspiring together, brought about the Fall of Man. It is upon

[4] Plate 75 of *Jerusalem* shows two women in the coils of a serpent with seven heads, and the text on the page begins, "Rahab, Babylon the Great, hath destroyed Jerusalem." The drawing for the title page of "Night the Eighth" of Young's *Night Thoughts* (reproduced in color in Keynes, *Blake's Illustrations to Young*) depicts the Whore sitting on the beast with seven monstrous heads. All the heads are crowned save one which has a helmet and another with a biretta; the triple crown is also seen and another head has a bishop's mitre and a double crown. This design dates from 1796-1797. Also in the British Museum is a watercolor (dated 1809) of "The Whore of Babylon" (Figgis, *Paintings of William Blake*, plate 86) which is quite different from the present illustration. The beast is not a serpent, but a monstrous human crawling on all fours. The Whore sits on his back and from her cup (note its classical design and serpentine handles) the Daughters of Albion carry down small cups of the wine with which they incite warriors who battle fiercely on the earth below.

[5] The significance of the cup should be clear from the following quotations:
> He saw the Harlot of the Kings of Earth, & saw her Cup
> Of fornication, food of Orc & Satan, press'd from the fruit of Mystery.
>
> Four Zoas VIII, 589-590 (p. 346)
> "O Mystery," Fierce Tharmas cries, "Behold thy end is come!
> Art thou she that made the nations drunk with the cup of Religion?"
>
> Four Zoas IX, 655-656 (p. 366)

[6] One of the strongest weapons by means of which religious systems enslave mankind is sexual repression; hence the brambles (see discussion of the twentieth illustration above). Note the similar juxtaposition of brambles and a serpent in the bottom margin of the fifth Job engraving.

this tree that the Son of Man must be crucified to reveal to Fallen Man that the Moral Law breeds death and that only by the sacrifice of the selfhood can he be redeemed.[7] It is also the tree that originally sprang up from under the heel of Urizen as he wrote the laws of the false religion of vengeance for sin.[8]

> The Spectre saw the Shade Shiv'ring over his gloomy rocks
> Beneath the tree of Mystery, which in the dismal Abyss
> Began to blossom in fierce pain, shooting its writhing buds
> In throes of birth; & now, the blossoms falling, shining fruit
> Appear'd of many colours & of various poisonous qualities,
> Of Plagues hidden in shining globes that grew on the living tree.
>
> Four Zoas VIIa, 211-216 (p. 315)

We saw in our discussion of the preceding design that Blake identified Beatrice with Vala. She now sits under the Tree of Mystery as a sign of submission to the Moral Law of Urizen which is supreme in the Fallen World. Beside her are the Daughters of Albion holding the closed book of the Law.[9] In the Harlot and the Giant we have a vision of the monstrous evil of the Fallen World which follows upon the dominance of the Female Will. Self-righteous and externalized religion—with which Blake identifies Beatrice and to which, in his opinion, Dante had given full allegiance—is the worship not of God but of Satan. The result is that now "The Beast & the Whore rule without control."[10]

[7] In plate 76 of *Jerusalem* Christ is shown crucified upon a tree which bears large fruits like those seen here.

[8] *Ahania*, lines 103-129 (pp. 237-238).

[9] Note that while the text (XXXII, 95-97) describes Beatrice as attended by seven women with torches, Blake shows only three with a book. He thus makes clear that he intends to represent the Daughters of Albion as in the preceding design and *not* the Daughters of Beulah as in Drawing 87.

[10] Annotation to Watson's *Apology for the Bible*, p. 750. In the passage quoted, Blake is referring to the politically expedient opposition of organized religion in his own day (Dr. Watson was Bishop of Llandaff, Wales) to social betterment. Among Blake's comments is, "To defend the Bible in this year 1798 would cost a man his life."

3

PARADISO

~~~~~~

Now I a fourfold vision see,
And a fourfold vision is given to me;
'Tis fourfold in my supreme delight
And threefold in soft Beulah's night
And twofold Always. May God us keep
From Single vision & Newton's sleep!

Poem in a letter to Thomas Butts,
22 November, 1802 (pp. 861-862)

~~~~~~

90. DANTE ADORING CHRIST

THE FIRST DESIGN for the *Paradiso* illustrates Canto XIV. Having traversed the Spheres of Air and Fire, and the Heavens of the Moon, Mercury, Venus, and the Sun, Dante and Beatrice now pass upward into the Fifth Heaven, that of Mars, in which are the souls of Warrior Saints and Martyrs. Dante beholds a vision of their spirits forming a cross of light in the shape of a figure of the crucified Christ.

As leads the galaxy from pole to pole,
Distinguish'd into greater lights and less,
Its pathway, which the wisest fail to spell;
So thickly studded, in the depths of Mars,
Those rays described the venerable sign,
That quadrants in the round conjoining frame.
Here memory mocks the toil of genius. Christ
Beam'd on that cross; and pattern fails me now.
But whoso takes his cross, and follows Christ,
Will pardon me for that I leave untold.

Paradiso XIV, 90-99

The figure of Christ occupies most of the drawing. It floats high on the page, facing us with the arms outspread in the form of a cross. No actual cross, either of wood or of light, is shown. Christ stands on a flaming sun and two more appear behind His hands, which are held palms outward in such a manner that they suggest the nailing of them to the cross. From all three suns, rays and flames shoot out, enveloping most of the design. Dante kneels at the foot of the page, facing Christ, and looking up at Him in adoration. He also holds his arms outspread and rays of light from the figure stream down upon him.

We may well ask ourselves why Blake made no illustrations at all to the first thirteen cantos of the *Paradiso*, and chose this passage to begin with. The answer is that Blake

175

himself once had much such a vision as that described by Dante. Such parallel mystical experiences of creative artists were to Blake affirmations of the eternal truth of inspired vision, and as such this passage of Dante's poem had particular interest for him.

Soon after his arrival at Felpham in the early autumn of 1800, Blake had been sitting by the sea on a fine day when he had suddenly experienced a moment of illumination which profoundly influenced the whole further course of his thought and which provided him with a central focus for his belief which he had lacked up to that moment. All his early prophecies had ended either with revolution or with the triumph of evil. As a result of this vision by the sea, he became convinced of the reality and nature of Apocalypse, and it is on this note that his three greater prophecies end. A few days later he described his experience to Thomas Butts in a letter:

> To my Friend Butts I write
> My first Vision of Light,
> On the yellow sands sitting.
> The Sun was Emitting
> His Glorious beams
> From Heaven's high Streams.
> Over Sea, over Land
> My Eyes did Expand
> Into regions of air
> Away from all Care,
> Into regions of fire
> Remote from Desire;
> The Light of the Morning
> Heaven's Mountains adorning:
> In particles bright
> The jewels of Light
> Distinct shone & clear.
> Amaz'd & in fear
> I each particle gazed,
> Astonish'd, Amazed;
> For each was a Man
> Human-form'd . . . . . .
>   . . . .
> My Eyes more and more
> Like a Sea without shore
> Continue Expanding.
> The Heavens commanding,
> Till the Jewels of Light,
> Heavenly Men beaming bright,
> Appear'd as One Man,
> Who complacent began
> My limbs to infold
> In his beams of bright gold;
> Like dross purg'd away
> All my mire & my clay.

Soft consum'd in delight
In his bosom Sun bright
I remain'd. Soft he smil'd,
And I heard his voice Mild.
October 2nd, 1800 (pp. 846-847)

This vision of the spiritual nature of all things and of their ultimate unity with God in Eden[1] became the central theme of Blake's philosophy from now on. *The Four Zoas, Milton,* and *Jerusalem* all end with visions in which all living forms become one with Christ in the Apocalypse which follows upon the attainment of complete spiritual and mental liberty.

The significance of this scene for Blake should by now be clear. The poet kneels in adoration as he sees the vision of Christ in Eden as the center from which all light—which is divine energy—radiates, and as the unity into which all things are absorbed and in which even the Blessed Trinity, here symbolized by the three fiery suns, is made One.[2]

There are a number of similar representations of this adoration of the Divine Vision by the poet in Blake's work. The most notable is the full-page illustration of plate 76 of *Jerusalem* in which Albion beholds Christ crucified upon the tree and himself extends his arms in the same manner as here.[3] Having shown in the *Jerusalem* design God's sacrifice of Himself to save Man, Blake now depicts the fruit of that sacrifice, Man made One with God through Divine Love.[4] This is the final instant in which is made real that unity with Divine Vision of which the poet is aware in all of his inspired moments during his life in the Fallen World.

Of the Sleep of Ulro! and of the passage through
Eternal Death! and of the awaking to Eternal Life.

This theme calls me in sleep night after night, & ev'ry morn
Awakes me at sun-rise; then I see the Saviour over me
Spreading his beams of love & dictating the words of this mild song.

. . . .

"I am not a God afar off, I am a brother and friend:
Within your bosoms I reside, and you reside in me:
Lo! we are One, forgiving all Evil, Not seeking recompense."
Jerusalem 4, 1-5; 18-20

It was his faith in this vision which gave to the last thirty years of Blake's life its entire direction and which formed the course of all his thought and art. This scene

[1] Note Blake's remark, made in 1825 in conversation with Henry Crabb Robinson: "We are all co-existent with God—members of the Divine body." (Symons, *William Blake,* p. 255.)

[2] As a possible further extension of the significance of the three suns, see Blackstone, *English Blake,* p. 407: "Throughout Blake's work the sun is present in his triple aspect of light, heat and motion, the trinity of energy."

[3] See also the watercolor, "David Delivered out of Many Waters," and the tempera, "The Agony in the Garden" (reproduced in Laurence Binyon, *The Drawings and Engravings of William Blake,* London, 1922, plates 9 and 55).

[4] See Damon, *William Blake,* p. 219: "Plate 90 shows Dante adoring Christ; this is the ecstatic counterpart of the tragic crucifixion in *Jerusalem.*"

from Dante is, therefore, for Blake an affirmation of that spiritual confidence which had made it possible for him to triumph over neglect, poverty, human tragedy, and the many disappointments which had been his lot in the world.

> . . . Los beheld the Divine Vision among the flames of the Furnaces.
> Therefore he lived & breathed in hope.
>
> *Jerusalem* 62, 35-36

This is a very unfinished wash drawing, only the head and upper part of the body of Christ being in a more developed state. Some details are still in pencil. The number "97" which appears in the upper right corner is puzzling to explain. Perhaps this was the ninety-seventh sheet as the pages were originally arranged, or it may refer to line 97 of Cary's translation of this canto, as quoted above.

91. A DESIGN OF CIRCULAR STAIRS

BLAKE has written lightly in the upper right of this drawing "Par Canto 19."[1] In spite of this, it is not easy to identify the design with any particular passage. However, it probably illustrates in Blake's terms lines 59-63 and represents Divine Intelligence manifesting itself in the world.[2]

> . . . Light is none,
> Save that which cometh from the pure serene
> Of ne'er disturbed ether: for the rest,
> 'Tis darkness all; or shadow of the flesh,
> Or else its poison.

The drawing is entirely in pencil and very sketchy. At the bottom, an arc of a circle suggests this world. From it a flight of stairs rises in five decreasing spirals to the top of the page. Near the bottom may be seen a group of people ascending and others—who, as we shall see in a moment, are probably angels—descending. They are so slightly indicated that, save for one group of a mother and child, it is impossible to make them out in any detail. Alongside the stairs in the middle of the page four stars are shown; at the sides clouds are also suggested.

The clue to this illustration is to be found by comparing it with the watercolor, "Jacob's Ladder,"[3] which dates from about 1800. Jacob, who is to be identified with Albion, lies on the couch of death, which is shown as the circle of this world. The separation of his mortal from his eternal self is indicated by the wisp of cloud which floats in the sky just above his body. He sees in his dream a spiral ladder ascending

[1] The "9" is not very distinct and might perhaps be a "7"; this does not, however, clear up any difficulties in identifying the passage illustrated.

[2] Attention should also be called to *Paradiso* X, 79-84, and XXI, 22-38, where celestial stairways figure in the imagery of the poem. There are, of course, cases—such as Drawing 34—where incorrect inscriptions appear on these illustrations. W. M. Rossetti, in his catalogue of the Dante drawings in Gilchrist's *Life*, II, p. 234, says: "Canto XIX, to which Blake has referred this design, does not contain anything closely corresponding with it. Perhaps it symbolizes the relation, as in descending grades, between the divine and created intelligences."

[3] Figgis, *Paintings of William Blake*, plate 80. Formerly in the collection of W. Graham Robertson, this drawing is now in that of the Department of Prints and Drawings of the British Museum.

in five turns,[4] as here, through the night of Beulah—also in this case indicated by stars —to the sun of Eden at the top of the page. Upon the ladder figures are ascending, of whom several are women who hold children by the hand. Angels also descend bearing gifts for the restoration of the sleeping humanity.[5]

Blake probably has a similar idea in mind in this sketch. The Inferno, or this world, is connected by the spiralling path of Purgatory or Beulah (God's love and mercy) to the Paradise of Eden, the burning heaven of eternal imaginative life. Up this stairway man's happier instincts, personified by the children who are still in a state of innocence, mount to be met and sustained by the pitying Daughters of Beulah. This is in a sense a schematic diagram of the entire *Divine Comedy,* and the gradation of the celestial spheres in the *Paradiso* would probably suggest the idea to Blake again.[6]

The stars, besides indicating that the spiral stairway is to be thought of as existing in Beulah, have additional connotations. "*Stars,* whatever else they may symbolise, are the point of contact between the spiritual and corporeal visions of life, or the irreducible minimum of spiritual reality which even the corporeal vision cannot quench; the fragments of universal light which Night itself cannot drown."[7] The number four, as has several times been noted, is associated with the eternal life of Eden. Thus it is appropriate that beside the stairway of God's mercy reaching from the Eternal to the Fallen World, there should be four stars.

> Thus were the stars of heaven created like a golden chain
> To bind the Body of Man to heaven from falling into the Abyss.
> Four Zoas II, 266-267 (p. 274)

[4] The five circles of the spiral probably symbolize the five senses, as in the following passage:
> . . . when the five senses whelm'd
> In deluge o'er the earth-born man; . . . . . .
>
> . . . .
>
> The ever-varying spiral ascents to the heavens of heavens
> Were bended downward.
> Europe, lines 137-138; 140-141 (p. 216)

[5] These gifts include bread, and also the arts (books) and sciences (compasses), all knowledge being a gift of God to open man's eyes to Eternity. "What is the Life of Man but Art & Science? . . . To Labour in Knowledge is to Build up Jerusalem." (*Jerusalem,* p. 77.)

[6] A spiral stairway also figures in the watercolor, "Meditations Among the Tombs," in the Tate Gallery (Figgis, *op. cit.,* plate 89). The symbolism is, however, rather different from that of "Jacob's Ladder" to which the present illustration seems much more clearly linked.

[7] Wicksteed, *Blake's Vision of the Book of Job,* p. 94.

92. THE RECORDING ANGEL

WHEN DANTE AND BEATRICE ascend to the Sixth Heaven, that of Jupiter, they find the spirits of those who excelled in the maintenance of justice. Each of these spirits appears as a light and they group to form an eagle, the emblem of the Holy Roman Empire, which Dante believed God had ordained to maintain justice among men.[1]

[1] Traces of faint pencil lines can be seen beneath the washes of the sky and indicate that the wings of the figure were originally intended to be larger and that more stars were shown. The number "65" appears faintly on the ground at the bottom left near the star, and has been covered with watercolor; as in the case of similar numbers found on illustrations 45, 54, and 90, its intention is obscure.

The eagle speaks, prophesying the fate of unrighteous rulers. At the beginning of the list of ones then living, which it proceeds to give, is a very indirect reference to the Recording Angel; it is on the basis of this that Blake conceived the present illustration.

> "What may the Persians say unto your kings,
> When they shall see that volume, in the which
> All their dispraise is written, spread to view?
> There amidst Albert's works shall that be read,
> Which will give speedy motion to the pen."
>
> Paradiso XIX, 111-115

The angel occupies most of the page. A bearded figure with a firm but placid expression, he is seated on a throne, only the lower wings of which are visible. He wears a long garment, from beneath which his left foot protrudes; his large wings rise behind him and meet at a point over his head. He gazes thoughtfully upward as he writes with a quill pen upon a scroll which lies in his lap. Beneath his feet appears the arc of the Fallen World. Where the two wings of the throne meet the ground, stars are to be seen; a third star is between the angel's wings and immediately over his head. Traces of clouds appear at the sides of the page in the lower portion.

From his appearance, from the fact that only his left foot is shown,[2] and from his activity of writing, it is clear that this figure is intended to represent Urizen in the guise of the "angel" of convention and tradition who upholds the Moral Law. This illustration is the "contrary" to Drawing 90. In that, Christ appeared as the Divine Vision, surrounded by the three suns of creative imagination. Here we have Jehovah-Urizen, the God of This World, which is "built at the level of the stars—for the stars are third and last in the order of heavenly illumination."[3] While, as we have seen in connection with the preceding design, the stars are symbols of God's light still shining in darkness, we must be able to recognize them as such; the worship of the stars for themselves is a philosophy of rationalism, in love with the regularity of their motion rather than with the Divine Love which is the source of their light.[4] As God of the Moral Law, Urizen sits on a rock—which doubtless explains the shape of the visible part of his throne in this drawing—and writes in a book.[5]

> For when Urizen shrunk away
> From Eternals, he sat on a rock
> Barren: a rock which himself
> From redounding fancies had petrified.
>
> .   .   .   .
>
> .   .   .   .   .   he wrote
> In silence his book of iron.
>
> Ahania 103-106; 111-112 (pp. 237-238)

[2] Wicksteed, *Blake's Vision of the Book of Job*, pp. 133-136.

[3] Percival, *Blake's "Circle of Destiny,"* p. 60. It will be recalled that in Drawing 90 two suns were placed above and one below; the arrangement of the stars here is just the reverse.

[4] Schorer, *Politics of Vision*, p. 251. Urizen placed here in the midst of the stars recalls *Jerusalem* 91, 36-37: "Los reads the Stars of Albion, the Spectre reads the Voids Between the Stars."

[5] See also *Urizen* 75-91 (p. 222) and the design of the title page of the same book.

Salvation in Blake's eyes comes from active love and forgiveness, not from passive observance of Moral Law; thus the spirit who, instead of pardoning error keeps track of it so that it may later be punished, is evil—Satan in this world.[6] Here again we have an example of Blake, from all of the many descriptions of the *Paradiso*, picking out one of the least obvious because it happens to suggest one of the cardinal points of his own belief.[7]

> Urizen answer'd: "Read my books, explore my Constellations,
> Enquire of my Sons & they shall teach thee how to War.
>
> . . . .
> . . . . for I am God
> Of all this dreadful ruin."
>
> Four Zoas VIIa, 90-91; 93-94 (p. 311)

[6] To emphasize further the Satanic character of this figure, Blake has covered the drapery of the legs with a scaly pattern, a regular attribute of such figures in his work (e.g. see Drawing 28 of the present series; the fifth, sixth, and sixteenth Job engravings; *Europe*, plate 5; etc.). Compare *Four Zoas* VI, 298 (p. 308): "A spectre Vast appear'd, [the] feet & legs with iron scaled."

[7] It will be noted that recording angels appear in the upper margin of the fifteenth Job engraving; however there, according to Wicksteed (*op. cit.*, p. 106), they do not have Urizenic connotations.

93. BEATRICE AND DANTE IN GEMINI AMID THE SPHERES OF FLAME

DANTE AND BEATRICE have now reached the Eighth Heaven, that of the Fixed Stars, where they enter the constellation of Gemini under which Dante was born. Beatrice and he look back through the seven transparent spheres which they have traversed and see the earth far below. Dante is then accorded a vision of the Triumph of Christ and of the Virgin Mary; afterward he is examined by St. Peter on the subject of Faith, by St. James on Hope, and by St. John the Evangelist on Love. The present illustration shows Dante and Beatrice surrounded by the spirits of the Blessed just before St. Peter appears to question Dante.

> . . . the rejoicing spirits, like to spheres
> On firm-set poles revolving, trail'd a blaze
> Of comet splendour: and as wheels, that wind
> Their circles in the horloge so work
> The stated rounds, that to the observant eye
> The first seems still, and as it flew, the last;
> E'en thus their carols weaving variously,
> They, by the measure paced, or swift, or slow,
> Made me to rate the riches of their joy.
>
> Paradiso XXIV, 11-19

This drawing is little more than a faint sketch. Two spheres are seen which overlap, the upper one being to the right and transparent so that the other can be seen through it. Beatrice, still crowned as Blake showed her when she first appeared to Dante on the car, stands in the center of the right sphere in a frontal pose. Her hands are raised, palms outward, to the level of her shoulders. Near her, but in the center of the sphere to the left, is Dante; he repeats Beatrice's gesture, but his figure is seen from behind. He looks intently at Beatrice, who gazes upward with a thoughtful expression. Around the edges of the spheres numerous angels are very faintly sketched.[1]

The twin spheres are, of course, suggested by the twin stars of Gemini. After the soul leaves Eden and enters into the repose of Beulah—of which the moon and stars are the symbols—the unified personality divides and sexes are formed. Here we see the poet and his inspiration in the harmony of Beulah.[2] Their spheres, once united in the sun of Eden, are now separate, but still closely and harmoniously linked. The Daughters of Beulah guard the spheres with loving care.

Blake portrays in this drawing the ideal relationship between the Identity and the Emanation. Neither seeking to dominate, their mutual love provides repose from the warfare of Eden, while the angels watch tenderly over them. In due time, the spheres will reunite to form the intense spiritual sun of Eden, and the divided Identity will then become one with itself and with God.[3] This is the contrary aspect of that depicted in Drawing 88 when the Female Will was dominant and the Imagination humbled itself before her.

It will again be noted how relatively little connection there is between this design and the text of Dante's poem and how Blake picks up the least suggestion that will give him an opportunity to develop a relationship between Dante's vision and his own. The draperies of both figures are especially successful here, being full of grace and light movement which suggests the joy and beauty of the heavenly sphere as described by the poet.

[1] If they were more complete, it is probable that they would be much like the angels of the title page for the Job engravings.

[2] Dante and Beatrice are, of course, to be identified here with Los and Enitharmon.

[3] The illustration recalls strikingly the reunion of Los and Enitharmon as described at the Last Judgment:

> . . . their bodies lost, they stood
> Trembling & weak, a faint embrace, a fierce desire, as when
> Two shadows mingle on a wall.
>
> Four Zoas IX, 26-28 (p. 348)

94. ST. PETER, BEATRICE AND DANTE

THIS ILLUSTRATION is based upon Canto XXIV, 20-151. St. Peter, detaching himself from the whirling spheres of flame, approaches Dante. Beatrice requests him to question Dante concerning Faith, which he proceeds to do.

St. Peter appears in a flame from above, holding his key in his right hand. He recalls lines 20-22:

> From that, which I did note in beauty most
> Excelling, saw I issue forth a flame
> So bright, as none was left more goodly there.

The saint is a large bearded figure who appears head downward in the flame. He looks toward Beatrice as she floats toward him from the lower right, her hands raised in supplication. Balancing the figure of Beatrice, Dante floats upward from the left corner toward the center. He looks in wonder at St. Peter and gestures as though in surprise. From the tapering flame which swathes the saint, light radiates throughout the design.

This illustration is closely related to the two which follow. Its general meaning seems to depend upon the identification of Faith—the subject on which St. Peter examines Dante—with reason in its enlightened or unfallen aspect. Urizen is here benevolent in appearance and gives off rays of light. Reason properly controlled provides illumination in man's search for truth; it is only when it usurps control of all the functions that it becomes an evil which is worshipped in the place of God. In the Eternal World we know that Urizen "is the Prince of Light, driving the chariot of the sun . . . It is more important to remember that he is faith and certainty."[1] To him Beatrice and Dante turn as they seek reunion in the Eternal World.

The woman reaches out toward St. Peter eagerly, while the man seems to hesitate slightly. Perhaps this indicates Blake's belief that woman is more likely to depend upon traditional religious forms, as symbolized by the key of God's Kingdom on Earth, than is man, the more creatively imaginative of the two.

[1] Percival, *Blake's "Circle of Destiny,"* p. 21.

95. ST. PETER, BEATRICE, DANTE WITH ST. JAMES ALSO

ST. PETER having questioned Dante concerning Faith, St. James appears. After the two saints have greeted each other, St. James, in response to Beatrice's request, examines Dante on the subject of Hope.

> Next from the squadron, whence had issued forth
> The first fruit of Christ's vicars on the earth,
> Towards us moved a light, at view whereof
> My Lady, full of gladness, spake to me:
> "Lo! lo! behold the peer of mickle might,
> That makes Galicia throng'd with visitants."
> As when the ring-dove by his mate alights;
> In circles, each about the other wheels,
> And, murmuring, cooes his fondness: thus saw I
> One, of the other great and glorious prince,
> With kindly greeting, hail'd; extolling, both,
> Their heavenly banqueting.
>
> Paradiso xxv, 15-26

There are now two flames similar to the one in the preceding drawing, their pointed ends reaching to the upper corners of the page. St. Peter is swathed in the flame at the left; he holds his key in his left hand and makes a sign of benediction with his right. Toward him floats St. James, with a gesture of greeting. Rays of light emanate from each figure and fill the entire design. Beatrice and Dante are again shown below but, instead of facing each other as in the previous illustration, their positions are now reversed. Dante floats beneath the figure of St. Peter and looks across at St. James. Beatrice, while placed underneath the form of St. James, gazes at St. Peter.

The poet and his inspiration are now joined by a second figure who represents Hope in the poem. Whereas Faith—who carries the key signifying the Kingdom of God on

Earth—is concerned with the operations of grace in the Fallen World, Hope leads us to be confident of eternal life and ultimate salvation.[1] As Faith may be compared to the unfallen reason, so Hope corresponds to the unfallen emotional life (Luvah). As such, it is associated with the intended function of women, which is to be the "comforters of Men"[2] in Beulah. Thus it is that Beatrice appears beneath St. James, while Dante is shown below St. Peter.[3] However, in the ideal state man requires the support of woman's love, while woman needs man's intellectual energy as her guide; hence Beatrice and Dante each look up at the figure which is opposite to them rather than to the one above.[4]

[1] This is a possible explanation for the fact that the flame which encloses St. Peter's figure appears wholly within the page, whereas that surrounding St. James trails beyond the bounds of the design.

[2] See reversed inscription at bottom of plate 72 of *Jerusalem*.

[3] "The mind and the emotions are the male and female of many systems." (Percival, *Blake's "Circle of Destiny,"* p. 29.)

[4] From a purely formal point of view, the composition requries these diagonal accents to give it balance, just as it requires that Dante and Beatrice move away from each other to contrast with the direction of movement of the saints.

96. ST. PETER, ST. JAMES, DANTE, BEATRICE WITH ST. JOHN ALSO

. . . Amidst them next,
A light of so clear amplitude emerged,
That winter's month were but a single day,
Were such a crystal in the Cancer's sign.
Like as a virgin riseth up, and goes,
And enters on the mazes of the dance;
Though gay, yet innocent of worse intent,
Than to do fitting honour to the bride:
So I beheld the new effulgence come
Unto the other two, who in a ring
Wheel'd, as became their rapture. In the dance,
And in the song, it mingled. And the dame
Held on them fix'd her looks; e'en as the spouse,
Silent, and moveless. "This is he, who lay
Upon the bosom of our Pelican:
This he, into whose keeping, from the Cross,
The mighty charge was given." Thus she spake:
Yet therefore nought the more removed her sight
From marking them: or e'er her words began,
Or when they closed. As he, who looks intent,
And strives with searching ken, how he may see
The sun in his eclipse, and, through desire
Of seeing, loseth power of sight; so I
Peer'd on that last resplendence.

Paradiso xxv, 99-122

DANTE AND BEATRICE kneel in the center foreground facing each other. They are surrounded by three figures each of which is enclosed in a disk which emits rays. St. Peter kneels within the sphere at the left, his key in his left hand. In another sphere at the right kneels St. James. Both look upward and toward the center at the figure of St. John, who is seen hovering above the heads of Dante and Beatrice. The Evangelist is shown head downward and the disk in which he is enclosed slightly overlaps the other two. A semicircular arc of color divides the page horizontally, passing above the sunlike spheres of Peter and James, but intersecting that of St. John. Along its rim may be seen eight stars, four on each side of the center.

It is clear that St. John, who in the *Divine Comedy* now proceeds to question Dante concerning Love, is here identified by Blake with the Poetic Genius.[1] Only through God's love, as revealed in the Divine Imagination, can mortal life escape from the bounds imposed upon it by the Mundane Shell and comprehend the glory of the Eternal World. It will be noticed that Reason and Feeling are here shown within the Mundane Shell and beneath the stars which are its symbol. The sphere of St. John, however, breaks through the boundary between the Created and Eternal Worlds and overlaps the spheres of St. Peter and St. James as well. Reason and Feeling are man's guides in the Fallen World, but only through Imagination can he regain immortality.

This drawing, therefore, presents the final stage in the gradually expanding degrees of perception which formed the subject of the two preceding illustrations. The poet has attained to the point of fourfold vision, on which plane of Eden he is about to reunite with his Emanation. Thus Beatrice and Dante are shown close to each other, making complementary gestures. It will be recalled that Blake considered that there are two avenues by means of which man in the Fallen World may communicate with Eternity: creative art and an ideal sexual relationship. Both of these are here symbolized by the poet and his Emanation.

The present illustration is in many respects the antithesis of that of plate 92 of *Jerusalem*, in which Jerusalem appears in despair surrounded by the half-buried forms of the Fallen Zoas. Now Jerusalem is shown just at the instant of her reunion with Albion, who is to be thought of at the same time as both Dante and Tharmas. She is thus shown at the center of the harmonious conclave of the Zoas, for Urizen and Luvah flank her on either side, and Los descends from above to form the essential link between this world and Eternity.

The presence of the eight stars is, of course, explicable on the basis that Dante and Beatrice are now in the Eighth Heaven, the region of the Fixed Stars, and St. John comes to them from the highest sphere of all, which is still above them. However, Blake doubtless thought in his own terms as well, in which he places Eternity above the stars. Four is for Blake the number of infinite extension and is therefore associated with Eden; here the group of four stars appears twice, once above each half of the design.[2] Their presence serves to recall the most famous of the Job series, "When

---

[1] The figure seen plunging head downward within the disk of the sun in the watercolor, "The River of Life," (reproduced in Figgis, *Paintings of William Blake*, plate 5) is much like that of St. John in this drawing; both are doubtless to be identified with Los.

[2] Similarly the three suns are to be associated with those which surround the figure of Christ in Drawing 90.

the Morning Stars Sang Together," in which the stars are symbolized by four angels.[3] In the Job illustration as well, man and woman in the Fallen World are shown at the moment of receiving a glimpse of Eternity through the agency of the Divine Imagination. In each case the figure which pierces the veil is flanked by personifications of Reason and Feeling which are above the generated level but beneath the Eternal one.

In a sense also, this drawing is a pictorial rendition of the same concept which Blake presents in diagrammatic form on plate 36 of *Milton*, in which the path of the Poetic Genius is shown as he penetrates the Mundane Shell between the overlapping spheres of Urizen and Luvah to bring light to the sleeping Humanity.[4]

Although the washes are still in an unfinished state, this drawing is exceptionally brilliant in its coloring. St. Peter wears a blue garment; the disk which encloses him shades from red-violet in the upper left to a high value of an orange tone. St. James is clad in red-violet and his sphere is colored blue. The disk in which St. John appears is yellow with a splash of orange and red at the right. Yellow rays shoot from the lower spheres and red from the upper one. Dante wears red, and Beatrice yellow-green. The background has bright variegated colors.[5]

[3] It will be noted that in the case of the present drawing Blake apparently considered representing the stars in similar fashion by four figures of angels, but later painted them over. They can be faintly seen standing on the rim of the arc by the stars, two on either side of the sphere of St. John.

[4] Reproduced in *Poetry and Prose*, p. 421. In the diagram, Milton's destination is seen to be Adam, the limit of contraction. It must have been of significance to Blake, therefore, that in the *Paradiso* Adam appears to Dante immediately following St. John (XXVI, 79-141).

[5] Anthony Blunt has called attention to the similarity of the overlapping disks in this drawing to a common decorative motif of medieval stained glass and manuscript illumination. ("Blake's Pictorial Imagination," *Journal of the Warburg and Courtauld Institutes*, VI, 1943, p. 199.)

97. THE DEITY, FROM WHOM PROCEED THE NINE SPHERES

IN CANTO XXVIII of the *Paradiso*, Dante is accorded a vision of the Deity, who appears as a point of light of intense brightness surrounded by nine concentric rings. The nearer these rings are to the center, the more swiftly they revolve and the more brilliant is their light. Associated with each circle is one of the orders of the heavenly Intelligences, from the Seraphim, who are nearest to God, to the angels in the outermost ring of those around the throne.

Blake, instead of showing the vision as Dante describes it, with God in the center, depicts rather the pathway of Dante's journey from the earth at the bottom to God in the outermost circle. It will be noted that it is the Created World—the arc of which is seen at the bottom of the page just on the point of sinking beneath the waters of Ulro—that is the focus around which all revolves and that God is farthest from the center. Blake was evidently thinking of the penciled notation which he had made on the seventh illustration, along the margins of which is a rough diagram of the spheres of the *Paradiso* in the order in which they are shown here: "Every thing in Dante's Comedia shews That for Tyrannical Purposes he has made This World the

Foundation of All." Now to Blake, of course, this world is Hell and Satan is its God. It is in this guise that he appears at the top of the page—an ancient, hopeless, bearded figure peering down upon the Fallen World of his creation. His wings are spread behind him and he raises his right hand in a weak gesture of blessing. Urizen here is truly "The Son of Morn in weary Night's decline"; he seems to be aware of the failure of the elaborate system of law which he has built in order to attempt to salvage something from his fall, and appears much as we would expect him to at the moment when he exclaims, "I am God of all this dreadful ruin."[1]

It is thus that Blake conceived of Dante's acceptance of traditional Catholic dogma, which to him was "the Religion of the Enemy & Avenger and not of the Forgiver of Sin."[2] Throughout the *Divine Comedy* it is emphasized how many suffer forever in Hell or for long periods in Purgatory, and how few attain to a state of eternal bliss. Dante is continually calling upon his readers to note in this fact the operation of divine justice. Dante was thus guilty, in Blake's eyes, of the supreme error of confusing God with Satan. Hence it is Satan's realm which he diagrams here—"the Mundane shell builded by Urizen's strong Power"—and at the top of the page we see "the King of Light on high upon his starry throne."[3]

In the very regularity of heavenly motions, Blake saw an unyielding mechanistic principle opposed to freedom and imagination. Thus the essence of Urizen's creation is its mathematical precision of movement:

> Each took his station & his course began with sorrow & care.
> In sevens & tens & fifties, hundreds, thousands, number'd all
> According to their various powers, subordinate to Urizen
> And to his sons in their degrees & to his beauteous daughters,
> Travelling in silent majesty along their order'd ways
> In right lined paths outmeasur'd by proportions of number, weight,
> And measure, mathematic motion wondrous along the deep.
>
> Four Zoas II, 268-274 (pp. 274-275)

The relationship of the present drawing to the Fallen World of Urizen is made abundantly evident in the following passage:

> . . . then all the eternal forests were divided
> Into earths rolling in circles of space, that like an ocean rush'd
> And overwhelmed all except this finite wall of flesh.
> Then was the serpent temple form'd, image of infinite
> Shut up in finite revolutions, and man became an Angel,
> Heaven a mighty circle turning, God a tyrant crown'd.
>
> Europe, lines 145-150 (p. 216)

Within each circle between the earth at the bottom and the Deity at the top, Blake

---

[1] *Gates of Paradise*, p. 579; *Four Zoas* VIIa, 93-94 (p. 311). This representation of Urizen should be compared with that of the third design of this series. A similar anguished figure with wings, shown looking over the rim of the globe in much the same manner as here, appears at the top of plate 62 of *Jerusalem*.

[2] *Jerusalem*, plate 52.

[3] *Four Zoas* II, 248 (p. 274); III, 1 (p. 279).

has shown the various "stars of Urizen in Power."[4] Nine concentric arcs are drawn across the page. In the middle of each arc appears the heavenly body ascribed by Dante to that particular sphere and at the sides of the page in each tier are seen the different orders of heavenly Intelligences associated with each circle. Reading from the bottom upward, the heavenly bodies and the grades of divine beings paired with them are as follows:

Moon	Angels: young, female figures who are probably to be associated with Daughters of Beulah.
Mercury[5]	Archangels: handsome, young male figures with haloes.
Venus	Principalities: young, female figures with flowing hair.
Sun (shown emitting rays)	Powers: more austere and middle-aged female figures, with expressions which are at once anguished and severe. Perhaps personifications of the Female Will.
Mars (symbolized by a cross in a circle)	Virtues: male figures with helmets. Dante places Soldiers of the Faith in this sphere; the mere association of religion and war would, of course, imply the Fall to Blake.
Jupiter	Dominions: elderly, bearded figures.
Saturn	Thrones: even older and more heavily bearded figures, with their heads bent in weariness.
Fixed Stars[6]	Cherubim: two groups of three youthful, female figures (Daughters of Albion); the figure nearest the center in each group gestures toward Urizen.
Primum Mobile	Seraphim: the bearded figure of Urizen appears in the center of this arc; the Seraphim are suggested at the sides, but are too sketchy to be made out in detail.

It will be noted that the youthful spirits, with the exception of the Daughters of Albion, are at the bottom of the page near the earth—closest to Fallen Man and farthest from the Angry God of This World. The Daughters of Beulah, who watch over the Sleeping Humanity, are nearest to the earth; as the spirits approach Urizen, they become increasingly aged and either hopeless or sinister.

Thus again does Blake transpose Dante's vision into his own terms.

The entire scheme of the drawing is clear, although numerous details are unfinished. Pencil, india ink, and washes have been used. Some of the heads, particularly those in the center of the page, have taken form to a considerable degree. Others are merely sketched, that of Urizen being one of the least finished. The group of five heads from the middle of the page to the bottom on the left side are all quite fine and expressive, and are effectively modeled.

[4] *Four Zoas* viib, 213 (p. 328).

[5] Note that all of the planets are surrounded by atmospheres, cloudy layers which act to shut off vision. Compare *Jerusalem* 7, 21-22.

[6] Shown as two small figures of angels; a lightly penciled star may be seen at the extreme right edge of this circle. Note along the right side of the page the indication of clouds; these emphasize that this is the system of the Fallen World and is shut off from Eternity.

98. DANTE IN THE EMPYREAN, DRINKING AT THE RIVER OF LIGHT

>   . . . I look'd;
> And, in the likeness of a river, saw
> Light flowing, from whose amber-seeming waves
> Flash'd up effulgence, as they glided on
> 'Twixt banks, on either side, painted with spring,
> Incredible how fair: and, from the tide,
> There ever and anon, outstarting, flew
> Sparkles instinct with life; and in the flowers
> Did set them, like to rubies chased in gold:
> Then, as if drunk with odours, plunged again
> Into the wondrous flood; from which, as one
> Re-enter'd, still another rose. "The thirst
> Of knowledge high, whereby thou art inflamed,
> To search the meaning of what here thou seest,
> The more it warms thee, pleases me the more.
> But first behoves thee of this water drink,
> Or e'er that longing be allay'd." So spake
> The day-star of mine eyes: then thus subjoin'd:
> "This stream; and these, forth issuing from its gulf,
> And diving back, a living topaz each;
> With all this laughter on its bloomy shores;
> Are but a preface, shadowy of the truth
> They emblem: not that, in themselves, the things
> Are crude; but on thy part is the defect,
> For that thy views not yet aspire so high."
> Never did babe, that had outslept his wont,
> Rush, with such eager straining, to the milk,
> As I toward the water; bending me,
> To make the better mirrors of mine eyes
> In the refining wave: and as the eaves
> Of mine eye-lids did drink of it, forthwith
> Seem'd it unto me turn'd from length to round.
> Then as a troop of maskers, when they put
> Their vizors off, look other than before;
> The counterfeited semblance thrown aside:
> So into greater jubilee were changed
> Those flowers and sparkles; and distinct I saw,
> Before me, either court of Heaven display'd.
>
>   Paradiso xxx, 59-96

THE SOURCE OF LIGHT, which is the lower half of the sun, appears at the top of the page with rays streaming from it. Out of the bottom of it the river of light pours straight downward. It passes completely through the middle of the design, crossing as it does so the boundary between this world and that of vision, seen as a dividing line about two-thirds of the way up the page. The river of light is full of small angelic

189

forms of "infant joys" which, like the "sparkles instinct with life" of the poem, come tumbling out of the river on both sides.

To the right of the river of light, as one looks at it, are two female figures, one above the other. The upper is aged and sits in a crouched position, a veil over her head and her hand resting on a tablet. Below her sits a young woman, with clinging garments and floating hair, who is looking at herself in a hand mirror. Around her on all sides fly a host of the angelic graces which have issued from the stream.

On the opposite bank of the river are four groups of figures, also one above another. At the top is seated an aged, bearded poet, garlanded and surrounded by oak leaves; he looks up at the sun and writes on a scroll. Beneath him is a very lightly sketched group showing figures engaged in artistic pursuits:[1] a man bends over an engraver's press and an angelic figure, holding a palette, stands before an easel. A little below, Dante kneels by the river of light, drinking from a shallow bowl which he holds with both hands in the heavenly stream. Behind him in the left corner of the page are several growing plants, some with flowers and buds; from these plants two small human forms are seen partially emerging.[2]

Again, it is apparent that Blake has introduced quite a number of details which have no connection with the text, although the illustration as a whole is clearly based upon the poem. We must expect to find in Blake's own corpus of belief an explanation for these additions. The similarity of Beatrice to representations of Vala,[3] the presence near Dante of the group engaged in artistic activities, and the fact that men are shown on one side of the stream and women on the other, would suggest that Blake intends this design to represent Nature and Art, both perfected through the power of Divine Vision which pours down upon this world from Eternity.

The natural aspects of this life, as always with Blake, are personified as feminine, while the figures representative of mental and artistic pursuits are masculine. Also, if we take the Spiritual Sun itself as a point of reference, we shall see that the masculine side is to the right, and the feminine to the left. All this is in accord with Blake's basic theories concerning the masculine and feminine principles.

Turning to the individual figures, the aged woman is evidently Enion, the Earth Mother and Emanation of Tharmas. In the Fallen World the generative instinct comes to be regarded as a sin through the cruelties of the Moral Law—represented by the book or tablet on which her hand rests. "Blind & age-bent," Enion is driven forth to the farthest wastes of Ulro, where she becomes a "Spectrous form in the Void."[4] There from the dark deep she wails the magnificent lament which closes the Second Night of *The Four Zoas*:

> "What is the price of Experience? do men buy it for a song?
> Or wisdom for a dance in the street? No, it is bought with the price

---

[1] W. M. Rossetti, in his catalogue of the Dante drawings in Gilchrist's *Life*, ii, p. 234, mentions in connection with this design that "one finds operations of pictorial art represented." In the same notation, he very rightly remarks that the illustration also has details introduced by Blake in accordance with his "Doctrine of Correspondences."

[2] This detail is, of course, suggested by *Paradiso* xxx, 64-67, as quoted.

[3] Beatrice, it will be recalled, is identified with Vala in Drawing 88.

[4] *Jerusalem* 87, 1; *Four Zoas* ii, 424 (p. 279).

Of all that a man hath, his house, his wife, his children.
Wisdom is sold in the desolate market where none come to buy,
And in the wither'd field where the farmer plows for bread in vain."

Four Zoas II, 398-402 (p. 278)

Eventually, however, Enion ceases to bewail the terrors of the Fallen World and begins to prophesy that there will someday be a Regeneration and that the Golden Age will return.

"Listen. I will tell thee what is done in the caverns of the grave.
The Lamb of God has rent the Veil of Mystery, soon to return
In Clouds & Fires round the rock & the Mysterious tree.
And as the seed waits Eagerly watching for its flower & fruit,
Anxious its little soul looks out into the clear expanse
To see if hungry winds are abroad with their invisible array,
So Man looks out in tree & herb & fish & bird & beast
Collecting up the scatter'd portions of his immortal body
Into the Elemental forms of every thing that grows.

. . . .

. . . . wherever a grass grows
Or a leaf buds, The Eternal Man is seen, is heard, is felt,
And all his sorrows, till he reassumes his ancient bliss."

Four Zoas VIII, 550-558; 576-578 (pp. 345-346)

Thus we find in this design both the lamenting Enion and, in the lower left corner "Man looks out in tree & herb." Enion's prophecy is fulfilled; under the life-giving influence of Divine Energy which streams from the Spiritual Sun, and is received as the draught of imaginative vision by the poet, Nature is made young and beautiful again in the person of Vala, and the infant loves play around her. The feminine side of this illustration once more bears Blake's message that unselfish love, even in its physical aspects, is divine in its origin and provides one of the pathways by which human beings in a Fallen World can rise out of themselves momentarily and catch glimpses of the joys of Eternity.

Turning now to the other side of the page, we find that just as Enion is restored to youth through Divine Love, so is the patriarchal poet made young again by partaking of the River of Life. The aged figure with oak leaves and scroll is, of course, Urizen. However, under the guidance of Imagination he is a benevolent figure. Through drinking at the fountain of Divine Inspiration, he is rejuvenated, and as the Fallen Enion has her counterpart in the Eternal Vala, so does the Fallen Urizen become renewed in the likeness of Los. While dominant Reason is an evil, intellectual warfare is the rightful occupation of the Poetic Genius. Thus it is that when Urizen denies his selfhood, he rises from his aged form in a new aspect of radiant youth.[5]

Upon the masculine side of the design, we find symbolized the other avenue of

[5] *Four Zoas* IX, 161-192 (pp. 351-352). The ancient poet and the youthful one of the present drawing doubtless represent a contrast between poetry which follows traditional forms mechanically, and that endowed with creative originality.

communication by means of which Fallen Man can retain the vision of his Immortal Life. Just as love can lead to a direct perception of God, so can creative art. Hence we find the painter busy at his easel and the engraver at his press.[6] These figures, together with Dante who represents poetry, personify the arts which were Blake's own means of creative expression.

Thus Nature and Art are both raised to the Eternal World by the agency of the Divine Imagination. In the Fallen World, unselfish love and creative art keep the Divine Vision and are the means by which "The Eternal Man is seen, is heard, is felt, And all his sorrows, till he reassumes his ancient bliss." It is to remind us of this, that the human forms appear among the foliage in the immediate foreground, close to the figure of the poet who drinks of the river of light.[7]

This drawing thus evidently presents in pictorial form Blake's theory of the four stages of vision. Enion represents Single Vision, which is pure physical sensation. Vision becomes twofold when we see spiritual forms in material objects, as the human figures in the plants.[8] Through love this vision becomes threefold: the spiritual forms are seen to exist not only as symbols in this world, but as realities in Eternity with which man can identify himself and thus escape from the bonds of the Fallen World even while his physical self still lives below. Finally, there is the supreme moment of creative exaltation when the artist becomes one with God as he drinks of the river of light and experiences Fourfold Vision.

Two of the great visionary experiences of Blake's life, both of which took place at Felpham, are reflected in this drawing. In the first, as already brought out in the discussion of the ninetieth illustration, he saw that all the objects of nature have spiritual forms and that these forms unite to make the body of Jesus; in the second, he was made aware of the four stages of perception of which man in this world is capable. The human forms in the river of light, as seen here, are a pictorial presentation of the first of these visions.

> In particles bright,
> The jewels of Light
> Distinct shone & clear.
> Amaz'd & in fear
> I each particle gazed,
> Astonish'd, Amazed;
> For each was a Man
> Human-form'd. Swift I ran,
> For they beckon'd to me
> Remote by the Sea,

[6] In the eighteenth engraving to Job, Blake as here introduces the tools of his own craft and shows his palette and brushes in the bottom margin. "The Whole Business of Man Is The Arts, & All Things Common." (Notes on the Laocoön Group, p. 582.)

[7] To emphasize further the divine nature of intellectual pursuits, Blake in this drawing shows two infant loves just beneath the figure of Dante who are engaged in reading a large open book which lies on the ground before them; below Beatrice another small figure reclines as though reading.

[8] See Schorer, *Politics of Vision*, p. 5.

Saying: "Each grain of Sand,
Every Stone on the Land,
Each rock & each hill,
Each fountain & rill,
Each herb & each tree,
Mountain, hill, earth & sea,
Cloud, Meteor & Star,
Are Men seen Afar."

> From a letter to Thomas Butts,
> October 2nd, 1800 (pp. 846-847)[9]

As the poet drinks of the river of light, comes the realization of Fourfold Vision:

Now I a fourfold vision see,
And a fourfold vision is given to me;
'Tis fourfold in my supreme delight
And threefold in soft Beulah's night
And twofold Always. May God us keep
From Single vision & Newton's sleep!

> From a letter to Thomas Butts,
> November 22nd, 1802 (pp. 861-862)

It is this multiple vision, represented here by the figure of the poet holding the bowl in the stream of light, that is so beautifully and expressively described in the famous lines from "Auguries of Innocence":[10]

To see a World in a Grain of Sand
And a Heaven in a Wild Flower,
Hold Infinity in the palm of your hand
And Eternity in an hour.

[9] The next two lines following those quoted are particularly reminiscent of the present design: "I stood in the Streams of Heaven's bright beams" . . .
[10] *Poetry and Prose*, p. 118.

99. THE QUEEN OF HEAVEN IN GLORY

AFTER DANTE has drunk of the river of light, his eyes are opened and he beholds the eternal abode of the Blessed rising like a great rose from a luminous sea. Beatrice resumes her seat within the Celestial Rose; St. Bernard then directs Dante's gaze to the most remote circle of the heavenly flower, where he beholds the Virgin Mary, surrounded by a host of angels. St. Bernard prays to the Virgin to grant that Dante may see the face of God. In answer to the prayer, he is vouchsafed a vision of the Blessed Trinity united in the person of Christ. At this point the *Divine Comedy* ends.

Blake again departs from the literal text and composes a design based largely on his own beliefs. This illustration has been described by S. Foster Damon:[1] "Plate 99, the Rose of Heaven, is the most paradoxical of all the designs, for it clearly represents the evil dominion of the Female Will. At the top sits Mary, naked, holding a sceptre and looking-glass (evidently the symbols of sex). Below her, to left and right, crouch

[1] *William Blake*, pp. 219-220.

the two sphinxes of 'Laws' and 'Dominion' upon the two Testaments, 'chain'd round,' while Aristotle and Homer are wide open. Lower yet are the petals of the Rose, each of which contains embracing figures, or others playing upon lyres. We must presume this picture to symbolize Blake's conception of the evil effects of the dogmas of the Immaculate Conception and the Virgin Birth."

The large flower fills the entire design. Mary kneels in the upper center, in the middle of the flower. She is not naked, but clad in a thin garment. In her right hand she holds a scepter and in her left a looking glass.[2] A halo of light sets off her head and her entire figure is also surrounded by a circle of small flying cherubs. From her appearance, from the symbols which she holds, and from her transparent garment, it is apparent that Blake here shows us Vala, the Goddess of Nature. As Damon says, the scepter and looking glass are sexual symbols; however, in addition they must be thought of as being attributes proper to the triumphant materialism which characterizes the Female Will. The scepter, of course, represents the worldly systems of authority through which she maintains her control and the mirror—the "Vegetable Glass of Nature"[3]—signifies her contemplation of purely material things. To recall again the inscription on the seventh design of this series: just as the ninety-seventh illustration showed that "for Tyrannical Purposes he has made This World the Foundation of All," so does this one continue the statement of Blake's feelings concerning Dante and the *Divine Comedy* by presenting in pictorial form the idea that Dante has also made "the Goddess Nature Mistress; Nature is his Inspirer & not the Holy Ghost."

Just beneath the Virgin sits the handsome naked form of Beatrice. As the Emanation and Inspiration of Dante, she looks over her left shoulder at the Female Will above her and raises her right hand in a gesture of tribute. Surrounding Beatrice on the petals of the flower is a circle of other female figures. While, of course, suggested by the group of Eve and other women of the Old Testament who attend the Virgin in Dante's poem, it will become apparent later in the discussion that they must also be thought of as the Daughters of Albion, or of Memory.

To the right and left, on the petals of the flower close to the female figures who flank Beatrice, lie open books. That on the left is marked "Homer" and that on the right "Aristotle." Beyond these, and at the edge of the flower on each side, are closed books bound around by chains. Near each of them Blake has written "Chain'd 'round" and, on the one at the right, "Bible." As Damon says, they evidently represent the Old and New Testaments. Upon each of the chained books sits a figure which is hard to make out, but which is in all probability some sort of sphinx, as Damon suggests. Above that at the left appears the word which Damon interprets as "Laws," but which appears rather to be "Thrones." Taken in conjunction with "Dominions," which is written above the other sphinx, we have the names of two of the higher orders of angels who inhabit paradise. Angels who have names associated with positions of worldly authority are, of course, the "angels" of convention and tradition of *The*

[2] Blake has identified this figure and the objects she holds by writing "Mary," "Scepter," and "Looking Glass" nearby.
[3] *Vision of the Last Judgment*, p. 639.

Marriage of Heaven and Hell, and as such are appropriate attendants for the Female Will.

The rest of the illustration is briefly described. In other petals, additional attendant figures are lightly sketched; they are all too indistinct to make out Blake's intention, save for those along the front edge of the flower which are clearly female angels playing upon harps—the angels of convention engaged in the pursuits of a conventional heaven. Leaves appear around the edge of the flower below, and circling it above are a number of heavenly bodies.

We have here, then, the world beneath the stars "in its vegetated mortality."[4] The Female Will is enthroned upon it to signify that in the Fallen World it is material Gods that are worshipped. The most potent weapon which woman has at her command to enforce her authority over man is that of the denial of sex. In Blake's opinion, worldly systems in general and particularly the church aid woman in this respect by forbidding sexual freedom. Woman, through jealousy and because of the desire for dominion over her mate, thus becomes the great supporter of conventional morality, so that her husband may not be able to escape from her authority and obtain sexual satisfaction elsewhere. Hence the Female Will here holds the sexual emblems which have the double significance of suggesting worldly power and materialism. It will be noted too that Blake has departed from Dante's description even with respect to the flower, which is not a rose at all, but a *sunflower,* which throughout Blake's work is always a sexual symbol.[5] In short, Blake is here once again presenting his opinion that, just as organized religion has set Satan up for worship under the name of God, so in the Madonna cult—with its attendant doctrines of the Immaculate Conception and the Virgin Birth—the church elevates Vala-Rahab and honors as the Queen of Heaven the Queen of the Fallen World.[6]

In order to maintain its sway, tyranny must deny access to inspired writings. Hence in the Fallen World practical rationalism is exalted and imagination suppressed. Blake firmly believed in the divinely prophetic origin of the Bible, but maintained that classical literature and philosophy were, in the main, wholly materialistic.[7] Thus the writings of Homer and Aristotle lie open, while the Testaments are chained shut and monsters, which bear the names of forces of earthly authority, sit upon them. Thus does Blake present pictorially his conviction that organized religion, while outwardly paying lip-service to the Bible, deliberately misinterprets it as a document of law and punishment instead of as one whose inner message is that of love, forgiveness, and freedom in the widest sense for all men.

[4] Letter to John Flaxman, September 21, 1800 (p. 844).

[5] For the sunflower, see the discussion of Drawing 20; also the poem, "Ah! Sun-flower." (*Poetry and Prose,* pp. 73-74.)

[6] It will be noted that the head of the scepter in the drawing is shaped like a lily, symbol of the Virgin Birth. In Blake's eyes, sex is holy and the gift of God; hence any doctrine which attempts to explain the birth of Christ as any other than natural, in effect implies the creation of evil by God, and is therefore blasphemous. The perversion of God's gifts is attributable solely to man's error in his fallen state. See *The Everlasting Gospel,* pp. 139-143; *Jerusalem* 61, 1-52; Damon, *op. cit.,* pp. 191 and 457; Frye, *Fearful Symmetry,* pp. 388-393.

[7] See Blackstone, *English Blake,* pp. 346-366, 424-429.

Blake states these opinions frequently in his writings, and one passage in particular is of great importance for its close connection with the present drawing:

> The Stolen and Perverted Writings of Homer & Ovid, of Plato & Cicero, which all men ought to contemn, are set up by artifice against the Sublime of the Bible; but when the New Age is at leisure to Pronounce, all will be set right, & those Grand Works of the more ancient & consciously & professedly Inspired Men will hold their proper rank, & the Daughters of Memory shall become the Daughters of Inspiration.
>
> Milton, Preface

We are now in a position to identify the women who surround Beatrice as the Daughters of Memory, or Daughters of Albion, for "The Greek Muses are daughters of Mnemosyne, or Memory, and not of Inspiration or Imagination."[8] Furthermore, when we recall that "Israel deliver'd from Egypt, is Art deliver'd from Nature & Imitation,"[9] the significance of the sphinxes which sit upon the Testaments immediately becomes clear.

It is apparent, therefore, that Blake had reservations concerning the inspired nature of Dante's final vision. After Dante drank of the river of light, he beheld heaven as a vegetable form in which were those who had successfully run the obstacle course of the Moral Law; here they are arranged in respect to each other with the precision of a diagram and pay court to the Female Will. Now to Blake, "The Gods of Greece & Egypt were Mathematical Diagrams," and he was convinced that, "If Morality was Christianity, Socrates was The Saviour."[10] The diagrammatic arrangement in Dante's poem of those Blessed in the terms of the Law, taken in connection with the vegetated world and the Female Will, made it clear to him that Dante had mistaken a vision of Ulro for a vision of Eden. It is this conviction which he presents in this illustration.[11]

[8] *A Descriptive Catalogue*, p. 595.

[9] Inscription on the engraving of the Laocoön Group, p. 580.

[10] *ibid.*, p. 581, and an annotation to Dr. R. J. Thornton's *New Translation of the Lord's Prayer*, p. 825.

[11] Symbolically, this drawing has much in common with the design on page 53 of *Jerusalem*: a female figure, wearing the triple crown of ecclesiastical power in the temporal realm, appears seated upon a sunflower which rises from the waters of Udan-Adan; behind her is a mandorla of the same shape as the head of the scepter in the present illustration. Both designs show the Fallen World as the realm of "the delusive Goddess Nature & her Laws." (Letter to George Cumberland, April 12, 1827, p. 927.)

4

ADDITIONAL DRAWINGS

꧁꧂꧁꧂꧁꧂꧁꧂꧁꧂꧁꧂꧁꧂꧁꧂꧁꧂꧁꧂꧁꧂

THE THREE FOLLOWING DRAWINGS cannot be connected directly with any specific passages in the *Divine Comedy* and are not included in William Michael Rossetti's catalogue of the Illustrations to Dante in the second volume of Gilchrist's *Life*. However, they clearly belong with the series and are similar in style and format. They passed with the other Dante drawings to Linnell after Blake's death. Although all apparently relate to the *Inferno*, they are placed at the end of the National Art-Collections Fund portfolio, and are so placed here in conformity with the usually accepted numbering of the designs.

꧁꧂꧁꧂꧁꧂꧁꧂꧁꧂꧁꧂꧁꧂꧁꧂꧁꧂꧁꧂꧁꧂

100. MALE FIGURE RECLINING

TWO ARCHES of rock, like those shown in many of the *Inferno* designs, form the setting. In the cavern-like opening of that in the foreground to the right, an aged bearded male figure has fallen asleep upon a stone lectern. A book is seen beneath his head, and scrolls trail down to the right of the desk; in his right hand is a pen. Directly in front of him, the body of a beardless young man lies flat on its back, with the head near the feet of the aged man.

Urizen, writing in his book of laws with his iron pen, has given up in despair over the hopelessness of his task.[1] At his feet lies the sleeping body of the Fallen Albion. All around are the barren wastes of the created world.

Numerous passages in Blake's prophetic writings suggest this scene. As Albion sinks to sleep, he calls upon Urizen to rule over the Fallen World:

> Take thou possession! take this Scepter! go forth in my might,
> For I am weary & must sleep in the dark sleep of Death.
> > *Four Zoas* II, 5-6 (p. 267)

Urizen institutes his repressive rule of law, but in the course of time comes to recognize the futility of his attempt to impose a purely negative authority. In despair, "Urizen sat stonied upon his rock, Forgetful of his own Laws."[2] He is grimly determined, however, never to renounce the Moral Law, for then his dominion would end:

> But still his books he bore in his strong hands, & his iron pen,
> For when he died they lay beside his grave, & when he rose
> He siez'd them with a gloomy smile; for wrap'd in his death clothes

[1] For Urizen writing, see Drawing 92 and the accompanying discussion. It will be recalled that human forms enclosed in caverns have figured in a number of the other Dante drawings, and are a common motif in Blake's symbolism.

[2] *Four Zoas* VIII, 415-416 (p. 342). See also *Urizen*, 449-453 (p. 232), as quoted in the Introduction.

197

He hid them when he slept in death, when he reviv'd, the clothes
Were rotted by the winds; the books remain'd still unconsum'd,
Still to be written & interleav'd with brass & iron & gold,
Time after time, for such a journey none but iron pens
Can write And adamantine leaves recieve, nor can the man who goes
The journey obstinate refuse to write time after time.

Four Zoas VI, 167-175 (p. 305)

This design should be compared with that of plate 64 of *Jerusalem*, in which a female figure at the top of the page lies asleep upon a stone altar and dreams of her lost immortal life, while at the bottom Urizen reclines beside his open book and looks up in contentment at her apparent passivity under his rule of law, being unaware of her dream.

We have here what seems to be a comment by Blake in his own terms upon the *Inferno*, or perhaps upon the *Divine Comedy* as a whole. He probably means to imply that, through his attempt to justify the ways of the Angry God of This World and to set forth the punishments for violating his laws, Dante has in fact slain the Divine Humanity.

O Human Imagination, O Divine Body I have Crucified,
I have turned my back upon thee into the Wastes of Moral Law.

Jerusalem 24, 23-24

101. DIAGRAM OF HELL-CIRCLES

This is not properly a drawing at all, but a diagram of the most sketchy sort of the nine circles of the Inferno—shown rising like a spiral—with quite a few notations in Blake's handwriting. Many of the inscriptions are so faint and hastily written as to be very difficult to decipher. The only figure is a crudely drawn angel who is shown as though standing inside the ninth spiral with traces of the lower parts of his body within a couple of the circles below. As his name written on his left wing attests, this represents Lucifer.

Most of the inscriptions in the center are purely descriptive in character and, unlike the drawing of the spheres of the *Paradiso* (Drawing 97), the diagram itself is based directly on Dante's scheme without other connotations. The two inscriptions in the lower left and right corners are, however, very important for understanding Blake's opinions concerning Dante and Dante's beliefs. They have already been discussed in Chapter 3 of the Introduction, but are quoted here for reference.

In the lower left:
   It seems as if Dante's supreme Good was something Superior to the Father or Jesus; for if he gives his rain to the Evil & the Good, & his Sun to the Just & the Unjust, He could never have Built Dante's Hell, nor the Hell of the Bible neither, in the way our Parsons explain it—It must have been originally Formed by the devil Himself; & So I understand it to have been.

In the lower right:
   Whatever Book is for Vengeance for Sin & Whatever Book is Against the Forgiveness of Sins is not of the Father, but of Satan the Accuser & Father of Hell.

1 9 8

Also written outside the circles, this time along the right margin, is another inscription which refers purely to the scheme of the *Divine Comedy* and to the fact that, after passing the center of the earth at the bottom of the infernal regions, the direction of gravity changes, so that Dante and Virgil have to turn upside down to right themselves. To this Blake appends a brief note which suggests that to him Dante's Hell and Purgatory are pretty much the same, both being places where the Angry God of This World exacts punishments.[1]

> This is Upside Down When view'd from Hell's gate, (which ought to be at top,) /
> But right When View'd from Purgatory after they have passed the Center.
> In Equivocal Worlds Up & Down are Equivocal.[2]

Beginning at the bottom, each circle is numbered and has one or more brief inscriptions of a factual sort dealing with the nature and inhabitants of the various zones. Some of these reveal confusion about the exact details of Dante's scheme, which is not surprising considering that certain features of the infernal regions as Dante describes them are not easy to make out and that Blake did not, of course, have the benefit of the many full commentaries on the subject which are available today. These inscriptions are here given under the number of the circle in which they occur.

1. Limbo. Charon.
2. Minos.
3. Cerberus.
4. Plutus & Phlegyas.
5. City of Dis. Queen of Endless Woe.[3] furies &. . . .[4] Lesser Circle Point of the Universe.[5] Canto Eleventh Line 68.
6. Minotaur. The City of Dis seems to occupy the space between the Fifth & Sixth Circles or perhaps it occupies both Circles with its Environs.
7. Centaurs. Most Likely Dante describes the 7, 8 & 9 Circles in Canto XI v 18. 3 (Compartments?). Dante calls them *Cerchietti.*[6]
8. Malebolge. Geryon. Containing 10 (gulfs?).
9. Lucifer. Containing 9 Round(s?).[7]

---

[1] This inscription is written in such a way that the first part must be read with the page held so that the right margin becomes the top. At the point indicated by the slant mark (/), the page must be reversed in order to read the rest. It will be noted also that the words enclosed in parentheses are in small printed letters rather than in script, and may not have been written by Blake.

[2] Frye, *Fearful Symmetry*, p. 275, remarks in connection with this sentence: "The fallen world knows nothing of position or direction; its center is anywhere and its circumference nowhere, as in some definitions of God."

[3] Quoted from line 45 of Cary's translation of Canto IX of the *Inferno*.

[4] Another word (perhaps "Gorgon"?) follows, but has been so covered over by one of the pale washes which tint some of the circles that it is indecipherable.

[5] Quoted from lines 67-68 of Cary's translation of Canto XI.

[6] This word occurs in *Inferno* XI, 17. Cary renders it in line 18 of his translation by "close circles."

[7] Apparently this notation is based inaccurately upon the "argument" given by Cary at the beginning of his translation of Canto XXXI, where he speaks of "the ninth circle, in which there are four rounds."

102. FEMALE FIGURES ATTACKED BY SERPENTS

SEVEN large naked female forms fill the page. They stand, sit and lie in contorted poses on what appears to be hot sand. Most of them have anguished expressions and some have their eyes shut. Among them are three serpents, two of which glide suggestively across the genitals of the recumbent figures at the right. Between the two forms on which the serpents prey, a small stream runs through the sand and the farther figure has her legs in the water.[1]

This drawing does not illustrate any recognizable incident of the *Inferno*, although it recalls a number of the illustrations based upon the twenty-fourth and twenty-fifth cantos, in which the thieves are attacked by serpents. It will be remembered that the events in the seventh trench of the Eighth Circle had a peculiar fascination for Blake, as he made no less than eight designs to illustrate them. In the discussion of the forty-seventh drawing, the symbolism of serpents in Blake's work is considered at some length.

Again, this illustration seems to be a general comment upon the *Inferno*. As Drawing 100 portrayed the downfall of masculine reason in a fallen world, so does this show that the attempt of the Female Will to dominate ultimately brings disaster upon itself. Having accepted the offer of the serpent in order to enslave men to their will, the Daughters of Albion now find themselves wholly in the power of the evil forces of materialism. Sexual repression and jealousy, which they have made their weapons, have turned against them in the form of the Moral Law and have made their land a desert from which all happiness and love is banished. In the Fallen World, love ceases to be a source of spiritual joy and becomes all too often stealthy lust satisfying itself upon unwilling and exhausted bodies.

> . . . most thro' midnight streets I hear
> How the youthful Harlot's curse
> Blasts the new born Infant's tear,
> And blights with plagues the Marriage hearse.
> "London," from *Songs of Experience* (p. 75)

It has already been shown in the discussion of Drawing 99 that Blake placed much of the blame for this state of affairs upon the church with its unyielding laws of sexual prohibition. Inasmuch as the *Inferno* is the catalogue of the punishments which befall those who break Urizen's law, and the entire *Divine Comedy* is a presentation of traditional Roman Catholic dogma, Blake here shows his own version of the dreadful suffering that such a restrictive ethic inevitably brings to Woman in the Fallen World. The greatest evil that follows upon the fall from Beulah into Ulro is, in Blake's opinion, that love ceases to be a source of mutual joy which provides a way to Eden, and becomes surrounded with shame, guilt, and fear, enslaving both men and women.[2]

A number of passages in *The Four Zoas* which describe the sufferings of the Fallen World under the rule of Urizen's law, have imagery which suggests this design.

[1] Even in the original, this passage is hard to make out—the legs of the figure are apparently unfinished.

[2] See the discussion of Drawing 9, "Minos."

For Urizen beheld the terrors of the Abyss wandering among
The ruin'd spirits, once his children & the children of Luvah.

. . . .

. . . . some with crowns of serpents & some
With monsters girding round their bosoms; some lying on beds of sulphur,
On racks & wheels; he beheld women marching o'er burning wastes
Of Sand in bands of hundreds & of fifties & of thousands . . .

. . . .

Many in serpents & in worms, stretched out enormous length
Over the sullen mould & slimy tracks, obstruct his way
Drawn out from deep to deep, woven by ribb'd
And scaled monsters or arm'd in iron shell, or shell of brass
Or gold: a glittering torment shining & hissing in eternal pain;
Some, columns of fire or of water, sometimes stretch'd out in heighth,
Sometimes in length, sometimes englobing, wandering in vain seeking for ease.
His voice to them was but an inarticulate thunder, for their Ears
Were heavy & dull, & their eyes & nostrils closed up.
Oft he stood by a howling victim Questioning in words
Soothing or Furious; no one answer'd; every one wrap'd up
In his own sorrow howl'd regardless of his words, nor voice
Of sweet repose could he obtain, tho' oft assay'd with tears.
He knew they were his Children ruin'd in his ruin'd world.

               Four Zoas VI, 87-88; 104-107; 117-130 (pp. 302-304)

    I put not any trust in thee, nor in thy glitt'ring scales;
    Thy eyelids are a terror to me; & the flaming of thy crest,
    The rushing of thy scales confound me, thy hoarse rushing scales.
    And if that Los had not built me a tower upon a rock,
    I must have died in the dark desert among noxious worms.

               Four Zoas VIIb, 80-84 (p. 325)

In spite of unfinished details, chiefly in the upper left, this drawing is approaching completion. Although the poses are often extremely contorted, several of the figures are effectively and powerfully modeled—in fact, the finest nude female forms in any of the Dante designs, if not in Blake's entire production.[3]

[3] The results of Blake's studies of Michelangelo no doubt appear in the sculptural character of these forms. C. H. Collins Baker has made the interesting suggestion that the very contorted figure standing in the center is an adaptation of a figure which supports the Column of the Flagellation in the topmost zone of Michelangelo's Last Judgment ("The Sources of Blake's Pictorial Expression," *Huntington Library Quarterly*, IV, 1940-1941, p. 365).

APPENDICES, BIBLIOGRAPHY
AND INDEX

APPENDIX A

THE PAGINATION followed in all references to *Poetry and Prose of William Blake*, edited by Geoffrey Keynes, is that of the fourth and later editions. References can be located in the earlier editions, the pagination of which is different, by means of the following table. Numbers in the left column refer to pages in the fourth and later editions. In each case the first line on the page is taken as a point of reference and in the right column appears the number of the page in the earlier editions on which the same line will be found.

N.B. There being no significant differences in the first 150 pages of the two editions, they are not tabulated; also, as Blake's own pagination of *Milton* and *Jerusalem* is indicated in both editions, it is not necessary to tabulate the pages on which they appear.

4th edn.	earlier edns.	4th edn.	earlier edns.	4th edn.	earlier edns.	4th edn.	earlier edns.
150	150	255	282	360	442	730	927
155	157	260	290	365	450	740	937
160	165	265	298	370	457	750	949
165	172	270	306	375	464	760	959
170	178	275	313	* * *		770	970
175	183	280	320	570	754	780	980
180	189	285	328	580	764	790	991
185	194	290	336	590	776	800	1002
190	200	295	343	600	786	810	1012
195	206	300	351	610	797	820	1023
200	214	305	358	620	808	830	1034
205	222	310	366	630	819	840	1044
210	229	315	374	640	831	850	1055
215	236	320	381	650	842	860	1066
220	243	325	389	660	853	870	1077
225	248	330	396	670	864	880	1086
230	254	335	404	680	875	890	1097
235	259	340	411	690	886	900	1108
240	264	345	419	700	897	910	1120
245	270	350	427	710	906	920	1131
250	276	355	434	720	916	928	1139

APPENDIX B

THE PRESENT LOCATIONS of Blake's Dante drawings are here listed (numbers correspond to those given to the illustrations in the text).

National Gallery of Victoria, Melbourne.
1, 5, 9, 13, 15, 16, 19, 20, 25, 27, 28, 31, 34, 36, 37, 39, 47, 49, 51, 55, 56, 57, 59, 62, 63, 69, 73, 75, 76, 84, 85, 89, 90, 94, 95, 99.

Fogg Museum of Art, Harvard University, Cambridge, Massachusetts.
6, 7, 11, 17, 18, 22, 23, 26, 29, 30, 32, 33, 41, 43, 52, 54, 61, 64, 66, 67, 71, 77, 83.

Tate Gallery, London.
2, 4, 8, 12, 14, 24, 35, 40, 44, 46, 53, 58, 60, 70, 74, 78, 80, 88, 98, 102.

British Museum, London.
21, 38, 45, 48, 50, 68, 72, 82, 87, 91, 96, 100, 101.

City Museum and Art Gallery, Birmingham.
3, 10, 42, 65, 81, 92.

Ashmolean Museum, Oxford.
86, 93, 97.

Royal Institution of Cornwall, Truro.
79.

APPENDIX C

THE PRINCIPAL EXHIBITIONS at which a considerable number of the Dante drawings have been shown are here listed, together with the drawings exhibited. The numbers correspond to those given to the illustrations in the discussion of them in the text.

Royal Academy, London. Winter Exhibition, 1893.
4, 5, 9, 10, 11, 15, 20, 22, 31, 35, 43, 49, 51, 53, 57, 58, 60, 63, 74, 75, 77, 81, 82, 85, 86, 87, 88, 90, 93.

Tate Gallery, London, 1913 (also shown at Whitworth Institute, Manchester, Nottingham Castle Art Museum, and National Gallery of Scotland, Edinburgh, 1914).
2, 4, 8, 10, 17, 20, 25, 34, 40, 44, 53, 60, 63, 68, 70, 74, 82, 86, 87, 102.

Messrs. Scott & Fowles, New York, 1921.
6, 7, 11, 17, 18, 23, 26, 29, 30, 32, 33, 41, 43, 52, 61, 64, 66, 67, 71, 83.

Bibliothèque Nationale, Paris, 1937; also Albertina, Vienna, 1937.
3, 4, 10, 40, 42, 53, 58, 80, 81, 86, 88, 93.

Tate Gallery, London, 1947 (those given in parentheses were *not* included in the earlier exhibitions held in the same year in Paris, Antwerp, and Zürich).
4, (8), 10, (12), (14), 35, (53), 60, (70), (74), (78), (80), 88, (98), 102.

BIBLIOGRAPHY

See also Bibliographical Note following the Foreword

THE FOLLOWING BIBLIOGRAPHY lists all items cited in the text and footnotes. In addition, references of importance to Blake's Illustrations to Dante are given, even if not previously cited, and all items which contain such direct references to the Dante Illustrations are indicated by being preceded by an asterisk (*); in such cases page references are also given. Exhibition and sales catalogues are listed separately at the end of the Bibliography, by date rather than alphabetically.

When the city of publication is not mentioned in an entry, London is to be understood.

Alighieri, Dante. *Dante con l'espositione di Christoforo Landino et di Alessandro Velutello, Sopra la sua Comedia dell'Inferno, del Purgatorio, & del Paradiso*, Venice, Marchiò Sessa & fratelli, 1564 (another edn., 1578).

Alighieri, Dante. *The Divine Comedy* (translated by the Rev. H. F. Cary), The Everyman's Library, 1948.

Alighieri, Dante. *The Divine Comedy of Dante Alighieri*, edited by John D. Sinclair, 1948.

*Alighieri, Dante. *The Divine Comedy of Dante Alighieri, translated into English verse by Melville Best Anderson; with notes and elucidations by the translator, an introduction by Arthur Livingston, and thirty-two drawings by William Blake* . . . New York, The Heritage Press [1944].

*Alighieri, Dante. *The Inferno from la Divina Commedia of Dante Alighieri as translated by the Reverend Henry Francis Cary and illustrated with the seven engravings of William Blake*, New York, Printed by Richard W. Ellis for Cheshire House, 1931.

Baker, C. H. Collins. *Catalogue of William Blake's Drawings and Paintings in the Huntington Library*, San Marino, California, 1938.

Baker, C. H. Collins. "The Sources of Blake's Pictorial Expression," *Huntington Library Quarterly*, IV, 1940-1941, pp. 359-367.

Baker, C. H. Collins. "William Blake, Painter," *Huntington Library Bulletin*, X, 1936, pp. 135-148.

Binyon, Laurence. *Catalogue of Drawings by British Artists and Artists of Foreign Origin working in Great Britain, preserved in the Department of Prints and Drawings of the British Museum*, 1900.

Binyon, Laurence. *The Drawings and Engravings of William Blake*, 1922.

Binyon, Laurence. *The Engraved Designs of William Blake*, London and New York, 1926.

*Birnbaum, Martin. *Jacovleff and Other Artists*, New York, 1946, pp. 65-96 (largely reprinted from Scott & Fowles catalogue of 1921—q.v.).

Blackstone, Bernard. *English Blake*, Cambridge, England, 1949.

Blair, Robert. *The Grave, a Poem*, R. H. Cromek, 1808; another edn., R. Ackerman, 1813 (engravings by L. Schiavonetti from Blake's designs).

*Blake, William. *Illustrations to the Divine Comedy of Dante*, printed privately for the National Art-Collections Fund, 1922.

Blake, William. *Poetry and Prose of William Blake* (ed. Geoffrey Keynes), London and New York, 1927 and later edns.

Blake, William. *The Works of William Blake* (ed. E. J. Ellis and W. B. Yeats), 1893.

*Blake, William (subject). "Blake the Artist," *The Light Blue*, Cambridge, England, II, 1867, pp. 289-292. [The author, who signed himself simply "P.M.," had evidently seen the Dante drawings which belonged to Linnell and had never as yet been publicly exhibited.]

*Blake, William (subject). "Illustrations to the Divine Comedy of Dante by William Blake (1757-1827)," National Art-Collections Fund, *16th Annual Report*, 1919, pp. 40-44.

*Blake, William (subject). *The Literary Gazette*, August 18, 1827, pp. 540-541.

Blunt, Anthony. "Blake's 'Brazen Serpent,'" *Journal of the Warburg and Courtauld Institutes*, VI, 1943, pp. 225-227.

Blunt, Anthony. "Blake's Pictorial Imagination," *Journal of the Warburg and Courtauld Institutes*, VI, 1943, pp. 190-212.

Carroll, Rev. J. S. *Prisoners of Hope; an Exposition of Dante's Purgatorio*, 1906.

*Damon, S. Foster. *William Blake: His Philosophy and Symbols*, Boston, New York, and London, 1924, pp. 218-220.

Davies, J. G. *The Theology of William Blake*, Oxford, 1948.

*Eglinton, Guy. "Dante and Blake," an essay in *Reaching for Art*, Boston, 1931, pp. 106-120 (reprinted from *International Studio*, LXXX, 1924, pp. 239-248).

Ellis, Edwin J. *The Real Blake*, 1907.

Figgis, Darrell. *The Paintings of William Blake*, 1925.

Frye, Northrop. *Fearful Symmetry: A Study of William Blake*, Princeton, New Jersey, 1947.

*Gilchrist, Alexander. *Life of William Blake with Selections from his Poems and Other Writings*, 2nd ed., 1880, I, pp. 375-378; II, pp. 227-234 (catalogue of the Dante drawings by W. M. Rossetti).

Grigson, Geoffrey. *Samuel Palmer, the Visionary Years*, 1947.

*Hoff, Ursula. "William Blake's Illustrations to Dante's Divine Comedy," in *Masterpieces of the National Gallery of Victoria*, Melbourne and London, 1949, pp. 91-97.

Jung, Carl Gustav. *Psychological Types or the Psychology of Individuation*, New York, 1933.

Keynes, Geoffrey. *A Bibliography of William Blake*, New York, 1921.

Keynes, Geoffrey. *Blake's Illustrations to Young's "Night Thoughts,"* Cambridge, Massachusetts, 1927.

Keynes, Geoffrey. *Blake Studies*, 1949.

Keynes, Geoffrey. *The Note-Book of William Blake called the Rossetti Manuscript*, 1935.

Keynes, Geoffrey. *Pencil Drawings by William Blake*, 1927.

Keynes, Geoffrey. *William Blake's Engravings*, 1950.

Nanavutty, Piloo. "A Title-Page in Blake's Genesis Manuscript," *Journal of the Warburg and Courtauld Institutes*, X, 1947, pp. 114-122.

Palmer, A. H. (ed.). *The Life and Letters of Samuel Palmer, Painter and Etcher*, 1892.

Percival, Milton O. *William Blake's "Circle of Destiny,"* New York, 1938.

Preston, Kerrison (ed.). *The Blake Collection of W. Graham Robertson described by the Collector*, edited with an introduction by Kerrison Preston. Published for the William Blake Trust, 1952.

Richardson, Jonathan. *A Discourse on the Dignity, Certainty, Pleasure, and Advantage, of the Science of a Connoisseur*, 1719.

*Robinson, Henry Crabb. *Diary, Reminiscences, and Correspondence of Henry Crabb Robinson* (ed. Thomas Sadler), 1869 and later edns. [More reliable are the references to Blake as published in Part II of Symons, *William Blake*—q.v.—and in *Crabb Robin-*

son, *Blake, Coleridge, Wordsworth, Lamb, Etc., being Selections from the Remains of Henry Crabb Robinson*, ed. Edith J. Morley, Manchester, 1922.]

Rossetti, William Michael. *The Rossetti Papers, 1862-1870*, 1903.

Rossetti, William Michael. *Some Reminiscences of William Michael Rossetti*, New York, 1906.

Russell, Archibald G. B. *The Engravings of William Blake*, 1912.

Russell, Archibald G. B. "The Graham Robertson Collection," *Burlington Magazine*, XXXVII, 1920, pp. 27-39.

Russell, Archibald G. B. *The Letters of William Blake together with a Life by Frederick Tatham*, 1906.

Schorer, Mark. *William Blake, the Politics of Vision*, New York, 1946.

Sloss, D. J., and Wallis, J. P. R. *The Prophetic Writings of William Blake*, Oxford, 1926.

Smith, John Thomas. *Nollekens and his Times*, 1828, vol. II.

Story, Alfred J. *The Life of John Linnell*, 1892.

Swinburne, Algernon Charles. *William Blake, a Critical Essay*, 1868 and later edns.

Symons, Arthur. *William Blake*, 1907.

Thornton, Robert John. *The Pastorals of Virgil, with a Course of English Reading, Adapted for Schools*, 3rd edn., F. C. & J. Rivingtons, 1821 (contains engravings and woodcuts by Blake).

Todd, Ruthven. "The Techniques of William Blake's Illuminated Printing," *Print*, VI, 1948, pp. 53-65.

Toynbee, Paget. "Chronological List of English Translations from Dante from Chaucer to the Present Day," *Dante Society, Cambridge, Massachusetts, 24th Annual Report*, 1905.

*Toynbee, Paget. "Dante in English Art," *Dante Society, Cambridge, Massachusetts, 38th Annual Report*, 1919, pp. 13-24 and cross refs.

Toynbee, Paget. *A Dictionary of Proper Names and Notable Matters in the Works of Dante*, Oxford, 1898.

*Toynbee, Paget. "The Earliest English Illustrators of Dante," *Quarterly Review*, CCXI, 1909, pp. 395-417 (Blake's Dante illustrations, pp. 415-417).

Tozer, Rev. H. F. *An English Commentary on Dante's Divina Commedia*, Oxford, 1901.

Wicksteed, Joseph H. *Blake's Vision of the Book of Job*, London and New York, 1910 (2nd edn., 1924).

*Wilson, Mona. *The Life of William Blake*, 1927, pp. 296-297, 371 (2nd edn. without notes, 1932, pp. 290-291; 3rd edn., 1948, pp. 312-313, 391-392).

Witcutt, W. P. *Blake, a Psychological Study*, 1946.

Wolf, Edwin II. "The Blake-Linnell Accounts in the Library of Yale University," *Papers of the Bibliographical Society of America*, XXXVII, 1943, pp. 1-22.

Wright, Thomas. *Blake's Heads of the Poets*, Olney, Buckinghamshire, 1925.

*Wright, Thomas. *The Life of William Blake*, Olney, Buckinghamshire, 1929, II, pp. 84, 104, 111, 115, 156.

*Yeats, William Butler. "William Blake and his Illustrations to Dante," an essay in *Ideas of Good and Evil*, London and New York, 1903, pp. 176-225 (reprinted from *The Savoy*, II, 1896, no. 3, pp. 41-57; no. 4, pp. 25-41; no. 5, pp. 31-36; reprinted in *Collected Works*, 1908, vol. VI).

Young, Edward. *The Complaint, and the Consolation; or, Night Thoughts*, R. Edwards, 1797 (edition with engravings by Blake).

EXHIBITION AND SALES CATALOGUES

Burlington Fine Arts Club. Exhibition of the Works of William Blake. London, 1876 [introductory remarks by W. B. Scott].

*Exhibition of Works by the Old Masters and by Deceased Members of the British School including a Collection of Water Colour Drawings, &c., by William Blake, Frederick Calvert, Samuel Palmer, and Louisa, Marchioness of Waterford. London, the Royal Academy, 1893, pp. 41-45.

Carfax Exhibition of Works by William Blake . . . 14 June to 31 July 1906. Carfax & Co., Ltd., 24 Bury Street, St. James's, London, S.W.

*The National Gallery, British Art. Catalogue of Loan Exhibition of Works of William Blake. October to December, 1913, pp. 28-32. [Brief biography and notes on items by A. G. B. Russell. This exhibition was also shown at the Whitworth Institute, Manchester, in February and March, 1914, at the Nottingham Castle Art Museum in April 1914, and at the National Gallery of Scotland, Edinburgh, May 22 to July 4, 1914, at all of which catalogues were published.]

*Catalogue of the John Linnell Collection of . . . works by William Blake, Obtained direct from the Artist . . . which . . . will be sold by Auction by Messrs. Christie, Manson, & Woods . . . at . . . 8 King Street, St. James's Square, London, on Friday, March 15, 1918, pp. 16-19.

*Catalogue of an Exhibition of Original Water-Color Drawings by William Blake to Illustrate Dante with an introductory essay by Martin Birnbaum. New York, Scott & Fowles, 1921.

*Aquarelles de Turner, oeuvres de Blake. Paris, Bibliothèque Nationale, 1937, exhibit nos. 17-28. [Exhibition held January 15 to February 15, 1937.]

Staatliche Graph. Sammlung Albertina. Verein der Museumsfreunde in Wien. Ausstellung von Englischen Graphiken und Aquarellen, W. Blake und J. M. W. Turner. Wien, März-April 1937. [Exhibit nos. 17-28.]

A Descriptive Catalogue of an Exhibition of the Works of William Blake Selected from Collections in the United States. The Philadelphia Museum of Art, Philadelphia, Pennsylvania, 1939.

*William Blake, 1757-1827. Organized by The British Council, Paris, Antwerp, Zürich. Tate Gallery, 1947, pp. 22-23, 34-36. [An exhibition based upon one shown earlier in the same year on the Continent, but with additions from the W. Graham Robertson collection and from the permanent collection of the Tate Gallery. See also catalogue in French issued at the time of the exhibition at the Galerie René Drouin, Paris.]

Catalogue of Original Works by William Blake the property of the late Graham Robertson, Esq., which will be sold at Auction by Christie, Manson & Woods, Ltd., at Spencer House, 27, St. James's Place, St. James's Street, S.W. 1, on Friday, July 22, 1949.

The Tempera Paintings of William Blake. A Critical Catalogue with an Introduction by Geoffrey Keynes. Arts Council of Great Britain, 4, St. James's Square, London, S.W. 1, 1951.

INDEX

ILLUSTRATIONS

The order of illustrations has been adjusted to permit comparison of the engravings with drawings of the same subject.

The numbering of the plates is the same as that followed in the discussion of them in the Commentary, with the following three additions:

A. William Blake at Hampstead. Pencil drawing by John Linnell (c. 1825). By permission of the Syndics of the Fitzwilliam Museum, Cambridge.

B. William Blake in 1820. Pencil drawing by John Linnell. By permission of the Syndics of the Fitzwilliam Museum, Cambridge.

103. Head of Dante. One of a series of Heads of the Poets painted by Blake in tempera to decorate the library of William Hayley at Felpham, Sussex (1801-1803). By permission of the City Art Gallery, Manchester.

William Blake at Hampstead. Pencil drawing by John Linnell (c. 1825).
Reproduced by permission of the Syndics of the Fitzwilliam Museum, Cambridge.

William Blake in 1820. Pencil drawing by John Linnell.
Reproduced by permission of the Syndics of the Fitzwilliam Museum, Cambridge.

1. Dante Running from the Three Beasts.

2. Dante and Virgil Penetrating the Forest.

3. The Mission of Virgil.

4.   The Inscription over Hell-Gate.

5. The Vestibule of Hell, and the Souls Mustering to Cross the Acheron.

6. Charon and the Condemned Souls.

7.   Homer, Bearing the Sword, and his Companions.

8. Homer and the Ancient Poets.

9. Minos.

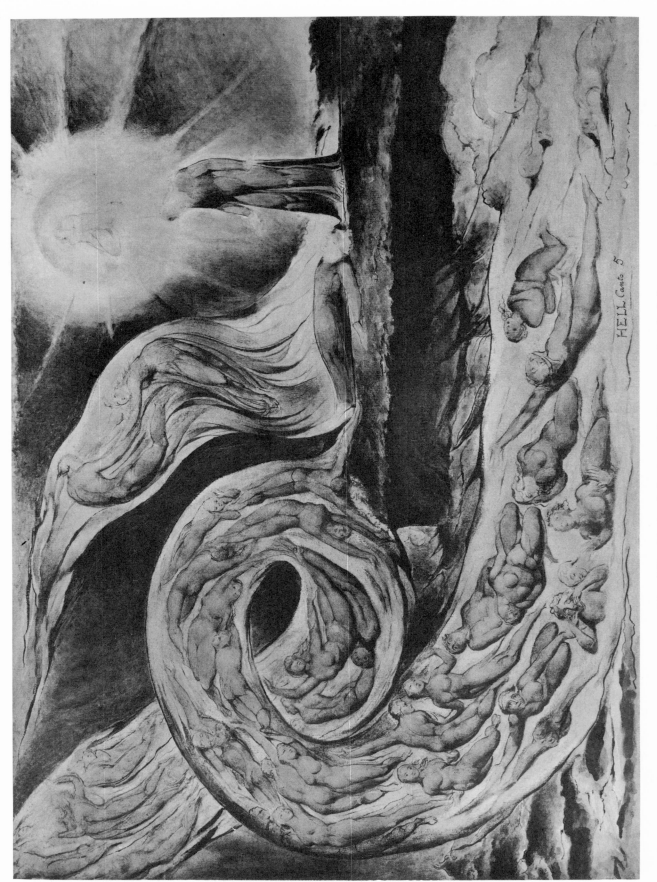

10. The Circle of the Lustful: Francesca da Rimini.

10E. The Circle of the Lustful: Francesca da Rimini (engraving).

11.   The Circle of the Gluttons with Cerberus.

12. Cerberus—first version.

13. Cerberus—second version.

14.   Plutus.

15.   The Stygian Lake, with the Ireful Sinners Fighting.

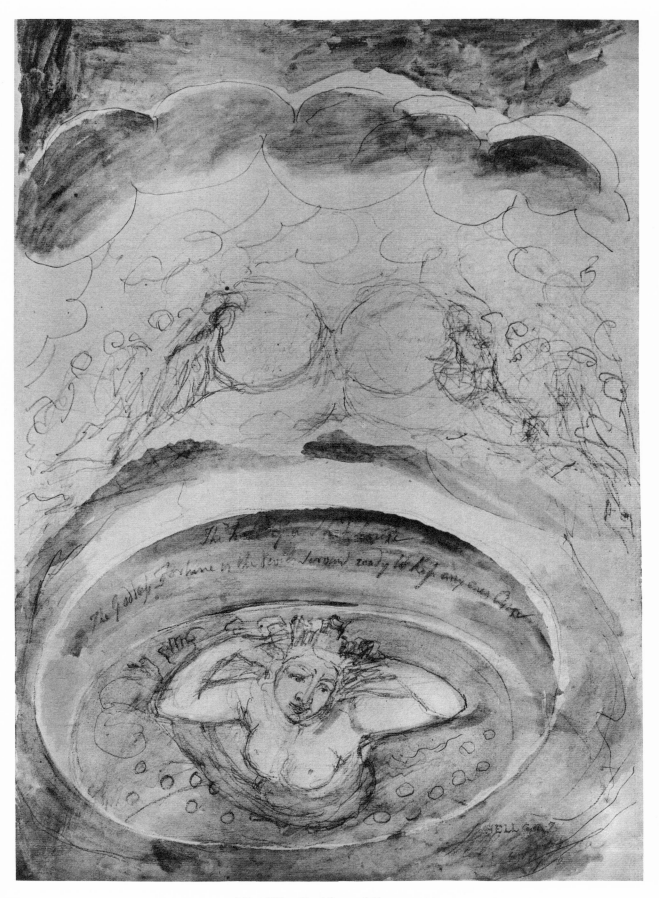

16. The Goddess of Fortune.

17. Dante and Virgil Crossing towards the City of Dis.

18. Virgil Repelling Filippo Argenti from the Boat.

19. The Angel Crossing Styx.

20.   The Gorgon-Head and the Angel Opening the Gate of Dis.

21. Farinata degli Uberti.

22. The Minotaur.

23. The Centaurs and the River of Blood.

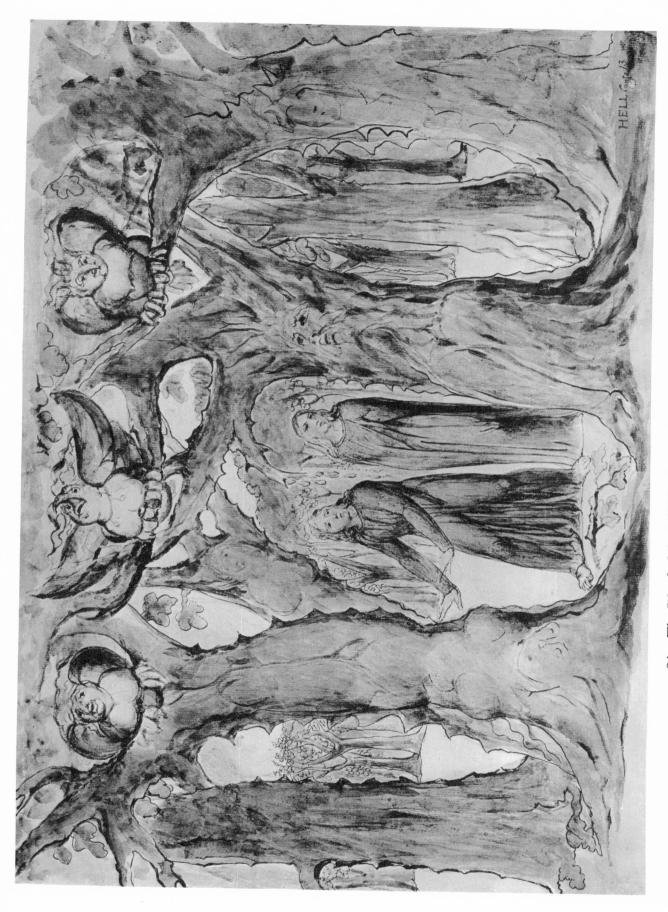

24. The Wood of the Self-Murderers: the Harpies and the Suicides.

25. The Hell-Hounds Hunting the Destroyers of Their Own Goods.

26. The Blasphemers.

27. Capaneus the Blasphemer.

HELL canto 14

28.   The Symbolic Figure of the Course of Human History Described by Virgil.

29. Jacopo Rusticucci and His Comrades.

30. The Usurers.

31. Geryon Conveying Dante and Virgil Downwards.

32.   The Seducers Chased by Devils.

33. The Flatterers.

HELL Canto 18

34. The Devils Under the Bridge.

35. The Simoniac Pope.

36.   The Necromancers and Augurs.

37.   The Devil Carrying the Lucchese Magistrate to the Boiling Pitch-Pool of Corrupt Officials.

HELL Canto 21

38. Virgil Abashing the Devils.

39. The Devils Setting Out with Dante and Virgil.

HELL Canto 22.

40.   The Devils, with Dante and Virgil, by the Side of the Pool.

41. Ciampolo Tormented by the Devils.

41E. Ciampolo Tormented by the Devils (engraving).

42. Baffled Devils Fighting.

42E. Baffled Devils Fighting (engraving).

HELL Canto 23

43. Dante and Virgil Escaping from the Devils.

44. The Hypocrites with Caiaphas.

45.   The Laborious Passage Along the Rocks—first version.

46. The Laborious Passage Along the Rocks—second version.

HELL Canto 24

47. The Thieves and Serpents.

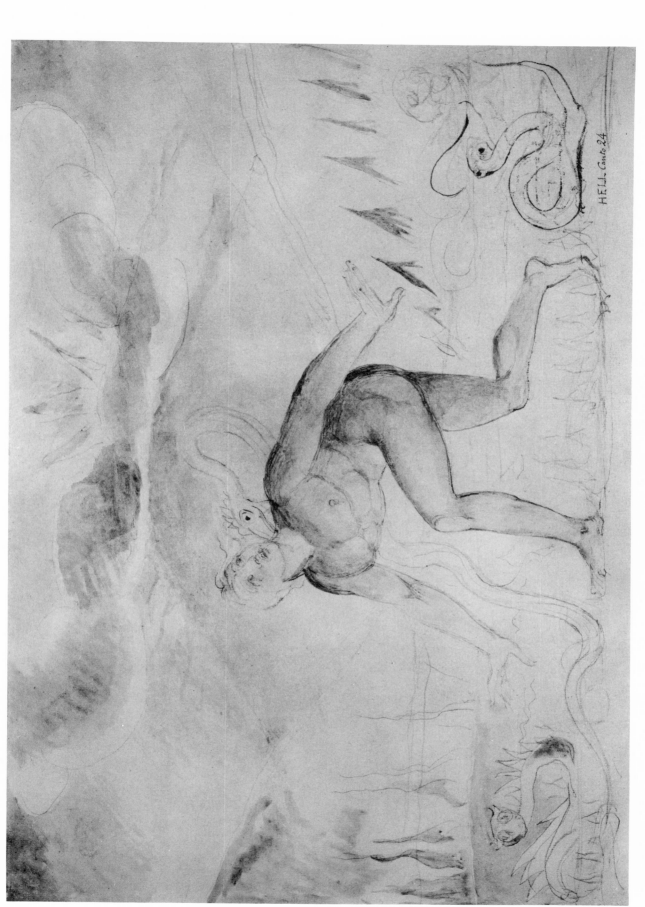

48.   The Serpent Attacking Vanni Fucci.

49. Fucci "Making the Figs" Against God.

50. Cacus.

51.   The Six-Footed Serpent Attacking Agnolo Brunelleschi.

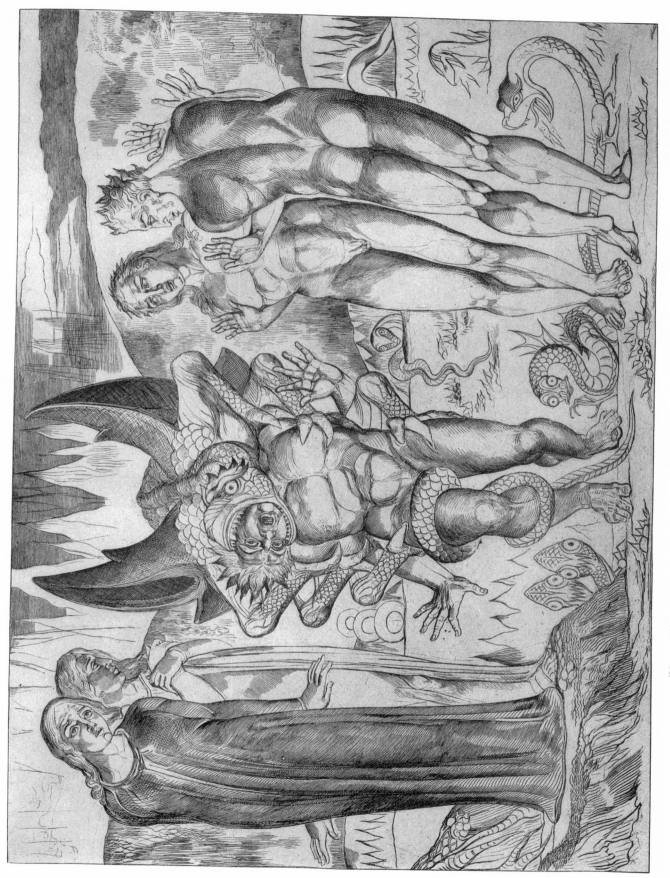

51e.　The Six-Footed Serpent Attacking Agnolo Brunelleschi　(engraving).

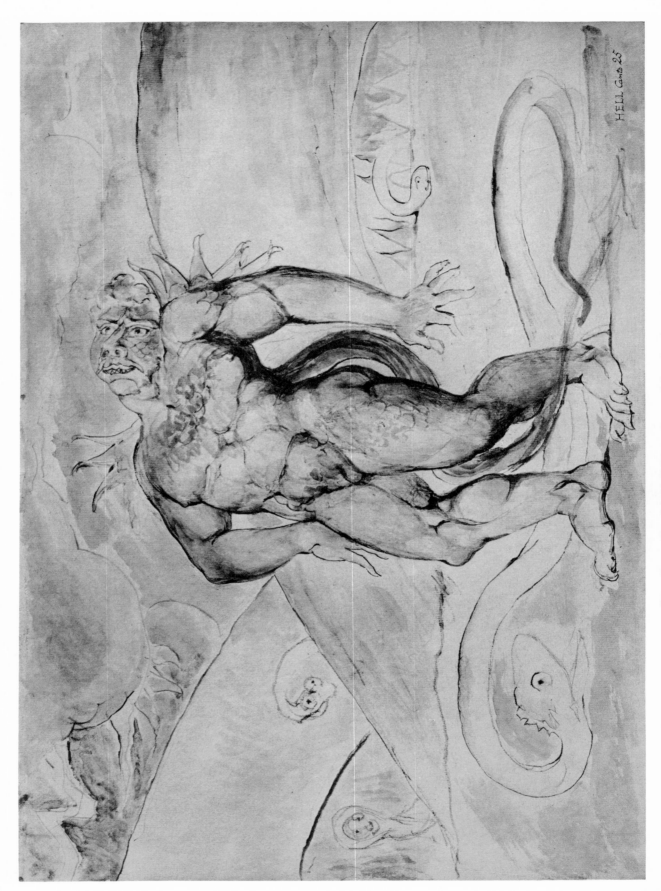

52. Brunelleschi Half Transformed by the Serpent.

HELL Canto 25

54. Donati Transformed into a Serpent: Guercio Cavalcanti Retransformed from a Serpent to a Man.

53 and 53E follow.

53.   The Serpent Attacking Buoso Donati.

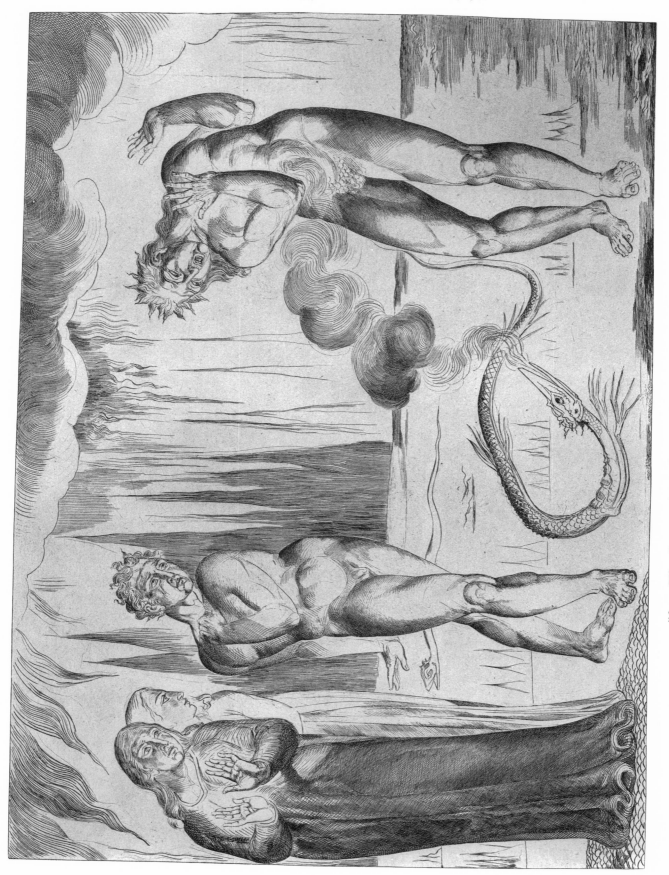

53E.   The Serpent Attacking Buoso Donati (engraving).

55.   Ulysses and Diomed Swathed in the Same Flame.

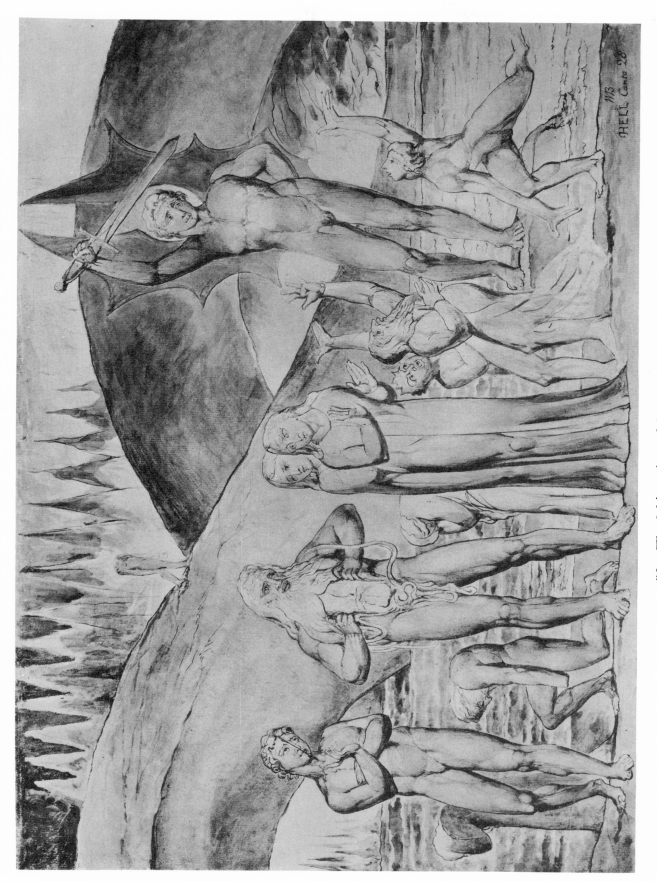

56.   The Schismatics and Sowers of Discord.

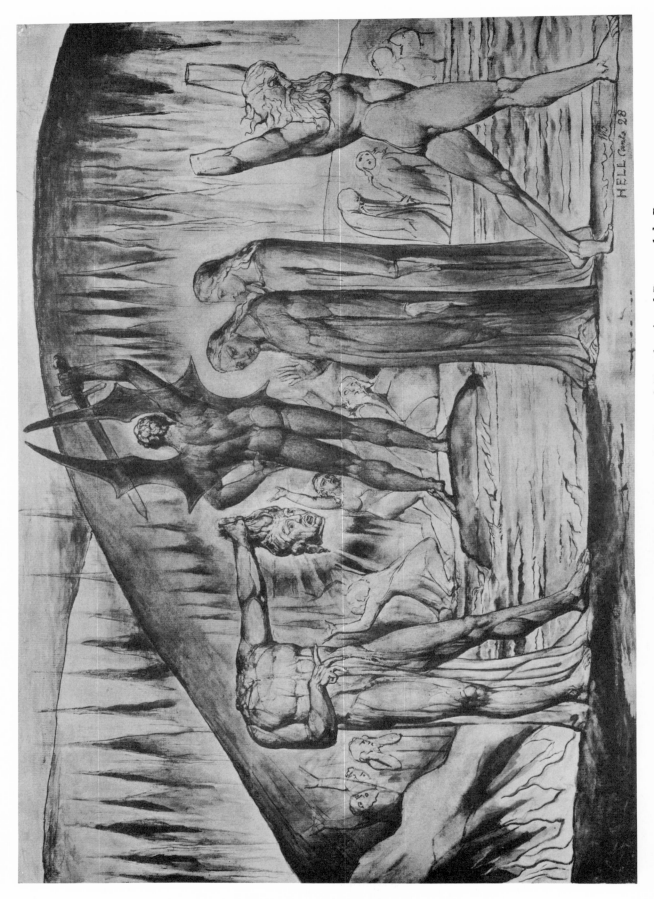

57. The Schismatics and Sowers of Discord: Mosca de'Lamberti and Bertrand de Born.

59.   The Pit of Disease: Gianni Schicchi and Myrrha.

58 and 58E follow.

58. The Pit of Disease: the Falsifiers.

58E. The Pit of Disease: the Falsifiers (engraving).

HELL Canto 31

60. Primeval Giants Sunk in the Soil.

61. Nimrod.

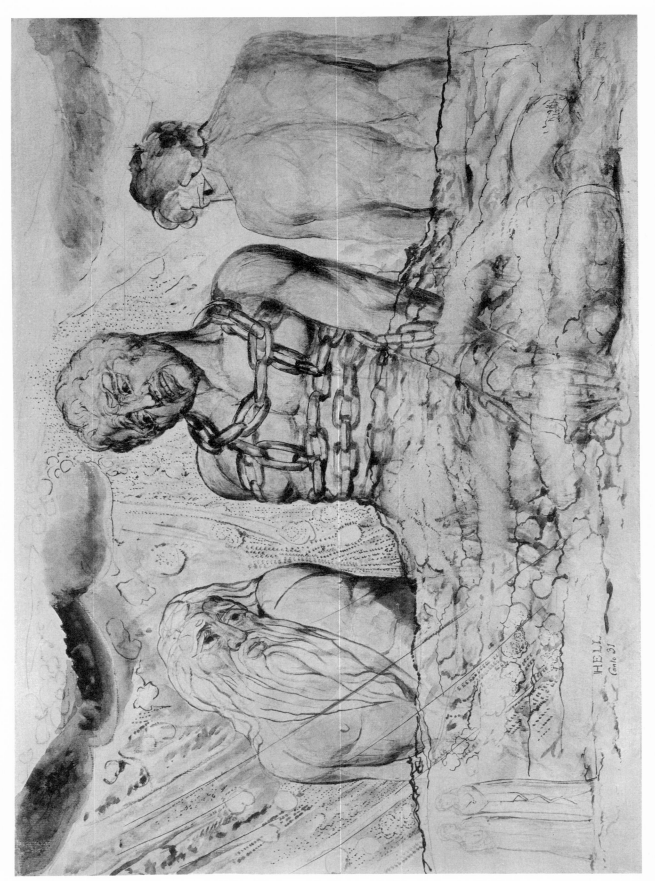

62.   Ephialtes and Two Other Titans.

63.   Antaeus Setting Down Dante and Virgil.

HELL Canto 32

64. The Circle of Traitors: the Alberti Brothers.

HELL Canto 32

66.   Dante Tugging at Bocca's Hair.

65 and 65E follow.

65.   The Circle of Traitors: *Dante Striking Against Bocca degli Abati.*

65E. The Circle of Traitors: Dante Striking Against Bocca degli Abati (engraving).

67. Ugolino Relating His Death.

68.   Ugolino in Prison.

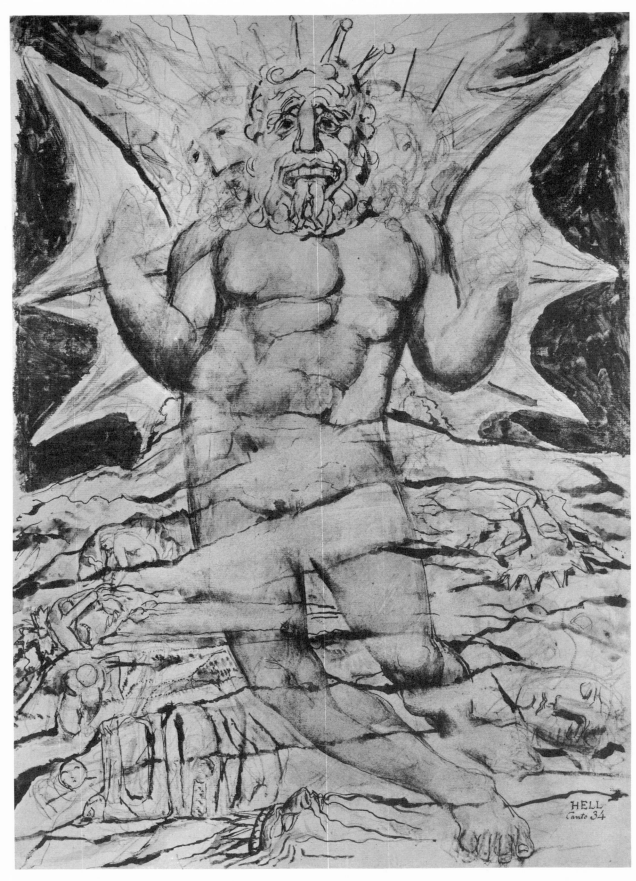

69.　Lucifer.

P-g Canto I

70.   Dante and Virgil again Beholding the Sun as They Issue from Hell.

P-g Canto. 1

71.   Dante, Virgil, and Cato.

72. The Angelic Boat Wafting Over the Souls for Purgation.

P—g Canto 4

73.   The Mountain Leading to Purgatory.

74.   Dante and Virgil Ascending the Mountain of Purgatory.

75.   The Souls of Those Who Only Repented at the Point of Death.

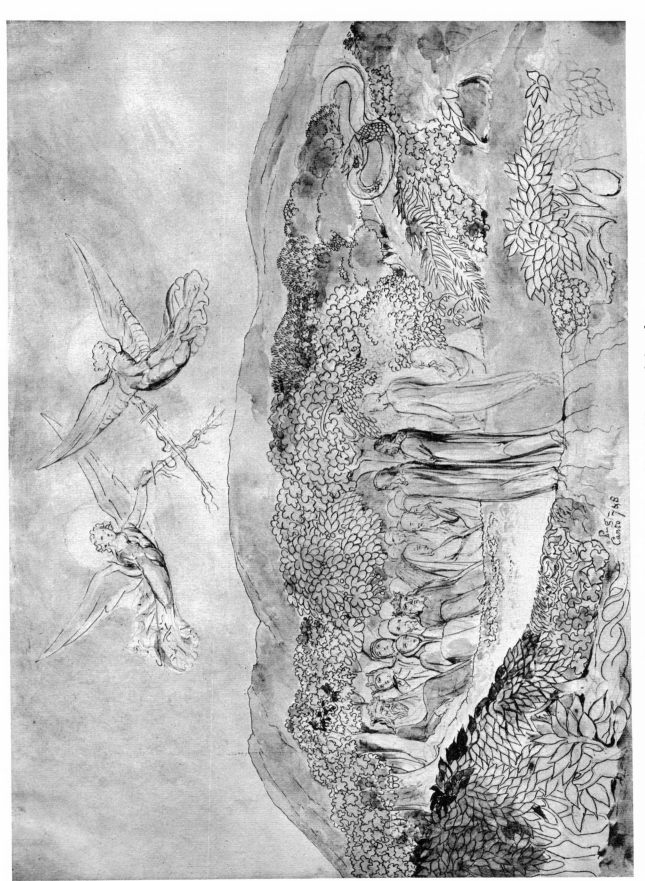

76.   The Lawn with the Kings and Angels.

77. Lucia Carrying Dante in His Sleep.

P—g—
Canto 9

78.   Dante and Virgil Approaching the Angel Who Guards the Entrance of Purgatory.

79. The Angel Marking Dante with the Sevenfold "P."

80. The Rock Sculptured with the Recovery of the Ark and the Annunciation.

81.   The Proud Under Their Enormous Loads.

82. The Angel Descending at the Close of the Circle of the Proud.

83.   The Souls of the Envious.

84.   The Angel Inviting Dante to Enter the Fire.

85.　Dante at the Moment of Entering the Fire.

86.   Dante and Statius Sleeping, Virgil Watching.

P. g. Canto 29

87. Beatrice on the Car, Dante and Matilda.

P.g Canto 29 & 30

88. Beatrice Addressing Dante from the Car.

P-g Canto 32

89. The Harlot and the Giant.

90. Dante Adoring Christ.

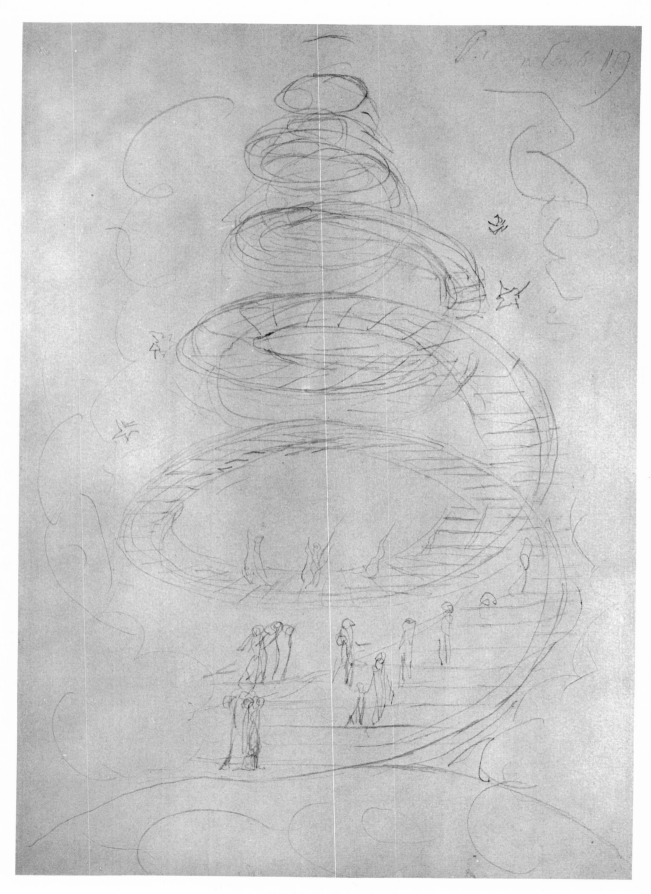

91.   A Design of Circular Stairs.

92.   The Recording Angel.

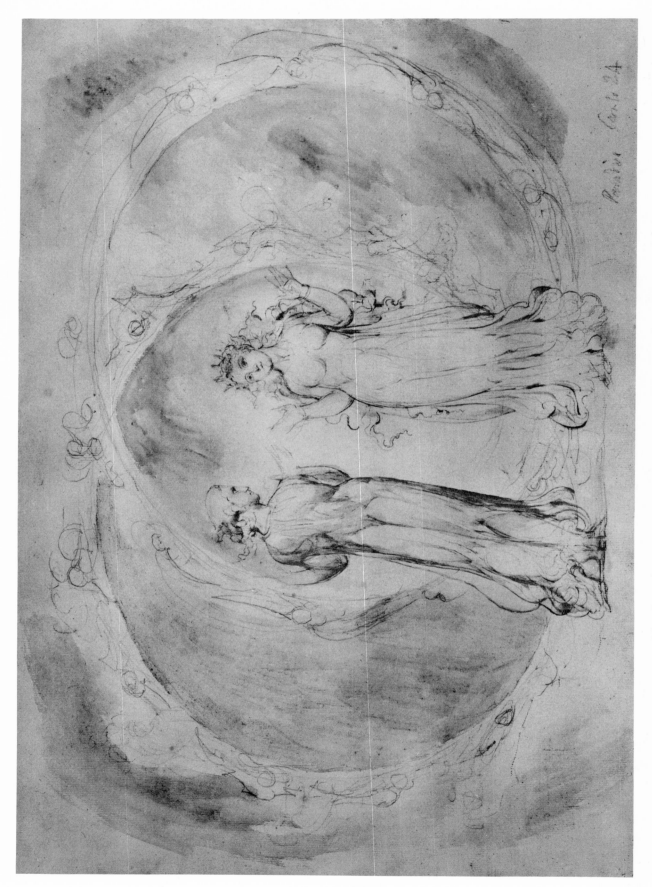

93.   Beatrice and Dante in Gemini Amid the Spheres of Flame.

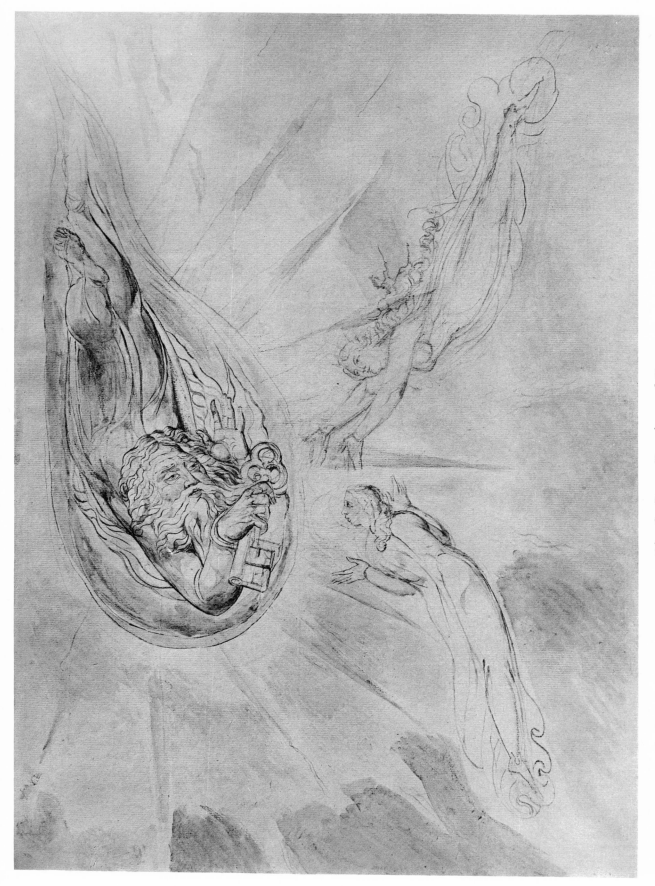

94. St. Peter, Beatrice, and Dante.

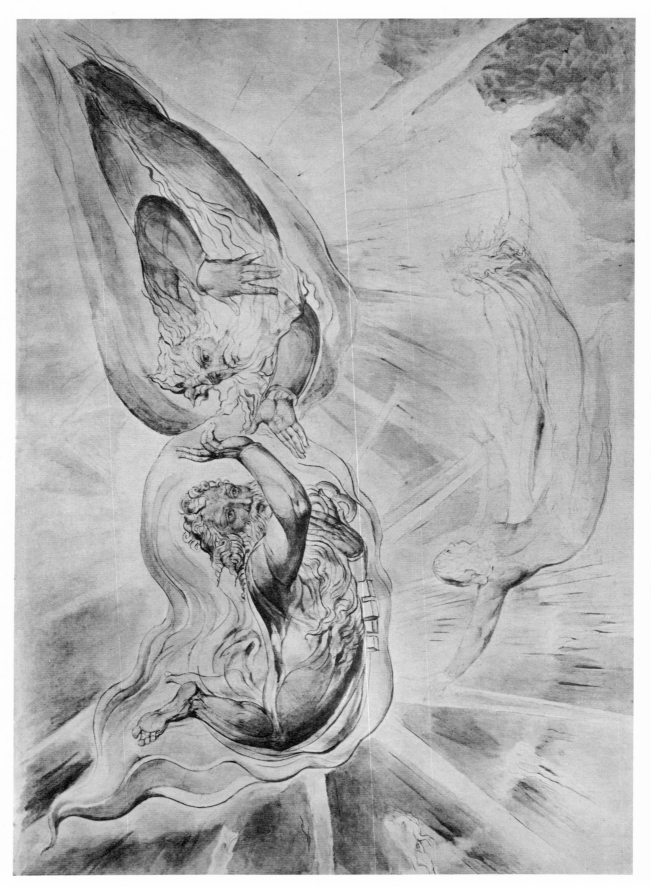

95. St. Peter, Beatrice, Dante with St. James Also.

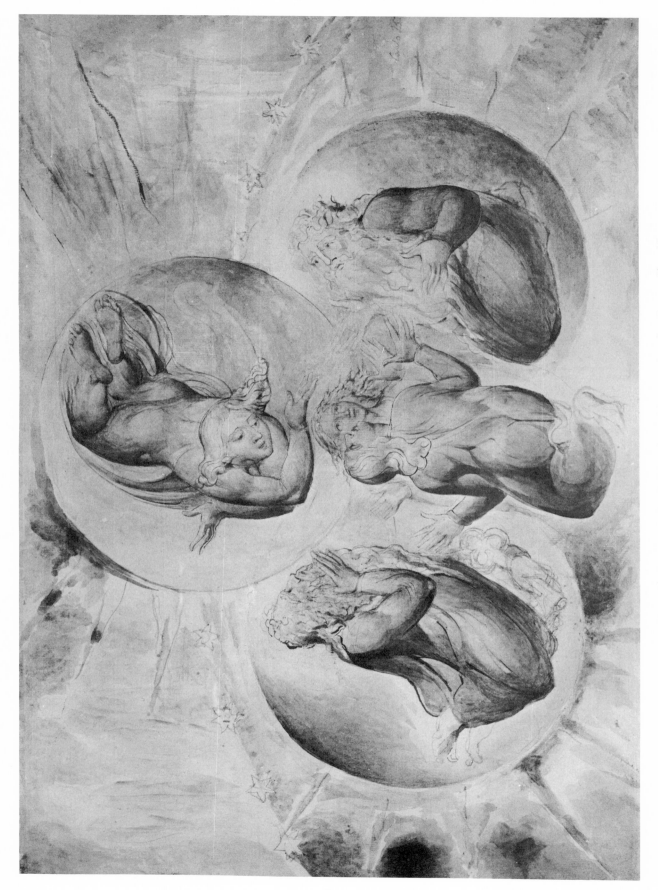

96. St. Peter, St. James, Dante, Beatrice with St. John the Evangelist Also.

97.   The Deity, from Whom Proceed the Nine Spheres.

PAR. *Canto 30*

98.   Dante in the Empyrean, Drinking at the River of Light.

99. The Queen of Heaven in Glory.

100.   Male Figure Reclining.

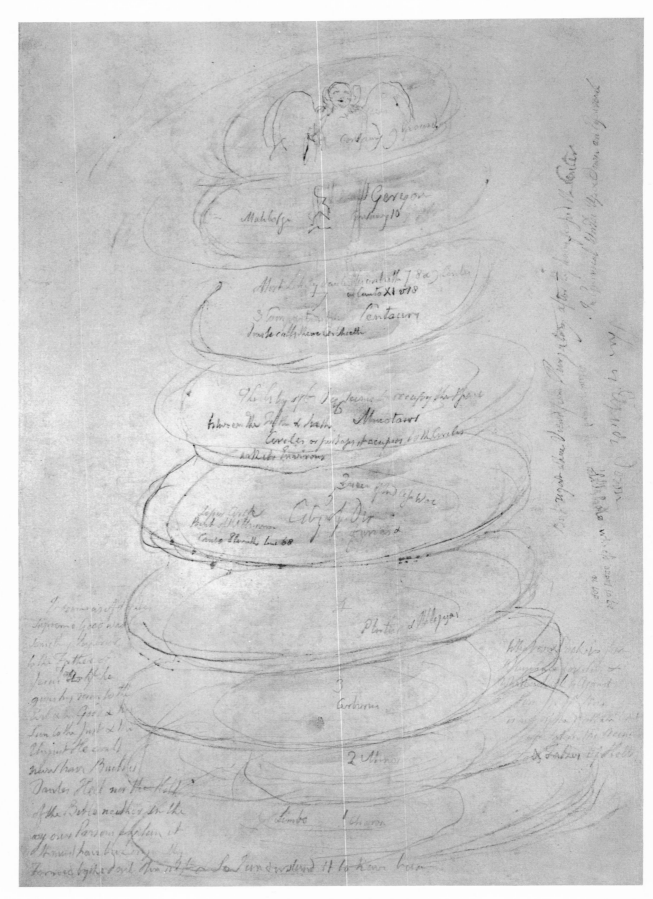

101. Diagram of Hell-Circles.

102. Female Figures Attacked by Serpents.

103.   Head of Dante. One of a series of Heads of the Poets painted by Blake in tempera to decorate
the library of William Hayley at Felpham, Sussex (1801-1803).
By permission of the City Art Gallery, Manchester.